PALACES AND PROGRESSES OF
ELIZABETH I

THEOBALDS

BIRD'S EYE VIEW FROM THE EAST

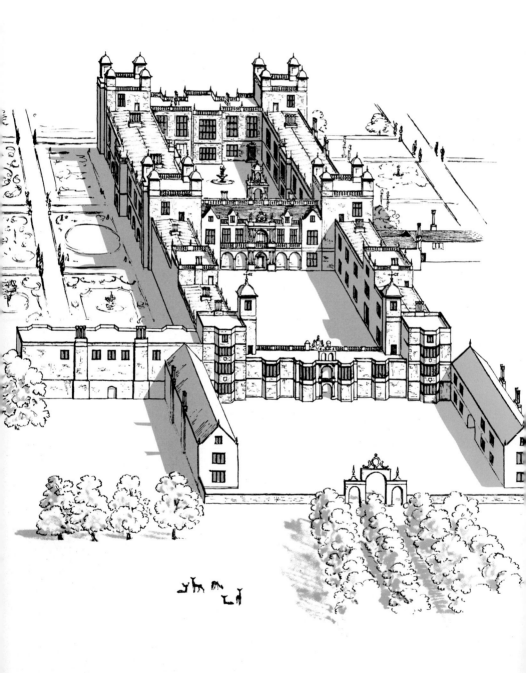

IAN DUNLOP

PALACES
& PROGRESSES *of*
ELIZABETH I

TAPLINGER PUBLISHING COMPANY
NEW YORK

FIRST PUBLISHED IN THE UNITED STATES IN 1970
BY TAPLINGER PUBLISHING CO., INC.
29 EAST TENTH STREET,
NEW YORK, NEW YORK 10003
© 1962 BY IAN DUNLOP

SBN 8008 6209 0

Library of Congress Catalog Number 72 107009

PRINTED IN GREAT BRITAIN

CONTENTS

ILLUSTRATIONS

ACKNOWLEDGMENT

I would like to thank the Marquess of Salisbury for putting at my disposal the material in the library at Hatfield House, and for allowing me to work there. It has been no small advantage to this book that much of it should have been written in such appropriate and inspiring surroundings. I am most grateful to Miss Clare Talbot, librarian at Hatfield House, for her help and encouragement.

I would also like to thank Sir John Summerson for allowing me to use his material for the chapter on Theobalds and for much constructive advice, and Martin Biddle and John Dent of the Nonsuch Palace Excavation Committee for their help and for permission to use their translation of Dr Watson's Latin description of Nonsuch. I am grateful to John Dent for the loan of the photograph on Plate 18 (*top*).

To
DEIRDRE
with all my love

PROLOGUE

WOODSTOCK: THE REMAINS OF DISTANT TIMES

> There is perhaps no one thing that the most polite part of Mankind
> have more universally agreed in, than the value they have ever set
> upon the remains of distant times.   SIR JOHN VANBRUGH

I T DOES not take long for a person to become a legend and for
the buildings with which that person was associated to become
places of pilgrimage. In the collection of papers known as the
Lansdowne Manuscripts there is an early account of a visit to one
of the houses with which Elizabeth I was most poignantly associated.[1] The author, who describes himself as a Gentleman of the
Army at Norwich, was passing through Woodstock during the
summer of 1634. The place had two features which might have
attracted a visitor: it had a royal palace rich in historic memories,
and it boasted an echo which would return as many as seventeen
syllables. The natural formation which produced this phenomenon
was the steep-cut valley of the River Glyme – in those days a mere
rivulet winding its way through a swampy bottom. Across the
low marshland ran a causeway, part of which survives as the
poplared island in Lancelot Brown's lake. The causeway connected
the town with its manor house – a large and castellated mansion
on the rising ground near what is today the north end of Vanbrugh's
bridge.

There was nothing unusual about a royal residence opening its
doors to visitors of respectable demeanour, but the Norfolk officer
was particularly fortunate, for the caretaker appointed her daughter,
a 'pretty, young and modest maiden', to be his guide – a service
which she proved as willing to offer as he was eager to accept;
'so up we mounted many fine steps of freestone into a spacious

---

[1] For details on sources, the reader is referred to the Bibliography, in which general sources,
special sources for each chapter and sources of miscellaneous quotations are listed.

Church-like hall'. The hall was of the medieval pattern, divided
down the centre with a stone arcade, so that it formed, as it were,
two aisles, and was hung with tapestry 'in which was wrought the
story of the wild boar'.

To the left of the hall was the chapel, a Norman structure with
seven round arches and many curious windows. Here the soldier
stopped awhile in prayer, and then with his companion 'nimbly
ascended' into the Guard Room, Presence Chamber and Privy
Chamber, from whose windows they looked out over the tennis
court to the town; on the other side were the withdrawing-chamber
and bedroom, from which they enjoyed 'the sweet prospect into
the Privy Garden'. The day was hot, and they took here a 'small
time of reposing', after which the caretaker's daughter resumed her
role of guide; 'she gently conducted me to the Queen's bedchamber,
where our late virtuous and renowned Queen was kept a prisoner.'

It had been in May of 1554 that Elizabeth had arrived here from
the Tower, under arrest for alleged complicity in the rebellion of
Thomas Wyatt. She had come by water to Windsor, and thence
'with much gazing of people' to West Wycombe, where she lodged
at Sir William Dormer's. From West Wycombe, where popular
interest was more intense, though still confined to gazing, she
proceeded to Lord Williams's at Rycote. The further from London
the convoy penetrated the more demonstrative the people became.
At Aston the bells had been rung, while at Wheatly and Stanton
St John there had been cries of 'God save your Grace!'

On arrival at Woodstock she was lodged in the gatehouse, the
newest built addition to the palace, for it dated only from the reign
of Henry VII. But the condition of the mansion was such as to
cause her custodian, Sir Henry Bedingfield, no little uneasiness. In
the whole building but four doors could be bolted and barred – a
defect which caused 'great disquiet and trouble of mind' to those
responsible. It was not only to guard against the possibility of her
escape that the fastness of the house was required; it might be
needed to protect the person. This proved no idle fear, for once,
during Sir Henry's absence, some two dozen ruffians were seen
loitering with evil intentions in the vicinity of Bladon Bridge, and
had tried to obtain access to the Princess.

There were four rooms allotted her, 'hung with the Queen's stuff', and she was to have liberty to walk in the upper and nether garden and the orchard. Still, her detention was irksome. Holinshed preserves in his *Chronicles* the tradition that on one occasion she heard through the window 'a certain milkmaid singing pleasantly' and envied her lowborn freedom. This is corroborated by Thomas Platter, a German visitor to England in 1599, who was told how 'she often declared that nothing would give her more happiness than to be a milkmaid like those whom she saw out in the field, so miserable and perilous was her captive plight.'

Elizabeth's confinement was fairly rigorous, but when she described her position as 'in worse case than the worst prisoner in Newgate', this must be taken as touching her legal and not her material condition. A fair hearing she might be denied, but it was the Queen's expressed intention that she should be served 'in such good and honourable sort as may be agreeable to our honour and her estate and degree'. In pursuance of this intention she was allowed three women of the Privy Chamber, two grooms of the same and a Yeoman of the Robes in personal attendance. She was, however, separated from her most trusted lady-in-waiting, Elizabeth Sands. Her complaints to the Queen and Privy Council were regular, but possibly not to be taken too seriously; she knew how to make things difficult, and was fairly secure in her own innocence. Her position was summed up accurately by the verses which she wrote 'very legibly' with a diamond on one of the window panes:

> 'Much suspected, of me
> nothing proved can be'
> Quoth Elizabeth, Prisoner

Right into the eighteenth century, sightseers could remember this room, with its 'arched roof of Irish Oak, curiously carved', painted blue and sprinkled with gold, and to the last retaining the name of 'Queen Elizabeth's Chamber'. Her stay at Woodstock was not a happy one, but in after life she occasionally indulged the whim of revisiting the scene of her captivity.

Out of the wardrobe court, the Norwich officer and his guide entered another hall, once used for Her Majesty's Guard, a council chamber 'curiously arched' and another neat chapel where the royal prisoner had made her devotions.

Next they mounted on the roof – the perfect climax to an interesting visit. Here, on the high leads of the gatehouse, a wonderful prospect was offered to their eyes. Below them lay the palace, 'strong, large and magnificent'. There, amid the jumble of towers and battlements, stone walls and leaden roofs, was the Prince's lodging, the hall and chapel, with the Bishop's lodging in convenient proximity; beyond the wardrobe court could be seen the 'fair staircase' they had so nimbly ascended, and the royal apartments behind that. To the east they looked over Tennis Court Mead to the roofs of Woodstock; to the north rose the high ground of Podge Hill, and the wider vista of the 'great and spacious walled park, the brave lawns and waters, and neat, finely built lodge, sweetly situated upon a hill'.

But Woodstock Palace had other memories than those of its captive Queen. Another prisoner of an earlier age had left her legend in the place – Rosamund Clifford, who was kept here tucked away by Henry II. No visit to Woodstock was complete that did not include a pilgrimage to Rosamund's Bower. Accordingly our officer now asked his 'pretty, willing guide' to show him where the jealous Queen had surprised her hide-out 'by a clue of silk'. In this, however, he was disappointed. 'I found nothing but ruins, but many strong and strange walls and windings, and a dainty, clear, square-paved well, knee-deep, wherein this beautiful creature sometimes did wash and bathe herself.'

The dilapidation of the palace was a long drawn out and intermittent process. Owing to the attractions offered by its hunting, Woodstock retained the royal favour long after it had ceased to be worthy of housing a Court.

James I made a visit here in 1603, much to the disgust of Robert Cecil. 'The King,' he wrote, 'regardless of the comfort of his courtiers, had it roughly fitted up for himself, while the household were obliged to lodge even in tents.' Such lack of consideration was in the best Henry II tradition, but this was no compensation. 'The place is unwholesome,' continued Cecil, 'all the house standing upon springs. It is unsavoury, for there is no savour but of cows and pigs. It is uneaseful, for only the King and Queen, with the Privy Chamber Ladies and some three or four of the Scottish Council are lodged in the house.' It is clear from this that the days of Woodstock as a royal palace were numbered.

During the Civil War the manor was besieged and badly battered, but there still remained enough for the Commonwealth Commissioners to find 'fitter to stand than to be demolished'. Time, however, was to continue what Cromwell's cannon had begun, and by 1709 a very picturesque little pile of sturdy walls and crumbling towers, their militant aspect somewhat softened by the presence of an elegant oriel window, still crowned the high banks of the north side of the River Glyme (Plate 1).

Across the valley, the enormous bulk of Blenheim Palace was taking ponderous shape amid the scaffolding and debris of Vanbrugh's builders. Vanbrugh's monumental layout comprehended a vast area round the actual precincts of the house. He had a veneration for the historic and a sharp eye for the picturesque. The manor house enshrined the memory of 'one of the bravest and most warlike of the English Kings'; suitably framed in a thicket of yew and holly it would present to the northern windows of the palace 'one of the most agreeable objects that the best landscape painters can invent'.

He took his pen and wrote an eloquent appeal to Duchess Sarah, pleading for 'the small remains of ancient Woodstock Manor'. He was at pains to compare travellers of his own day, who were drawn by the legend of Rosamund to the ruins of her Bower, with the generations of future visitors who would seek the memory of Marlborough among the porticoes of Blenheim. Altogether it was a carefully constructed and moving memorandum. The Marlboroughs, however, by this time deeply suspicious that Vanbrugh had private designs upon the manor house, were of another opinion. The ruins, they decided, were 'not in themselves a very agreeable sight'. Lord Godolphin, one of the many self-appointed arbiters of taste, likened the mound and its castle to a man 'with a great wen upon his cheek', and the buildings were doomed. Nevertheless, it was not until 1723 that the last remains were finally demolished.

Vanbrugh's appeal was unsuccessful, but in marshalling his

argument he makes a point which deserves to be quoted in full:

> There is perhaps no one thing that the most polite part of Mankind have more universally agreed in, than the value they have ever set upon the remains of distant times. Nor amongst the several kinds of those antiquities are there any so much regarded as those of buildings – some for their magnificence or curious workmanship, and others as they move more lively and pleasing reflections (than History without their aid can do) on the persons who have inhabited them.

These are the two sides of a topographer's business. On the one hand the magnificence and curious workmanship: the great houses of the Elizabethans, with their 'excess of magnificence and elegance even to ostentation', bred of their wealth, their self-confidence and the huge numbers of their households – these are the very stuff of topography. And yet no house or palace is just a soulless mountain of marble or 'laboured quarry above ground'; we all know the dullness of an empty house, and can understand how Pepys, when visiting Old Wanstead, found the place 'not being full of people, looked flatly'. For what are the Elizabethans' houses without the Elizabethans themselves? Without Burghley, tired and half blind with the cares of the State, riding the walks and alleys of Theobalds upon a little mule, or Elizabeth, weary, hot and faint with her journey, rolling into the courtyard in her gold and jewel-studded coach – without these 'lively and pleasing reflections', the houses may prove as uninteresting to read about as they can be wearisome to visit.

Unhappily a great number of Elizabethan palaces can no longer be visited except in the imagination. Too large to be adapted to eighteenth-century use, or too closely associated with the Crown to survive the Commonwealth, most of them have been demolished. There remain the few drawings and paintings of Wyngaerde and Wenceslaus Hollar, the few scattered descriptions, the details incidentally revealed in private letters or builders' accounts, from which a reconstruction often largely conjectural can be built up. But these shadowy resurrections reveal a vastness of conception and a richness of decoration not easily recaptured in the houses which survive. Their vanished glories have much to teach us about the architecture of the sixteenth century.

I therefore invite the reader to visit Elizabeth in her palaces of Hatfield, Greenwich, Whitehall, Richmond, Nonsuch, Newhall, Oatlands and Hampton Court among which she divided most of her time; to accompany her on progress, as she moved during the heavy, plague-ridden months of July and August round the larger houses of her richer subjects, and to share at first hand impressions of Tudor architecture such as might well have been received by a perceptive visitor.

PART ONE

THE PALACES

INTRODUCTORY

THERE were certain features of Elizabethan England which a perceptive visitor might have noticed as signs of the times. Some told of the passing of the age of ecclesiastical and baronial ascendancy; others of the rise of a new land-owning gentry; others again spoke of a stream of wealth, by-passing the landlords and flowing down to the cities of the coast, there to enrich and nourish a powerful merchant class.

He might have chanced, in some secluded valley where the grey walls rose from the green fields in a pleasant oasis of peace and isolation, upon the decaying hulk of some medieval abbey, lying exposed and neglected, its roofs a lead mine and its walls a quarry. On the hill-tops were further tokens of a passing age – the war-scarred ruins of some slighted castle, among whose foundations could still, perhaps, be seen 'sundry deep and horrible dungeons or prisons'. Such was the antiquary Norden's experience at Saffron Walden in 1594. But the significant feature of that place was no longer its abbey or its castle, but Audley End.

For there were signs, too, of a vigorous new order. Sometimes the traveller could have followed a trail of wagons carting away the stones from the abbey walls, and would have come upon the building of a nobleman's residence as capacious and imposing as the abbey itself. Nor were the new landlords contenting themselves with architecture, but were laying out the fields and woodlands into parks and chases which formed a striking contrast with their untamed or bleak surroundings. Lord Stourton, noted Aubrey in his *Brief Lives*, had made just such a metamorphosis of his lands, creating 'a most parkly ground and romancy pleasant place' out of what was 'heretofore all horrid and woody'. For much of England was still as rough and inhospitable as Caesar had found it, and there was a great emptiness about the land. Large tracts of country were 'villainous, boggy and wild ... very little inhabited and nearly waste', and travellers often mistook their way from mere want of anyone to inform them.

Against this background of hostile and intractable nature the wealth of England's fertile valleys was seen and appreciated, and Englishman and foreigner alike extolled 'the fruitfulness of their ground and soil, their lively springs and mighty rivers, their great herds and flocks of cattle'. Such was the wealth of the valley bottoms. On the short, tender grass of the treeless uplands there roamed immense numbers of sheep – the wonder of foreigners. 'This is the true Golden Fleece', exclaimed Paul Hentzner, 'in which consist the chief riches of the inhabitants.'

This richness was the most attractive feature of the land. 'I was totally inflamed with a love to see thoroughly all those parts of this your opulent and ample realm', wrote John Leland to Henry VIII. His *Itinerary* of 1546 remains as evidence of his passion, and was the first of a number of similar works. But despite what some historians have called 'the Elizabethan discovery of England', a great upsurge of topographical and antiquarian interest, it is not by the pens of Englishmen that the face of Elizabethan England was most vividly portrayed. The people who are at greatest pains to describe a country are usually foreigners. An ambassador trying to create for his prince a picture of the country of his mission, or a nobleman wishing to take away with him a memorial of his visit, is more likely to leave impressions which are at once general and picturesque than a native writer whose readers are already familiar with the objects he describes.

Foreign impressions of Tudor England varied considerably. The Duke of Württemberg discovered that in London the trades-people were 'extremely proud and overbearing', and their attitude towards foreigners offensive and insulting. Street boys and apprentices were known to offer physical violence to strangers, and being overwhelmingly superior in numbers, obliged them to put up with the insult as well as the injury.

A Dutch physician, Levinus Lemnius, received a different impression. He found his hosts careful to extend 'all points of most friendly courtesy', the more so because he was a stranger in their land. Perhaps because of his friendly reception, he was more disposed to praise the English people, whose clear, bright eyes 'gave out evident tokens of an honest mind'.

But diverse as their opinions on the English might be, foreign visitors were almost unanimous in their praise of England. 'The country', wrote a Venetian visitor in 1596, 'is the most lovely you can imagine in all the world.'

Perhaps no part of the English countryside appealed more directly to the imagination of the sixteenth century than that which immediately surrounded London, and more especially those lands which were watered by that 'sweet, clean and pleasant river', the Thames. Along its banks, continually bordered with delightful meadows, kings and courtiers, princes of the Church and rich merchants of the City had made their habitation, building and planting until the whole country 'shone with a lustre not to be described', so that it was impossible to view the prospect from any rising ground and not to be enchanted at the sight.

Nor did the cities of London and Westminster themselves attract less attention than their surroundings, being much esteemed for the beauty of their houses and for the grandeur of their palaces and churches. The river front from Westminster was an almost uninterrupted row of palaces, some whose walls dipped straight into the water, others which stood back behind the greenery of a riverside terrace, each with its jetty or 'bridge' to which was attached a cluster of wherries and barges.

The next most impressive feature was London Bridge. Eight hundred feet long and some thirty across, it was encumbered throughout its entire length with buildings and gatehouses, the latter bristling with pikes on which were exhibited the gruesome heads of decapitated traitors. There was much about Tudor London that would be extremely offensive to present-day taste, and the bridge served as an assembly centre for that most handsome of scavengers, the red kite. Great numbers of these birds could be seen in the air, hanging on motionless wings and displaying their matchless mastery over that element.

Architecturally, London Bridge was looked upon as a great

curiosity by strangers; to river travellers, however, it appeared as
a somewhat formidable obstacle, for the nineteen piers on which it
was carried occupied a considerable proportion of the riverbed,
and the narrowing of the channel caused an acceleration of the
current which made its navigation always difficult and sometimes
dangerous. The royal watermen received an extra bonus 'for a
barge beneath the bridge', and cautious travellers would alight at
Swan stairs and take ship again the further side, rather than risk
the shooting of the rapids.

Apart from this single hazard, the Thames provided by far the
easiest and most pleasant means of access to the capital, having a
tidal flow of some sixty miles 'for the great commodity of travellers'. At all times in the year, when it was not frozen, it was teeming
with vessels of every description, from the great ships of Drake
and Frobisher which discharged their ordnance in royal salute
beneath the windows of Greenwich Palace, to the thousands of
wherries and smaller craft which busied themselves about its
surface; from the cumbersome cargo boats which swung their
spreading canvas to the wind, to the glittering processions of state
barges which put off from Whitehall Stairs and troubled the
waters with their multitude of oars.

The pleasure and convenience of this waterway was such that
the main palaces of the Crown almost naturally sited themselves
at the extremities of the tidal flow. Greenwich (Plate 7) had been
the seat of Humphrey, Duke of Gloucester, and later Margaret of
Anjou, who called it 'Placentia' on account of its agreeable
situation. Under the Tudors it became the centre of naval and
military operations, guarding as it did the convergence of the River
Thames and Dover Road upon the capital. Henry VIII 'bestowed
great costs upon it, making it a pleasant, perfect and princely
Palace', adding in particular the armoury whose twin towers, overlooking the tiltyard, were the most conspicuous features of the
whole.

Yet in spite of its military and maritime associations, Greenwich
was very much the palace of Queens. From its pier Anne Boleyn
set out for her wedding, and on her last journey to the Tower.
Here both Mary and Elizabeth were born, and, in the reign of

Elizabeth, it became the favourite summer residence of the Court. From her Privy Chamber she could look out upon the Thames, its waters busy with the shipping which brought its peculiar greatness to her reign, and as her sailors passed out to sea, she bade them farewell 'with shaking her hand'. In later years the *Golden Hind* lay up upon the wharf, hired occasionally for parties, but suffering a slow and humid decomposition.

It was when leaving Greenwich in her barge to set out on her progress on July 17th, 1579, that Elizabeth nearly lost her life. She was heading, Stow records in his *Annals*, with Lord Lincoln and the French ambassador, for Deptford. 'It chanced that one Thomas Appletree, with two or three children of her Majesty's Chapel', was rowing up and down this reach with a caliver, 'shooting at random, very rashly'. He must have been unbelievably careless in his aim, for one of his random shots passed within six feet of the Queen, piercing one of her watermen clean through both his arms and knocking him out of his seat. This not unnaturally 'forced him to cry and screech out piteously, supposing himself to be slain'. Elizabeth showed herself equal to the occasion, and, seeing him maimed, 'she never bashed thereat, but bid him be of good cheer, and said he would want of nothing that might be for his ease.' Young Appletree, however, was given a terrible lesson. He was condemned to death, and four days later, brought to the gallows which had been set up by the waterside near the scene of his crime. But 'when the hangman had put the rope about his neck, he was, by the Queen's most gracious pardon, delivered from execution.'

Another accident, which could have been equally serious, is recorded by Lambarde of Queen Mary's reign. The master of a certain ship which passed by the palace while the Court was in residence, and 'meaning (as the manner and duty is) with sail and shot to honour the Prince's presence, unadvisedly gave fire to a piece charged with pellet instead of tampion'. The ball volleyed against the palace walls, 'ran through one of the Privy Lodgings and did no further harm'. There were certain hazards involved in living at such close quarters with one's subjects.

At the other end of the tidal reach stood the palace of Shene, 'a delightful mansion of curious and costly workmanship, befitting the character and condition of a king'. It had been burnt to the ground in 1498, but was 'raised again to a state of magnificence much superior to anything that had been seen here before' by Henry VII, who caused it to be called Richmond after his earldom.

How different was the outlook here from that of Greenwich. To pass from one palace to the other was to see all England. For next to Greenwich were docks and wharfs and customs houses; it was the focal point of trade and industry, naval and military, home and foreign affairs; here, better than anywhere else, could the sovereign keep his finger on the pulse of the nation. But at Richmond was the other England, the pastoral and aristocratic land, whose peace contrasted with the bustle and business of the East End. Here, among the broad acres and richly wooded slopes, the nobles built, and adorned the beauties of nature with the refinements of art.

For over a century there was nothing in England to equal the distant glories of these buildings. 'Take them in a remote view,' wrote Defoe, and the villas and palaces 'shine among the trees as jewels shine in a rich coronet ... at a distance they are all nature, near hand all art; but both in the extremest beauty.'

As a building, Richmond (Plate 12) was vastly superior to Greenwich – 'a splendid and magnificent house', Aubrey called it, 'which was after the most exquisite way of architecture of that age'. To the rather inadequate descriptions and drawings, the imagination must supply some of the intricate elegance of Henry VII's Chapel at Westminster. It was the largest of the royal palaces, and the most imposing, and had such unexpected conveniences as water conveyed by pipes to 'all the principal rooms'.

If Richmond had any rival in the land, it was Wolsey's palace of Hampton Court. Too sumptuous to remain for long a subject's house, it was the first of a succession of private palaces to become the property of the Crown. Three of the biggest houses to be built during the next hundred years, Theobalds, Holdenby and Audley End, were to fare likewise.

There is at first sight nothing remarkable about the position of Hampton – a flat and naked landscape which owes more to the improvements of man than to the endowments of nature. But a plain setting often becomes a rich jewel, and the elaboration of Wolsey's layout was greatly enhanced by the simplicity of the willows and water meads against the blue outline of the Surrey hills.

In spite of its enormous size, Hampton Court was a remarkably regular structure – 'a noble and uniform pile', as Evelyn puts it, 'and as capacious as any Gothic architecture can have made it'. Inside it was the palace of Midas. 'All the walls of this Palace', wrote Paul Hentzner, 'shine with gold and silver.' Everywhere were ceilings of gilded fretwork that traced its complex patterns against a ground of brilliant blue; gold and silver vessels furnished all the rooms; gold and silver thread was woven into the tapestries and embroidered on to the upholstery, while golden beasts held gilded weather-vanes high above the pinnacles and cupolas that lined the rooftops. The size and splendour of Hampton made it a palace suited to the festivities of the Court, and, on several occasions, Elizabeth kept Christmas or Shrovetide here 'with great and plentiful cheer'.

A few miles upstream from Hampton Court, and perched on the high ground that overtops the Surrey bank near Weybridge, was Oatlands (Plate 2), one of the largest of the Tudor palaces, which seemed consecrated by virtue of its position to the purpose of hunting. Commanding a delightful outlook over the long meanders of the River Thames between Staines and Shepperton, and enjoying a distant prospect of Windsor Castle, it was a situation entirely worthy of being a royal residence.

It is sometimes possible to evoke a whole landscape by the mention of some indigenous bird, and Oatlands has been associated by an eighteenth-century poet with that noisy, homely and essentially English bird, the rook. Rooks in those days enjoyed the protection of the aristocracy, 'the nobility priding themselves on seeing them in the neighbourhood of their villas, and looking upon them as birds of good omen; no one, therefore, is permitted to kill them, under severe penalties.'

It is best to imagine the place on a day when the year is still young; when the naked trees imbrown the hillside, and the clear, cold air opens the prospect to the blue horizon. From the topmost branches of the tall elms comes the incessant clamour of a rookery, breaking the deep silence of the countryside. Against the landscape can be seen a vast expanse of building, with rows and rows of gables and clustered chimneys. At first sight it would appear to be a closely packed village, but a further inspection would reveal the rose brick turrets of two lofty gatehouses, some taller castellated blocks and a great top-heavy octagon lantern which betray the presence of a noble mansion.

Built by Henry VIII in the nineteenth year of his reign, Oatlands is linked by tradition with the marriage of Anne of Cleves. Like Bridewell and Grimsthorpe Castle, it seems to have been an example of Tudor 'jerry-building', for the work was pushed on at a great speed. We read in the accounts of labourers being paid for working 'in the night times', 'in their drinking times', or 'in their own times' to assure 'the hasty expedition of the same'. Working with one's eye on the clock was not unknown, for there is mention also of the purchase of an hour-glass 'for workmen to keep their hours by'.

Advantage was taken of the dissolution of the Abbey of Chertsey to provide materials, which were supplemented by large orders of Reigate stone. This would have been for windows, doorways and other dressings, for, like Hampton Court, Oatlands was a palace of brick.

Its appearance is chiefly known from Wyngaerde's drawings, and from a rather crude bird's-eye view engraved by the antiquary Richard Gough. Although many foreign visitors of distinction included this palace in their round of sightseeing, none of them took the trouble to describe it. For, perhaps as the result of its hasty construction, the palace was architecturally unambitious. It covered a total area of nine acres by the simple expedient of surrounding its three main courts with what were little more than rows of cottages, set with their gable ends towards the court and their innumerable roof ridges at right angles to the main façades. Here and there a bow window or oriel, disposed without regard for symmetry, lent a little dignity to this unimpressive ensemble, but the only architectural effect worthy of the name was the typically Tudor alignment of the two gatehouses and the octagon tower.

The nine acres, measured by Mr Eric Gardner during recent excavations, no doubt included the outer courts, closed only on one side by lodgings; even so, Wyngaerde's drawing shows a very considerable mansion. Friedrich Gerschow, however, the Duke of Stettin's Secretary, who visited Oatlands in 1602, dismissed it as a 'cheerful hunting box' and noted that the 'common servants had set up their tents like a military camp, there not being enough lodgings'. But he was more interested in the sight of the Queen, who was in residence at the time, than in the appearance of her palace. She had been walking up and down in the Privy Garden, occasionally obliging the Duke and his suite by removing her mask for their benefit. At last, 'to show her Royal rank, she ordered some of the noble Lords and Councillors to approach, and they, in their stately dress, were obliged to remain on their knees all the time the Queen addressed them. Meanwhile the Queen uncovered herself down to her breasts, showing her snow-white skin.' Portraits of Elizabeth in her thirties had been shown to the Duke, from which he judged, as he was surely intended to, that there cannot have been many finer women in her time. 'Even in her old age, she did not look ugly,' he observed, 'when seen from a distance.'

It was for the hunting that the Court used to come to Oatlands, and it was here that John Selwyn, Under Keeper of the Park, performed a remarkable feat of huntsmanship which is recorded on a plaque in Walton Church. Leaping suddenly from his horse in mid-chase on to the back of a stag – 'both running at that time at their utmost speed' – he not only kept his seat but steered the animal by means of his sword to where the Queen was standing, and slew it at her feet.

Hunting was very different in those days from what it has become. Neumayr von Ramssla, who watched his master, the Duke of Saxe-Weimar, hunt with James I at Theobalds, describes it thus: 'The huntsmen remain on the spot where the game is to be found, with twenty or thirty dogs; if the King fancies any in particular among the herd, he causes his pleasure to be signified to the huntsmen, who forthwith proceed to mark the place where the animal stood; they then lead the dogs thither, which are taught to follow this one animal only ... Meanwhile the King hurries incessantly after the dogs until they have caught the game. There is, therefore, no particular enjoyment in this sport.'

Neumayr was more perceptive than most of his contemporaries as to the qualities of their sport. Jacob Rathgeb was less inclined to be critical of his master's amusements. When the Duke of Württemberg, to whom he was Secretary, visited Windsor in 1592, the huntsmen 'made some capital sport. In the first enclosure His Highness shot off the leg of a Fallow Deer, and the dogs soon after caught the animal.' Another beast was chased backwards and forwards for some time, but 'at length His Highness shot him in front with an English crossbow, and this deer the dogs finally worried and caught.' A third was overtaken so soon that it provided disappointingly little amusement.

Hunting and shooting were, in fact, combined, the dogs being used to make up for the deficiencies of the marksmen. But if the sport of the Tudors showed a deplorable ability to take pleasure in the sufferings of another creature, it was enriched by the most picturesque of pageantry and partaken of in the most attractive of surroundings. When Sir Thomas Pope took Princess Elizabeth to hunt at Enfield in 1557, they were awaited at the chase by fifty archers in scarlet boots and yellow caps and armed with gilded bows, and the arrows she shot were headed with silver and flighted with peacock's feathers.

The colourful paraphernalia of the hunt was greatly enhanced by its sylvan setting, and much of the beauty of England's countryside was due to the popularity of this sport. 'There were so many Forests, Chases and Parks,' claimed Aubrey, 'as were not to be matched in any Kingdom.' They extended to the very outskirts of the capital, and even when the Court was in London, it was not to be deprived of its favourite pastime.

It was a feature of certain English houses that the richness and magnificence of their apartments were in no way suggested by their plain and unpretentious exteriors, and Bacon's principle that use should be preferred to uniformity, except where both were to be had, was especially observed in the city palaces of the aristocracy.

above: WOODSTOCK   THE RUINS OF THE PALACE IN 1714
below: OATLANDS   PART OF THE PALACE FROM THE WEST, WITH INIGO JONES'S GATE

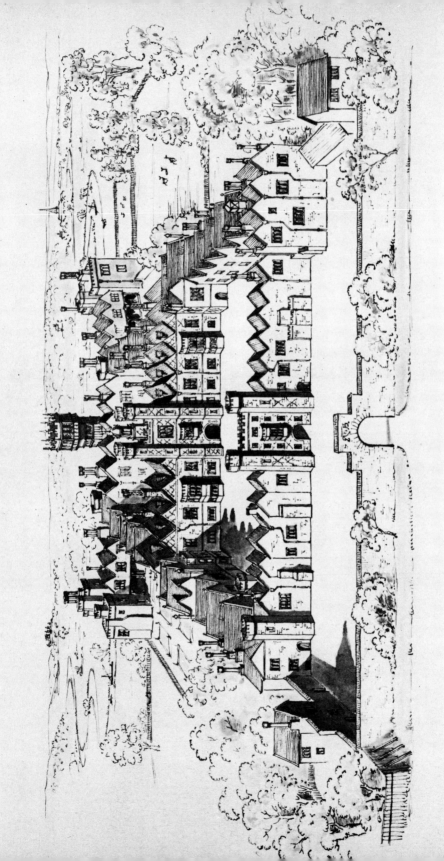

OATLANDS   THE PALACE FROM THE SOUTH

William Harrison, in his valuable *Description of England*, noted that 'many of our greatest houses have been outwardly very plain and simple to sight, which inwardly have been fit to receive a Duke and his whole train and lodge them at their ease.'

To this rule the royal palace of Whitehall was no exception. Samuel de Sorbière, who visited London in 1664, considered it to be 'nothing but a heap of houses, erected at divers times and of different models, which they made contiguous in the best manner they could for the residence of the Court'. But although it lacked any architectural coherence, he admitted it to be 'a more commodious habitation than the Louvre, for it contains above two thousand rooms, and that between a fine park and a noble river'. Its decoration seemed to many to be the most sumptuous in England; artistically it was the most distinguished, for Holbein had enriched some of the chambers with painted walls and ceilings.

Whitehall and Hampton Court were used by Cromwell, and so survived the Civil War. But a series of disastrous fires destroyed the greater part of Whitehall, while the royal apartments of Hampton Court were demolished to make way for Wren's imposing additions. By the end of the seventeenth century only one great palace of the Tudors survived in its entirety, and that was the palace of Newhall, near Chelmsford.

Newhall was bought at the Restoration by General Monk, Duke of Albemarle. He was one of the few men capable of maintaining so vast a mansion. 'He lives in a style equal to that of no other nobleman in the Kingdom', wrote one of his visitors, 'and is well able to keep up a splendid establishment, having an annual income of £20,000.' The visitor was Count Magalotti, one of the suite of the Duke of Tuscany who made a tour of England in 1669. He tells how they came from Chelmsford and, 'travelling the greatest part of the way through woods and meadows, descended into a valley which serves as a sort of receptacle to the streams of water that flow from the surrounding hills, forming a lake that approaches nearly to Newhall'.

The house had belonged to the Butlers and the Boleyns, but was purchased by Henry VIII in 1517, by whom it was 'incomparably adorned and beautified'. So pleased was he with the palace and its gardens and lakes that he called it 'Beaulieu', but the name of Newhall survived.

The house itself (Plate 3), 'a spacious and magnificent edifice, not only equalling but very much surpassing in extent and beauty almost every other in the Kingdom', made a great impression on Magalotti. Enclosing no less than eight courtyards, and presenting on the entrance front a façade of nearly five hundred feet, Newhall was another of those gigantic buildings in which the Tudors so much delighted. 'The *tout ensemble* of the structure', decided Magalotti, 'is of a high character; and although the architecture is not in that perfect style which is observable in modern buildings, yet it is by no means destitute of grandeur.'

Evelyn, who had been there a few years previously, was less enthusiastic. 'It is a fair old house,' he admits, 'built with brick, low, being only of two storeys as the manner then was; the gatehouse better; the court large and pretty; the staircase of extraordinary wideness ... The galleries are trifling; the hall is noble; the garden a fair plot, and the whole seat well accommodated with water; but above all I admired the fair avenue planted with stately lime trees, in four rows, for near a mile in length.' It is a quick 'thumbnail sketch', but he has characteristically picked out the important points: the attractive surroundings, the gatehouse and the hall.

Of all the embellishments which resulted from royal ownership, the great gatehouse had pride of place. The outward towers, which were really bay windows carried up to a third storey and crenellated, were backed and overtopped by the inward towers, standing further apart and raising their bulbous cupolas high above the rest of the building.

Secondary vertical accents, in the form of lofty and massive chimney-shafts, were placed to right and left of this impressive group, while at either end of the main front, two projecting wings advanced symmetrically and broke the line of the battlements with their decorated gables. It was as fine an example of Tudor architecture as was ever built, and unusually regular.

Behind the gatehouse lay the 'large and pretty court'. The eastern range incorporated the great hall, whose magnificent oriel looked into the quadrangle; the western range abutted the chapel, placed across its axis so that its window faced the east.

This window had a somewhat eventful history. Made in Dort for Henry VII's Chapel at Westminster, it was placed instead at Waltham Abbey. Here it would have been destroyed during the Civil War, had not Monk hidden it underground until times were safer for works of art. At the Restoration he set it up at Newhall, where it remained until the demolition of the chapel, when it finally found its way to Westminster, not to the Abbey, but to the Church of St Margaret's, where it remains today.

Across the courtyard opposite the gatehouse a flight of steps led up to a terrace, railed with a balustrade, behind which the north range of the quadrangle was built – a simple and rather monotonous row of bay windows. This wing was constructed, or remodelled, by Thomas Radcliffe, Earl of Sussex, to whom Elizabeth granted the palace in 1573. It was a princely present, and Sussex lost no time in putting up the inscription 'Viva Elizabetta' over the door. He also introduced a Renaissance touch in the porches round the quadrangle. His is the only portion of the building to survive, for after the death of Monk the fortunes of Newhall rapidly declined. In 1737 it was sold to John Olmius, later Lord Waltham, who took down about nine-tenths of the palace, including the hall, the chapel and the gatehouse. It is unfortunate that the wing which he retained for his own use should be architecturally the least interesting.

Newhall occupied an important position between London and Harwich. South of the capital, and beautifully situated amid the richly wooded hills between Ewell and Cheam, was Nonsuch, the most bizarre of the royal houses. Nonsuch also survived the Civil War, but not for long, and here in 1665 came Samuel Pepys 'with great trouble and discontent for the loss of our dog'. He was rewarded for his pains by the sight of 'a very noble house and a delicate park about it'. He noted the avenue – 'a great walk of an elm and a walnut set one after the other', and crossing the 'neat and handsome Bowling Green' which lay before the palace, he came to the massive gatehouse, 'looked through the great gates and found a noble court'.

Architecturally, Nonsuch was the most extraordinary achievement of its age. It was Henry VIII's last building venture, designed rather for his pleasure and retirement than to meet the needs of a full Court. It was built on a typical Tudor plan, with gatehouses and corner towers, but the façades of the royal apartments received an exuberant decoration of plaster reliefs in which the style of the French Renaissance was clearly reflected.

These garishly adorned façades were surrounded with such gardens and parks that it seemed a place 'pitched upon by Pleasure itself to dwell in along with Health'. This palace of Henry's old age made a deep impression on visitors, who recorded faithfully its 'excess of magnificence and elegance, even to ostentation'. There was often something distinctly vulgar about the lack of taste and restraint exhibited in Tudor buildings.

A love of display was, in fact, one of the characteristics of the time, and it very much impressed foreigners. Princes who visited England and ambassadors whose missions were accomplished were invited to make a tour of the royal residences – an invitation which it was a little difficult to refuse. Breuning von Buchenbach, over in England in 1595 to solicit the Order of the Garter for the Duke of Württemberg, found himself in just this predicament. He had already seen the palaces once, and his embassy having been unsuccessful, he was in no humour for sightseeing; it was impressed on him, however, that it would be undiplomatic to refuse; 'it might otherwise have been thought', he explained to the Duke, 'that I despised these houses as being insignificant.' Neither he nor his master thought them anything of the kind.

The magnificence of Elizabeth's palaces was even a factor in the complex structure of her marriage projects. In June 1559, Baron Breuner had come from the Emperor to negotiate an alliance between Elizabeth and Archduke Charles of Austria. In his first letter to the Archduke, he tells of the charms of the Queen: 'I believe that there is no princess of her compeers who can match her in wisdom, virtue, beauty and splendour of figure and form.' But, in case her spiritual and physical attractions were not found sufficiently persuasive, he goes on to enumerate her more sterling qualities. 'I have seen several very fine summer residences that belong to her ... and I may say that there are none in the world so richly garnished with costly furniture of silk, adorned with gold, pearls and precious stones. Then she has some twenty other houses, all of which might justly be called royal summer residences. *Hence she is well worth the trouble*' [my italic].

It was the opulent hangings and upholstery, embroidered with gold and studded with jewels, together with the great crowds of courtiers in their gorgeous costumes that most impressed visitors to the Court. Breuning had travelled much; he had visited the Courts of Germany, France, Italy and half the countries of the Middle East, and yet he could write in a confidential memorandum to his prince, 'at no other Court have I seen so much splendour and such rich clothes.' Although England was well behind the greater part of Europe in her attitude to Renaissance architecture, her palaces could nevertheless command the envy and admiration of her more sophisticated neighbours. 'I would not for a great matter have missed seeing this Kingdom', wrote Virginio Orsino, Duke of Bracciano, to his wife at the end of his visit in 1601. 'It seemed to me', he added later, 'that I had become one of the paladins who used to enter those enchanted palaces.'

In a more academic sense, the revival of learning was making good headway, and already a high standard, set by the scholars and admirably supported by the Royal Family, was beginning to spread. At the beginning of the century Erasmus had been delighted to find in England 'so much real learning, not commonplace and paltry, but profound, accurate and ancient Latin and Greek', and exclaimed in his enthusiasm, 'when I am listening to my friend Colet, I seem to be listening to Plato himself.'

The Court of Elizabeth was renowned for its erudition. Most of the ladies, Harrison claimed, had a sound knowledge of the classics, besides being fluent in Italian, Spanish and French, and in this they were little or nothing behind the gentlemen. Bibles, histories and other interesting and edifying literature were to be found in all the chief offices of a palace, and were read aloud, so that 'the stranger that entereth into the Court of England upon the sudden, shall rather imagine himself to come into some public school of the universities, where many give ear to one that readeth, than into a Prince's Palace.'

The house in which during Elizabeth's childhood this mixture of Court and college had been most pronounced was the royal nursery of Hatfield. Since the reign of Henry I, the bishops of Ely had owned a palace here – a convenient half-way house for one who divided his attention between the administration of his see and the government of the realm. The building as we know it is largely the work of Cardinal Morton, who 'bestowed great cost upon his house at Hatfield'. It was probably built between 1479 – the year of his appointment to the bishopric – and 1483, when he fled from Richard III, for soon after his restoration in 1485, he succeeded Bourchier at Canterbury and abandoned Hatfield for the greater glories of Knole.

Although it was not until 1538 that any legal conveyance was made, Henry VIII had, in fact, been using the bishop's manor as a royal nursery since 1533 and it witnessed some of the strange alternations of fortune in the lives of Mary and Elizabeth. They were worse for Mary, for she was old enough to feel the humiliations that were heaped upon her, and to feel them acutely. 'During the time of her averseness', writes Heylin in his *History of the Reformation*, 'the King sent certain of the Lords to remove her to Hatfield.' She went, obedient but protesting her legitimacy. Under Anne Boleyn, Mary tasted at Hatfield the bitterness of rejection. Her two remaining maids of honour were dismissed and 'only one common chambermaid' was set to serve her, and she dispensed with the precaution of tasting the food which was to be served to the degraded Princess. On one occasion she was 'against her will and by sheer force, placed in a litter with Anne's aunt, being in this manner obliged and compelled to pay her court to the said bastard'.

'The said bastard', better known as Elizabeth, enjoyed, in her turn, only too short a vogue, and the royal child, so lately paraded 'for the sake of pompous solemnity' through the streets of London as successor to the throne, was to be lodged at Hatfield in similar circumstances to her sister. Her governess, Lady Bryan, wrote a pathetic letter to Lord Cromwell, complaining of the want in which the Princess was kept, and asking 'that she may have some raiment; for she hath neither gown nor kirtle nor petticoat, nor no manner of linen for smocks nor kerchiefs'. A Mr Skelton, who was lording it over the household, was trying to force the young girl to dine and sup every day at the Board of Estate. 'Alas, my Lord,' wrote Lady Bryan, 'it is not meet for a child of her age to keep such rule.' It made it harder to discipline her, and she was 'as yet too young to correct greatly'. She was indeed too young – the poor Princess was still cutting her great teeth. Lady Bryan ends on a tender note: 'She is as toward a child and as gentle of conditions as ever I knew even in my life.'

Her towardness soon began to make itself apparent in her aptitude for learning. Following Roger Ascham's method of double translation, in which the pupil put a passage from the Latin or Greek into English and then back again into its original tongue, she attained to 'such a perfect understanding in both the tongues ... as they be few in number in both the Universities, or anywhere else in England, that are in both tongues comparable with Her Majesty'. How much she valued this gift which her tutor and his successors had bestowed upon her, may be judged from her words on hearing of his death. 'She would sooner have cast ten thousand pounds into the sea', she said, 'than have lost her Ascham.'

In 1543, the household at Hatfield was augmented by the arrival of the young Prince Edward. The accounts show a list of 'reparations done at the King's Manor of Hatfield against my Lord Prince's Grace coming thither'. Besides a long tale of minor adjustments in the kitchen and sculleries, payments were made for mowing the orchard, pairing the alleys, pruning the trees and casting the bakehouse pond. On Edward's birth, the rival claims of Mary and Elizabeth receded somewhat into the background, and, when he arrived at Hatfield with his tutor, Dr Coxe, the Old Palace became a happy and a studious menage.

One of the greatest attractions of Hatfield was its surrounding country. A survey made in 1538, when the manor was formally taken over by the Crown, shows it set in a great park seven miles in circumference, 'replenished with wood of great age' and abounding with deer. To this was added the Middle Park, a further three hundred and fifty acres, likewise planted with venerable oaks and beeches and likewise stocked with game.

Then there was the much smaller Innings Park – 'but the herbage of the same is very bare and mossy and [you] will scarce find the deer there.' To make up for the lack of deer, Innings contained a warren of coneys – the black variety of rabbit, as much esteemed for the warmth of its fur as for the quality of its meat. The rabbits of England, noted Fynes Moryson, were 'fat, tender and much more delicate than those of other lands'. They were in consequence, more highly prized than hares, whose flesh was thought to 'nourish melancholy'.

It was through this nobly wooded parkland that the palace and town of Hatfield were approached, the highway from London taking much the line of the present Agency Road. On the left was the George Inn (its name still preserved in 'George's Field'), built round three sides of a quadrangle and spanning the highway with its gibbet sign. Here the road parted into two ways, one dipping down the hill into the town (the present Church Street) and the other continuing straight on, skirting the eastern end of the churchyard and passing hard under the walls of gatehouse cottages.

Along the eastern side of the upper road ran a brick wall. The brick wall framed a plot of land covering some eight acres, and in the middle of the plot stood 'a very stately and goodly Manor Place erected and builded upon the side of an Hill ... commonly called the Bishop's Manor, constructed all of brick, and having in the same very stately lodgings'.

So many alterations have been made to the Old Palace (Plate 5) that it is difficult to picture its original appearance. The present alternation of windows and buttresses was achieved only by the conversion of the building into stables. When the stalls were set up, all ground floor windows were bricked in, and many of the buttresses were added as recently as 1830, by which time the drastic alterations had no doubt imperilled the stability of the structure.

In the process of conversion, many of the features typical of a fifteenth-century manor house were obliterated. Part of the charm of medieval architecture was in the distinctive appearance by which the several elements of a house could be identified. There is nothing today to indicate which side of the entrance tower at Hatfield was the great hall. In Tudor times, there could have been no doubt. It was marked by the inevitable lantern which crowned the roof ridge, and by the 'Great Window', a full length oriel which formed a luminous embrasure to the dais end. Both these features are mentioned in the accounts during the demolition, and the oriel is clearly marked on the only existing plan of the palace, made in 1608.

This plan shows the house to have been a simple courtyard, two hundred and eighteen feet square, with stables and a dove-house, 'builded all of brick', rambling away to the north. The south range contained the state apartments, which overlooked the gardens and orchard. The first view of Hatfield from the London road would have given the visitor a vista of red roofs and turrets and chimney stacks rising above the blossom of the orchards.

In spite of its many mutilations, it is still a strangely beautiful building. It is possible today, taking a remote view of the palace from the high ridge two miles to the westward, to see it nestling among the trees on the hillside, and to recapture some of its original atmosphere.

Little is known of the 'stately lodgings' it contained. Most of the rooms were lit from both sides, their windows looking out to the south over the knot garden and orchard, and to the north into the courtyard. This must have been a most attractive little quadrangle, but its appearance must remain largely conjectural. Each corner was taken up by a square projection housing a staircase – probably Tudor additions to the episcopal mansion – and they may have risen above the roof line to become the turrets mentioned in the accounts. All that is known about these turrets is that they were demolished in 1607. Across the east end of the quadrangle, and in plan again strongly suggestive of Tudor addition, was an inward-facing loggia of three arches. Through the central arch, one went out on to the green before the palace, and, from the green, by another distinctively Tudor archway, one gained the park.

The whole plan gives evidence of a trim and cosy seclusion and the architecture has an air of studious and collegiate simplicity –

for while there is great dignity and beauty in its conception, it is entirely free from superfluous ornament or ostentation. A visitor here might well have been in doubt whether he had come to a university college or a prince's palace. In important respects, Hatfield was both.

Roger Ashley, writing to Roger Ascham in 1552, recalls with nostalgia the learned and cloistered life they had shared at Cheston, Chelsea and here at Hatfield – 'our pleasant studies in reading together ... our free talk mingled always with honest mirth'. But the royal tutors were not the only studious persons at Hatfield. In the person of Sir Thomas Pope, Elizabeth's friend and custodian, the gravity of a college and the gaiety of the Court found a happy blend.

He and Elizabeth had much in common. They would discuss together his plans for Trinity College, Oxford, of which he was the founder and benefactor. 'She often asketh me about the course I have devised for my scholars,' he wrote to the President, 'and that part of my statutes respecting study I have shown her, which she likes well.'

On other occasions, he would give her some princely entertainment. In 1556, at Shrovetide, Sir Thomas 'made for the Princess Elizabeth, all at his own costs, a great and rich masking in the Great Hall at Hatfield'. There was a tourney in the palace yard, with a 'device of a castle of cloth of gold, set with pomegranates about the battlements'. At night, the hall was hung with the finest tapestries and there was a banquet given. There were seventy dishes served, and, at the side, the cupboard stood twelve tiers high, laden with gold and silver plate.

On November 17th, 1558, Elizabeth learned at Hatfield that she was Queen of England. The Earls of Pembroke and Arundel, Lord Clinton and five knights, amongst whom was Sir William Cecil, lost no time in riding to Hatfield, and here the first Privy Council was held. Cecil became her principal Secretary, and so began the partnership which was to last for the rest of his life.

On the same day the citizens of London heard their new sovereign proclaimed, and, in the afternoon, the bells rang out their joyous message. Elizabeth had always a fondness for church bells, and would cause her equipage to halt, in progress for Hatfield, to hear the bells of Shoreditch, 'much esteemed for their melody'. Perhaps, in her mind, they were associated with this hour of triumph. 'O Lord, Almighty and Everlasting God,' she prayed on entering the Tower a few days later, 'I give thee most hearty thanks that thou hast been so merciful unto me as to spare me to behold this day.' The joy was widespread, and brought home to every heart by those crazy pealing bells. When darkness began to fall, a thousand bonfires took up the sunset glow and filled the city with their gay, dramatic lighting, while, in the streets, tables were set and there was 'plentiful eating and drinking and making merry'.

Elizabeth's first move was to Lord North's at the Charterhouse, whence she rode, apparelled in purple velvet, by streets new-gravelled to the Tower, and as she went, there was a shout about her ears and a great shooting of guns – 'the like was never heard before.'

A public removal of the Queen was an extremely noisy affair. Going by water to the Tower a few days later, her barge was followed by that of the Mercers, which carried ordnance 'shooting off lustily as they went, with great and pleasant melody of instruments, which played in most sweet and heavenly manner'. During the first few days of her reign, she was constantly on the move amid this deafening uproar; trumpets blew, drums beat, flutes played, guns went off and squibs were hurled into the air as she went from place to place. It was a wise course of action; by showing herself freely to the people, she made herself dear and acceptable to them. Often she had no other motive in mind, but would spend the evening being rowed for her pleasure along the bankside, and always attended by an enthusiastic crowd of other craft.

In the following summer Elizabeth made her first progress, and her first move was to Greenwich, the picturesque, rambling riverside palace of her birth.

II

GREENWICH

IN 1662 a surveyor named Jonas Moore appended to his *Prospect and Map of London* a little pen-and-wash inset of Greenwich (Plate 6),[1] probably done by Wenceslaus Hollar. It has his characteristic combination of inaccuracy and charm. It gives a wonderful sense of the situation of this maritime palace, but little detail. Perhaps it was kinder thus; years of neglect had left their mark upon the fabric which a closer portrait might have revealed, for by this time the old palace was doomed. Henrietta Maria had resumed residence in the Queen's House, but Charles II had more grandiose projects for the site of the Tudor buildings. Two years later, Pepys recorded in his diary: 'At Greenwich I observed the foundation laying of a very great house for the King, which will cost a great deal of money.' It did cost a great deal, but the building which rose upon the site of 'Placentia' was never again to be the home of the King.

Hollar's picture has thus the importance of being the last glimpse of Tudor Greenwich. He has taken his viewpoint from the sea wall downstream, at a range remote enough to give the whole context. The atmosphere is admirably suggested. On the left are the water meadows of Greenwich Marsh – the sort of fertile fenland over which the lapwings cry and tumble. Behind them swells the green mound of Greenwich Hill, crowned with Duke Humphrey's Tower. At the foot of this hill lie the palace buildings, culminating in the high roofs of the great hall and Fountain Court and the tall gatehouse of the waterfront. The other half of the picture shows the river, separated from the marshes by the sea wall. It is obviously a choppy day, and one can almost hear the scream of gulls and the flap of rigging against the canvas. In the foreground,

[1] To be seen in the London Museum.

two ships are battling upstream, while beyond them a long procession of sails marks the course of the river round Limehouse
Reach.

The scene is delightful, but unfortunately Hollar is not to be
trusted. He has made the Queen's House like a toy fort – either by
exaggerating the chimneys or by including angle towers which
were never built, and he has drawn the hall roof too close to the
river front. Beyond stimulating the imagination, he does not help
us much with the reconstruction of Greenwich Palace.

It is an unfortunate fact that the exact topography of Greenwich
is not to be reconstructed. We can see the palace through a tele-
scope – a pleasant medley of roofs and towers – but lacking in
definition; or we can see it in vivid and fragmentary detail through
the magnifying glass of the surveyor's accounts: but there is no
means of seeing the whole clearly.

We can watch the carpenters making 'a new bay window with
a truss' in Anne Boleyn's bedroom, and the bricklayers 'beating
down a hole in the wall within the King's Bedchamber' to insert
another window there; but we cannot place either window in the
façade. We can follow the casting and setting up and gilding of
sixty-seven lead bosses and two hundred and eighteen buds
'turned and carved, for the fret in the King's Privy Chamber';
but we cannot picture the room as a whole. We know that the
conduit in the inner court was of Renaissance design, with cornice,
columns and spheres 'painted in fine jasper colour' and panels
enriched with heraldry and carved antique work; but we do not
know what the fountain looked like.

Sometimes the accounts can conjure up a whole landscape or
bring a flood of human interest into their tale of bricks and mortar.
What delightful invention, for instance, could have devised in the
King's garden a 'water maze'? Yet all we know of it is that its
paths were tiled. In another part of the gardens was erected a coop
for peacocks 'brought to the King out of the new-found land'. It
was an unsuccessful experiment, for payment is soon made for the
birds' removal 'because the Queen's Grace could not take her rest
in the morning for the noise of the same'.

The coming of Anne Boleyn was the occasion of the works to

which these accounts refer. She appears first under her own style of
'Lady Marquess of Pembroke', a title which gives place somewhat
uncertainly to that of Queen. In August, the carpenters were employed in making her 'a great bed of state' in her Presence Chamber,
and joiners were erecting an altar in her bedroom. All was in
readiness for the birth of her eagerly awaited child.

For it was here at Greenwich Palace, between three and four in
the afternoon on Sunday, September 7th, 1533, that Elizabeth was
born. 'The Queen was delivered of a fair lady,' runs a contemporary
description, 'for whose good deliverance Te Deum was sung in-
continently.' The birth of another girl was a great disappointment
to Henry, but the popular rejoicings were not to be denied, and
instant preparation was made for the christening. Twenty-nine
carpenters were kept busy 'framing and railing all the way from
the Hall door to the Friary Church', and eighteen pounds of candles
were bought to enable them to work by night. For the christening
took place on the Wednesday, only three days after the birth, 'upon
which day', runs the same account, 'the Mayor, Sir Stephen
Peacock, in a gown of crimson velvet ... and all the Aldermen in
scarlet with collars and chains, and all the Council of the City
with them, took barge at one of the clock and so rowed to
Greenwich.'

Meanwhile, in the Church of the Observant Friars, adjoining
the palace upon the west side, provision was being made for all
things necessary for the royal christening.

In the middle of the church, beneath a canopy of crimson satin
fringed with gold, was set the silver font, and near this 'a close
space with a pan of fire to make the child ready in'. With a scrupu-
lous regard for hygiene, it was arranged that 'divers gentlemen
with aprons and towels about their necks gave attendance about it,
that no filth should come to the font.' Rich cloth of arras had been
hung upon the walls of the church and along the passage which
connected it to the palace, and the way was strewn with green
rushes.

The assembly place was the great hall, and from here, the procession set out – 'first the citizens, two and two; then Gentlemen,
Esquires and Chaplains; next after them the Aldermen, and the

Mayor alone, and next the King's Council; then the King's Chapel in copes; then Barons, Bishops, Earls; the Earl of Essex bearing the covered gilt basins; after him the Marquess of Exeter with a taper of virgin wax; next him the Marquess Dorset bearing the salt; behind him the Lady Mary of Norfolk bearing the Chrisom which was very rich, of pearls and stones'. Next came Elizabeth herself, wrapped in a mantle of purple velvet and carried by the old Duchess of Norfolk, her long ermine train supported by two earls and a countess.

The party was met at the church door by the Bishop of London amid a company of bishops and abbots in their mitres. Thomas Cranmer, the Duchess of Norfolk and Lady Dorset stood sponsors. Immediately after the christening, 'Garter Chief King of Arms cried aloud, "God of his infinite goodness send prosperous life and long to the High and Mighty Princess of England, Elizabeth"; and then the trumpets blew.'

There had been many changes wrought in England during the twenty-five years which separated the christening of Elizabeth from her accession. She had been baptized with the full Roman rite, with salt and with oil, and there had been mitred abbots assisting at the ceremony. The service itself had taken place, not in the chapel, which occupied the eastern extremity of the waterfront, but in the Church of the Observant Friars, established there since 1482. Ten years later, the building was desecrated, and we read in the accounts of payments made 'for carrying of sawn timber from the sawpits into the Friars Church for the carpenters to work on'. The Friary Church had become a carpenter's shop.

In all other respects, Greenwich was enriched by the reign of Henry VIII. He made extensive additions and was constantly in residence, making it a favourite place to which to invite ambassadors, who would, no doubt, learn from what they saw here to respect the naval strength of a maritime nation. It is largely from their letters and dispatches that the picture of Greenwich has been built up. Gasparo Spinelli, Venetian Secretary, was present at an unusually lavish reception of the French ambassadors here in 1527, and was much impressed by the magnificence in all he saw.

Two temporary structures, one of them a banqueting house and the other in the form of an amphitheatre, were raised upon the tiltyard for this occasion. They are important in the history of English art, for, in the account books, there appears for the first time the name of Holbein.

Work was begun in January. About a dozen painters were engaged daily for wages between sixpence and a shilling *per diem*. A fortnight later, 'Master Hans' appears at four shillings a day – a modest enough beginning for the greatest artist who was to work in England during Henry's reign. An entry for 'senaper, lake and vermilion ... spent by Mr Hans and his company upon the roof' suggests a team of artists under Holbein's directions putting the finishing touches.

By March 11th, they were ready for Henry's inspection, and payment was made to ten men 'to hang the cloths in the King's sight and taking them down again'. In April and May, work continues day and night on the triumphal arch, right up till May 5th – the day before the banquet was held. The total cost for 'two arches triumphant antique wise' was £262.9.8.

The hall was a hundred feet long by thirty feet wide, the roof of purple cloth powdered with roses and pomegranates, the woodwork painted in blue and gold and the candlesticks polished like amber. 'The walls', wrote Spinelli, 'were hung with the most costly tapestry in England, representing the History of David, and there was a row of torches, closely set, illuminating the place very brilliantly.'

'The door of this Hall', he continues, 'was in the form of a very lofty triumphal arch, fashioned after the antique, beneath which were three vaulted entrances; through one passed the dishes for the table, through the other, they were removed, and, on each side of the centre one, which was the largest, stood two enormous cupboards bearing the wine to be served at table.' Over this triumphal arch, which clearly did duty for the hall screens, was a spacious balcony for musicians, bearing the arms of the King and Queen 'with sundry busts of Emperors and the King's motto "Dieu et mon Droit" and other Greek [*sic*] words'.

It was customary to display the gold and silver plate during a banquet, and Spinelli remarked on 'two cupboards reaching from

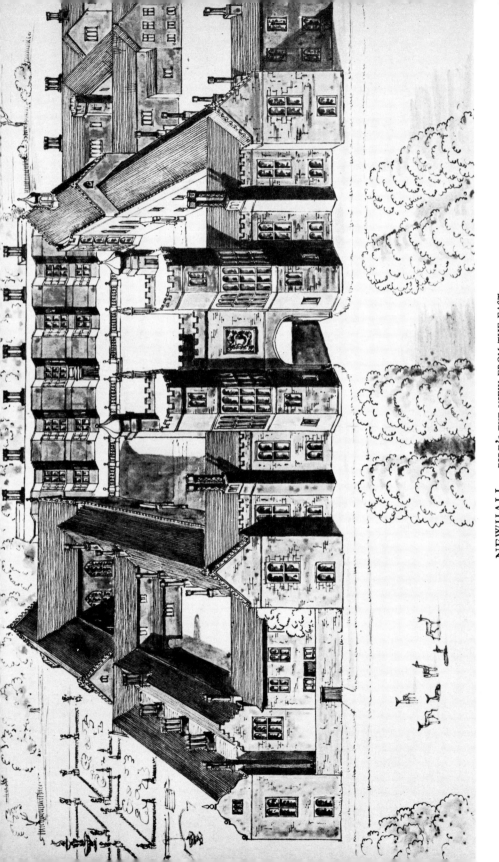

NEWHALL   BIRD'S EYE VIEW FROM THE EAST

The Plan of New Hall in Essex.

Formerly was an house which belonged to the Bullins Earls of Wiltshire, was purchased by King Henry VIII who built the great gateway and enlarg'd the House and Offices, the great Apartments next the garden was built by Queen Elizabeth. After the Restoration it was given to Gen.l Monke, and lastly in the possession of the Duke of Montague.

the floor to the roof, forming a semicircle, on which was a large and varied assortment of vases, all of massive gold, the value of which it would be difficult to estimate'.

Rising from dinner, the ambassadors were conducted along 'a corridor of no great length to the other Hall'. This was equipped with tiers of seats like an amphitheatre, the ceiling was painted with a map of the world, and the royal throne stood before an archway 'all gilt with fine gold, the inside of the arch being decorated with a number of beautiful figures in low relief.' Spinelli marvelled that it could have been raised in such a short time.

Meanwhile, the seats in the amphitheatre were filling up. 'All the spectators being thus methodically placed, without the least noise or confusion ... the entertainment began.' What seems to have struck the Italian most was the orderliness and discipline of the English Court. 'One thing above all surprised me,' he concludes, 'never having witnessed the like anywhere, it being impossible to represent or credit with how much order, regularity and silence such public entertainments are conducted in England.'

But well-conducted and orderly though they were, the revels continued all night, and before the entertainment had finished, the sun 'having perhaps had a hint from Mercury of so rare a sight', had risen into view over Greenwich Marsh, 'at which everybody thought it time to quit the royal chambers, returning to their own with such sleepy eyes that the daylight could not keep them open'.

Another Venetian Secretary, Niccolo Sagudino, witnessed at Greenwich in 1515 the ceremony of 'Bringing Home the May'. 'On the ambassador's arriving there,' runs his description, 'they mounted on horseback with many of the chief nobles of the Kingdom, and accompanied the Queen into the country to meet the King.' Katherine of Aragon, 'rather ugly than otherwise and supposed to be pregnant', was very richly attired and had with her twenty-five damsels 'mounted on white palfreys, with housings all of one fashion, most beautifully embroidered with gold'.

Ascending the hill behind the palace, the company proceeded to a wood, some two miles distant, where the King was awaiting them with his guard 'all clad in a livery of green, with bows in their hands', and about a hundred noblemen on horseback, all gorgeously arrayed. 'In this wood', continues Sagudino, 'were bowers filled purposely with singing birds which carolled most sweetly, and in one of these bastions or bowers were some triumphal cars on which were singers and musicians, who played on an organ, lute and flutes for a good while, during a banquet which was served in this place.'

The banquet over, the homeward procession began. It was accompanied by the sort of pageantry which has survived in the Lord Mayor's Show. 'Tall pasteboard giants, placed on carts and surrounded by the King's Guard, were conducted with the greatest order to Greenwich, the musicians singing all the way.' One can picture the colourful cavalcade making its unwieldy progress and winding its way down Greenwich Hill, with the King bringing up the rear 'in great state, being followed by the Queen and by such a crowd on foot as probably exceeded twenty-five thousand people'.

It was from the top of the hill, where Humphrey of Gloucester had built his little tower, that the most glorious view of Greenwich was to be obtained. Many have attempted to portray the scene, but none has left so vivid and pleasing a description as that of John Barclay which was published in his *Icon Animorum* in 1614.

'There is a hill that overtops the Palace', he begins, 'and at a moderate distance of height, takes a fair survey both of the town and river.' It was a favourite viewpoint for artists, too, and both Wyngaerde (Plate 6) and Hollar chose it for their panoramas. 'In a morning by chance I ascended thither; no man was near me to disturb the recreation of my thoughts, which wandered about with pleasing and delicious freedom. But the wonderful pleasure of the place had almost sooner ravished my mind than filled mine eyes with the fairest prospect, not only in Britain, but (it may be) in all Europe.' Another age would challenge his assertion, but it was typical of an Elizabethan to prefer his own country, and the tamer pastoral south at that, to more dynamic scenes. Men who live in troubled times are attracted by the friendly prosperity of a country; it is those who enjoy comparative security who seek the stimulus of more untamable landscapes. John Barclay was of the former type; his spirit was rejoiced by the green woods and fat pastures.

Across his landscape wound the River Thames, bringing its cargoes of wealth to the city, and 'filling the adjoining fields with a most pleasant fruitfulness'. There was infinite promise of riches and security about the green valleys of the south; navigation and irrigation were twin blessings which the great rivers of England bestowed upon her people. 'The whole coast is most sweetly verdant, and the profit of pasture has exempted it from tillage. The lands of private men are fenced with ditches, whose banks are adorned with rows of trees; especially the highways on each side are planted with poplars, so that the whole valley, to him that surveys it from the top of the hill, appears like continued gardens and walks of pleasure.'

The upland around him was the perfect complement to the fertile plain, contrasting its elevation with the other's flatness and echoing the windings of the river in the graceful sweeping contour of the Downs – 'those hills environing ... did neither suddenly debar the prospect, nor suffer the sight to be too much dispersed through the empty air', but framed before him 'the pleasant medley prospect of city, country, water and land'. But the most beautiful object was the view of London itself, 'esteemed among the fairest cities of Europe, a City of innumerable houses, yet scarcely able to contain her people'.

It was in summer that the Court was most at Greenwich. They came when it was still young, when the trees had not yet lost their varied tones, and the forecourts of the palace were white with blossom. On the first of May, the Queen and her Court would climb the hill and 'every man except impediment, would walk into the sweet meadows and green woods, there to rejoice his spirits with the beauty and savour of sweet flowers and with the harmony of birds, praising God after their kind.'

Seen from the hill behind, the palace was roughly T-shaped, the cross of the T being the buildings which lined the embankment, and the stem those which projected southward and divided the Privy Gardens from the tiltyard. The focal point of this irregular group was the great gatehouse, which towered above the halls and lodgings as the keep of a provincial castle rises from the houses and cottages clustered at its foot. To the left of the gatehouse, the hall

lantern and the slender *flèche* of the Observant Friars, and to the
right the twin towers and *poivrières* of the tiltyard, were the most
conspicuous features. Otherwise, the buildings of the palace were
almost indistinguishable from those of the two villages which
lay to east and west of it.

Before the palace was the Lawn – a wide expanse of open turf
which lent itself to military manœuvres. One of these demonstra-
tions was the occasion of Elizabeth's first visit to Greenwich as
Queen in July 1559. The militia had mustered on the Lawn, 'guns
were discharged on one another, the morris pikes encountered
together with great alarm; each ran to their weapons again, and
then they fell together as fast as they could in imitation of close
fight.'

The Queen watched from the gallery over the park gate, a
detached gatehouse (replaced by Inigo Jones's Queen's House)
which spanned the Woolwich road. This gatehouse was the scene
of the memorable occasion when Sir Walter Raleigh is said to have
spread his cloak before Elizabeth's feet.

Military reviews were by no means uncommon at Greenwich,
and it is probable that its strategic position, combined with the
facilities which it offered for this sort of demonstration, made it
a favourite place for the reception of foreign visitors and ambassadors. It was well they should be made aware of the potential
strength of the country, and the stately ceremonial of the Court
was designed to present the sovereign to them, as well as to her
own people, in as imposing a light as possible. They seldom failed
to record their impressions and their records make an important
contribution to the history of Greenwich Palace.

Henry Ramelius, ambassador from Denmark, Lupold von
Wedel, a nobleman of Pomerania, and Paul Hentzner, who all
visited the place between 1584 and 1598, describe their audiences
with the Queen.

It was usual to approach the palace by river, and Ramelius, being
an ambassador, had one of the Queen's barges sent to fetch him.
He does not describe it, but the defect can be made up from the
account of another ambassador who was taken to Windsor. It
was an eight-oared boat with a cabin 'divided from the rest by

contiguous doors' and covered with an awning of red satin. The interior was hung with coats of arms and the floor was strewn with flowers. In this, the ambassador travelled, 'seated in solitary grandeur' upon a bolster of cloth of gold.

The first view of Greenwich was of the long brick water-front (Plate 8) added by Henry VIII. It was a two-storeyed structure, turreted and embattled after the military fashion, but the large many-mullioned windows belied the fortress and the towers seemed to have been designed more for prospect than defence. The great gatehouse, taller by a storey than its surrounding buildings, spanned the embankment so that its walls and towers dipped straight into the river, and where it joined the main front, another tower, rising to five storeys in height, provided the most striking feature of this side of the palace.

Alighting here, Ramelius was conducted to the chapel, which was hung about with gold brocade. He was shown the gilded alcove in which the Queen waited to receive the Sacrament. Normally she attended divine service in the Holyday closet at the end of the gallery. The chapel was at the extreme eastern end of the river front, and, if the gallery thus adjoined, it must have extended along the same front overlooking the Thames.

The singing of the royal chapels attracted the frequent notice of visitors. Jacob Rathgeb, when visiting Windsor with the Duke of Württemberg, remarked on one of the choristers there who 'threw such a charm over the music with his little tongue that it was really wonderful to hear him'. At Greenwich, Ramelius listened to the office 'so melodiously sung and said ... as a man half dead might thereby have been quickened'.

There was, as might be expected, a great tradition of music at the Court of the Tudors. Under Henry VIII, Thomas Tallis had been organist at Greenwich, and, under Elizabeth, the Children of the Chapel were the pick of the choirboys of England. At the beginning of her reign, Richard Edwards was Master of the Children, and a warrant was issued 'for that it is meet that our Chapel Royal should be furnished with well singing children ... we do authorize our well beloved servant Richard Edwards ... to take as many well singing children as he shall think meet in all Cathedral

and Collegiate Churches.' It is small wonder the standard was so
high.

As the Queen left the chapel, presentations were made to her.
Eight trumpeters announced her coming 'with a blast very well
executed', and she advanced down the lane of kneeling subjects,
accepting petitions from rich and poor alike with a becoming
modesty, acknowledging their genuflection with the formula, 'I
thank you with all my heart.' Her air was stately, her look direct,
but her manner of speaking was mild and obliging. Her personal
appearance was carefully noted by Hentzner: 'Her face oblong, fair
but wrinkled [this was in her sixty-fifth year], her eyes small, yet
black and pleasant; her nose a little hooked, her lips narrow and
her teeth black' – a blemish not uncommon in the English from
'their too much use of sugar'.

Of her clothes and jewellery, no less than of her face and form,
visitors made the minutest observations. One of the most striking
accounts comes from Breuning von Buchenbach. 'Everything was
studded with very large diamonds and other precious stones', but
her customary extravagance was offset by a strange and most
macabre fancy: 'over her breast, which was bare, she wore a long
filigree shawl, on which sat a hideous large black spider that
looked as if it were natural and alive.'

It was not usual for visitors to be admitted to the Queen's dinner,
except at Christmas, but the elaborate preliminaries were carried
out under the gaze of all who came. Henry Ramelius, looking down
into a courtyard from an ante-room window, saw a procession of
'very personable young gentlemen' carrying covered dishes of
silver and gilt to the sound of drum and trumpet – 'a marvellous
delightsome thing to hear'. Lupold von Wedel was more fortunate,
for coming at Christmas he enjoyed the rare privilege of watching
the Queen at table.

She was served by a young man in black (for the Court was in
mourning for the Duc d'Alençon), her carver, and another who
served her beverages, kneeling all the while she drank. Around her
stood the great men of her realm; Lord Howard was there, of
Armada fame, and Leicester, the focus of curious eyes on account
of his reputation of being the Queen's lover; Lord Hertford, to

whose natural distinctions was added that of having some claim to
the throne, and Hatton, also surrounded by the aura of romance.
'All of them', noted von Wedel, 'had white staffs in their hands,
and were handsome old Gentlemen.' The Queen conversed freely
with them, each kneeling when he was addressed until bidden to
rise.

Meanwhile, the servants came and went with their courses. With
each dish that was brought, they bowed three times. 'They had
previously done the same', observed von Wedel, 'with the napkins
and all the table ware, although the Queen was not yet present.'
The ceremonial was enhanced by the Queen's musicians, who all
the while 'discoursed excellent music'. At the end of the meal, four
men approached the Queen with a large silver bowl and a towel;
she gave her ring to the Lord Chamberlain and washed her hands,
an operation which the absence of forks rendered a necessity. 'She
then took an earl's son by the cloak and retired with him to a bow
window. He knelt down before her and had a long talk.'

That was the most agreeable feature about the Elizabethan
Court; there was an atmosphere of friendly ease about it, which
appears to have been in no way cramped by the universal obligation
to kneel while speaking to the Queen. 'She chatted and jested most
amicably,' wrote von Wedel, 'and pointing with her finger at the
face of one Master or Captain Rall [Raleigh] told him there was a
smut on it. She also offered to wipe it off with her handkerchief,
but he anticipated her.' In the midst of all the gold and glitter of
Greenwich, with all its pomp and all its protocol, it was possible
to find the Queen seated informally on a cushion on the floor of
the gallery engaged in friendly conversation.

With a total population of only four and a half million people, it
was possible for Elizabeth to be in personal touch with a fairly
representative section of her people, and one of her most endearing
qualities was her readiness to meet her subjects face to face. When,
in 1601, Lambarde presented her with a copy of his *Pandecta*, she
gave him a typical reception in the Privy Chamber at Greenwich.
'You intended to present this book unto me by the Countess of
Warwick,' she began, 'but I will none of that; for if any subject of
mine do me a service, I will thankfully accept it from his own

hands.' She talked intelligently and at length, not without taking care to give the old scholar some opportunity of exhibiting his learning.

It was in the course of this conversation that she made her much quoted summary of the difference between the medieval age and her own: 'In those days force and arms did prevail; but now the wit of the fox is everywhere on foot.' Time passed, and she was called away to prayer, but not before she had taken leave of the old antiquary, forbidding him to fall on his knees: 'Farewell, good and honest Lambarde!'

That was the strength of Elizabeth. She knew when to be Queen and when to be even more commandingly human. She could let her royal pleasure be known, Sir John Harington declared, in terms 'which left no doubtings whose daughter she was', but her moods were like the climate of the land she ruled – varied and unpredictable; 'when she smiled, it was pure sunshine that everyone did choose to bask in if they could; but anon came a storm from a sudden gathering of the clouds, and the thunder fell in wondrous manner on all alike.' The portrait of her at Hatfield, holding a rainbow in one hand, seems to symbolize this mixture of temperament.

III

WHITEHALL

IT SOMETIMES took as much as two days for a ship to battle up from the mouth of the Thames to London. For the traveller who chose this route, the first important milestone was the sight of Greenwich Palace. Above its pink brick walls, the towers of the tiltyard moved in relation to the ship's progress, now hiding behind the gatehouse, now reappearing over the lower roofs of the outer court, suggesting an unexplored dimension and inviting a further visit. But the impression was only a fleeting one, an architectural overture to the city of London, which first came into sight as the palace began to recede into the background, its skyline pinnacled with the towers and spires of countless churches, and, in the middle, the impressive pile of St Paul's Cathedral rearing its great bulk high above the roofs and chimneys of the houses which clustered at its foot.

A popular inn for foreigners was the White Bear, and here, in August 1585, Lupold von Wedel made his headquarters. He lost no time in making a tour of the sights of the great city. There were many curious spectacles to be seen: a cow with six legs, a boy with his face speckled black and red like a pig's, a midget 'but six thumbs long ... her paces no longer than those of a cock'. On the south bank were the amusements of an unsqueamish age, the baiting of bulls and bears. The entertainment ended in a grand finale. 'A rocket was shot into a rosette which hung above the place'; from the rosette fell apples and pears among the crowd, and, as they scrambled for these, a salvo of fireworks fell among them, causing great panic and confusion – 'a mirth-provoking sight'.

The mirth of Merry England was not always edifying, for although the Elizabethans had all the charm and all the vitality of an

57

unsophisticated and uninhibited age, they tempered their enjoyment of plain and homely pleasures with the indulgence of a gross and sordid sensuality. The massacre and even torture of defenceless animals passed for sport, and enthusiastic crowds could be assembled to witness the flogging of an old, blind bear.

More directly sadistic impulses could be gratified at Bridewell. This building was of special interest to Germans, for it was said to have been run up in the space of six weeks by Henry VIII for the reception of the Emperor Charles V, and had served as a royal residence until King and Emperor fell out with one another, and Henry 'to spite him, put knaves and whores into this Palace'. So von Wedel was told, and, although the Emperor can hardly be supposed to have been deeply distressed by the fate of his erstwhile lodgings, the tradition persisted. Stow, however, knows nothing of it and dates the founding of the House of Correction in Edward VI's reign. According to his more probable account, it all started with a sermon preached by Nicholas Ridley before the young King, who was so moved by the bishop's eloquence that he founded Christ's Hospital for poor children, St Thomas's and St Bartholomew's for poor invalids, and Bridewell, 'where the vagabond and idle strumpet is chastised and compelled to labour' – a typically Tudor solution to the problem of the thriftless poor.

But, for whatever cause they came to be lodged in a palace, the wretched inmates were set to the treadmill and, unless they could purchase exemption, were flogged twice a week – a pitiful spectacle to which the public were admitted and which much appealed to the seamy side of their taste. ''Tis the best lechery', admitted Aubrey, 'to see them suffer correction.'

Von Wedel was more refined; he was interested in the architecture and marvelled much at this degraded mansion which had taken so short a time to build and known so brief a reign of splendour. 'It is a pity', he mused, 'that such a palace should be kept so ill.'

But there was no want of beautiful buildings which were not put to such a distressing use. There was the Tower, with its menagerie, its armoury and its mint; here could be seen the royal plate and many tapestries 'royally wrought in gold and silver'. In another room were 'many fine bedsteads, gilt all over, used when visitors of high rank arrive'. For the Tower was a storehouse for the Queen's furniture, articles being taken as required to whichever palace the Court happened to be using. The Crown Jewels were only on show when the Court was in London.

Then there was the Abbey, already crowded with tombs and monuments 'magnificently executed at great expense'. It was a treasure house in itself. Here was the sword of Edward I, so heavy that it seemed impossible to wield; there was the stone 'on which the Patriarch Jacob was said to have rested his head: believe it who will'. In the chancel the Coronation Chair was shown to trippers; von Wedel behaved like one, and sat in it himself. In Henry VII's Chapel were the memorials to the Royal Family, their effigies lying beneath canopies of marble and brass. 'Round each tomb kneel their children,' remarked von Wedel, 'likewise portrayed in their natural size. It is magnificent to behold'.

It was near this chapel, so the antiquary Norden informs us, that the ancient palace of Westminster had stood. From time immemorial Westminster had been the seat of government, and here too had been the chief residence of the King, 'though now brought to the ground, and green grass grows where it stood'.

There was nothing to command the attention of a tourist such as von Wedel, but, to the keen eye of an antiquary, 'the place which now carrieth the name of the Old Palace, showeth itself to have been in times past full of buildings', and Norden was able to discover 'apparent tokens in a wall yet standing, that there were many vaults, cellars and such like offices, in that place which is now a plain field', and adjoining the college wall, 'certain towers which seem to have been parcel of that Palace'. There was little to recall the Gothic glories of this medieval house and, as he paced about the site, Norden was moved to meditate upon the words of Juvenal, 'there is nothing but shall come to ruin, be it now never so glorious in the earth.'

Immediately adjoining the precincts of the Old Palace of Westminster was 'glorious Whitehall, a regal mansion situate upon the Thames, beautiful and large, adorned with many fair galleries' and containing within its irregular outline 'a most large and princely garden, full of pleasant walks and other delights, and an orchard also replenished with like treasures, though the place more solitary'.

Norden was, to say the least, uncritical of Whitehall. To the eyes of the Italian, Count Magalotti, who visited London in 1669, the palace appeared 'more remarkable for its situation than for the nobleness of its structure, being nothing more than an assemblage of several houses, badly built at different times and for different purposes', as the result of which it had 'nothing in its exterior from which you could suppose it to be the habitation of the King'.

Originally known as York House, Whitehall had been for centuries the London seat of the northern Primate. Under Wolsey, it had been greatly enlarged and enriched, notably by the building of the great hall, whose high-pitched roof stands out in the panoramas of the period. Although the house belonged to the See of York rather than to Wolsey in person, it was confiscated along with his private possessions and became the property of Henry VIII, who 'brought it, by great expense, unto its present princely form'.

This 'present princely form' can only be applied to the apartments, for happily the unimpressive and uncoordinated exterior concealed a rich and royal decoration. 'The inside of this house', wrote von Wedel, 'is regally and very beautifully furnished, though one would not judge so from the exterior, for the other houses in which I have been are outwardly far more beautiful, but inwardly not equal to this one.'

Like all royal palaces, Whitehall was regularly open to visitors. If the Queen was away, they were liable to be disappointed. 'When she is absent from her Palaces', complained Samuel Kiechel, 'all the fine tapestries are removed, so that nothing but the bare walls are to be seen.' For visitors of distinction, however, the hangings were specially replaced. There are occasional entries in the accounts such as one 'for making ready, by Her Majesty's commandment, of Whitehall for the coming thither of the Count of Emden and his train to see the magnificence of the same'. Von Wedel took advantage of the custom and has left an invaluable account of his visit. 'The Keeper of the Apartments', he writes, 'led us into the Palace and showed us round. First he led us up a straight staircase to a passage which runs alongside the Tiltyard.'

The tiltyard corresponded more or less with the present Horse

Guards, and the passage referred to was evidently the Tiltyard Gallery, 'a sumptuous Gallery', as Stow describes it, 'where the Princes and their nobility used to stand or sit at the windows to behold all the triumphant joustings and other military exercises'.

One of the most memorable had been the occasion of the visit of the Duc de Montmorency in 1559, when the joust was held by torchlight. The Queen had entertained the duke to a banquet in the gardens 'under the long and wide gallery on the ground floor, which was all hung with gold and silver brocade'. The gallery, which was known as the Stone Gallery, was 'closed with wreaths of flowers and leaves of most beautiful design, which gave a very sweet odour and were marvellous to behold'. The Venetian ambassador, Il Schifanoya, who describes the scene, was eloquent in praise of the 'large and excellent joints' with which they were served, but critical that the 'delicacies and cleanliness customary in Italy were wanting.' The whole Court sparkled with jewellery and golden collars, but the very exuberance of their costumes created a problem which was only with difficulty solved, for the ladies 'required so much space on account of the farthingales they wore that there was not room for all; so part of the Privy Chamber ate on the ground on the rushes'. The banquet ended, the Court came out into the upper gallery of the tiltyard, 'so that the said terrace was on all sides beset with Lords, Ladies and persons of quality, sumptuously apparelled and richly furnished; and among them, both above and under, stood many of the Guard in their rich coats, holding an infinite number of torches ... by which means those that beheld the terrace in this sort furnished, deemed it rather a Theatre Celestial than a Palace of earthly building.'

The Court being thus assembled, the Earl of Essex made his entry with twelve gentlemen 'armed at all pieces' – the Earl dressed in silver, his gentlemen all in white. Having saluted the royal party, he took up his stand at the east end of the Court. 'Forthwith entered the Earl of Rutland, with a like number in like sort armed, and apparelled all in blue.' At a signal from the Queen, they closed in combat by torchlight – 'a sight exceeding glorious to those that were below looking upward to the terrace ... as can hardly be seen the like in any Christian Court'.

The same tiltyard had witnessed an occasion of a rather more specifically Christian nature in the previous reign when the rank and file of Wyatt's rebellion were brought before Mary with halters round their necks, 'and between the two tilts the poor prisoners knelt down in the mire, and there the Queen's Grace looked out over the gate and gave them all pardon, and they cried out "God save Queen Mary!"'

The ceiling of the Tiltyard Gallery was ornamented with gold and the walls were hung with pictures. These included a portrait of Moses 'said to be a striking likeness', and Holbein's perspective portrait of Edward VI, which particularly intrigued von Wedel. 'To a person standing before it', he explains, 'it is so ugly and has such a long face and so long a nose, that it scarcely bears any resemblance to a human being.' After he had thus puzzled for a while, he was given by the guide 'a broad tin sheet, three spans long', with a little hole to look through, which revealed the 'fine, well-formed countenance into which the ugly face had been transformed. This really must be regarded', he concludes, 'as a great work of art.'

From the Tiltyard Gallery, the tour of the state apartments continued. In spite of the magnificence of the decorations, much of the interior was clearly in the medieval rather than the Renaissance tradition. 'The lodgements of this *palatio*', complained Gerschow, 'are almost all low and constructed with many recesses after the monkish way of building; the pavement is covered with neatly and tastefully plaited mats, which is a nice habit throughout England.'

Before attempting to follow von Wedel further on his tour of inspection, it will be helpful to form a general idea of the topography of the whole palace, for the confused jumble of buildings sprawled across a total area of twenty-three acres, and it is extremely easy for the imagination to get lost in it. It is best reconstructed in relation to present-day buildings and streets.

The palace spread round three sides of the Privy Garden, a rough square lying between the present Treasury and the river. The boundaries of this garden were to the west 'The Street', running between the corner of Downing Street and Dover House; to the south the Bowling Green, approximately on the site of Richmond Terrace; to the north the Privy Gallery, cutting at right angles across the end of the Banqueting House, and to the east, the Stone Gallery, midway between the Treasury and the Embankment.

To anyone approaching from Westminster, therefore, the buildings would be seen to group themselves into three blocks. To the left, on the site of the Treasury and Downing Street, were Henry VIII's additions – the tennis courts, the cockpit and the two gatehouses which stood at either extremity of The Street. To the right, across the garden, was the Stone Gallery with the Long Gallery above and various lodgings between these and the river. In front was the Privy Gallery, carried over The Street by means of the Holbein Gate; behind this and to the left was the tiltyard, and to the right, the chapel, hall and state apartments. We must now look in more detail at this last part, for it was the focal point of the whole palace.

Fortunately, there is a contemporary sketch by Wyngaerde (Plate 11) which will greatly assist the imagination. The artist has chosen an aerial view – which it would have been impossible to obtain in reality – from the river side. He shows the water gate in some detail, around which were grouped the royal apartments. To the left, the Privy Garden with the great fountain is just indicated, and behind it, the lofty tennis court, adorned with windows and turrets like a college chapel.

To the right of this is the Holbein Gate, and beyond that a polygonal structure which can only have been the cockpit. In fact, from this angle, the cockpit would have appeared behind the tennis court, but Wyngaerde must be excused for certain inaccuracies. It is extremely difficult to work out a bird's-eye perspective of an utterly irregular building.

At the foot of the Holbein Gate can be seen the posts of the tiltyard, and between the tiltyard and the state apartments an unpretentious little gatehouse. To fix these buildings in a modern orientation one has only to superimpose the Banqueting House, which adjoined this little gateway to the left and would have blotted out the Holbein Gate and cockpit from the view.

The little gatehouse gave access to the 'Sermon Court', around which lay the Privy Chamber, the Council Chamber, the Guard Room and the great hall, whose roof and lantern are clearly shown on the right of Wyngaerde's drawing. The chapel would have shown in front and slightly to the right of this.

With this framework in mind, we can now return to von Wedel and his guide and fill in some of the details, beginning with the Privy Garden.

The whole plot was marked out, as it were, by thirty-four high, painted columns surmounted by carved figures of animals 'with their horns gilt', carrying pennants with the Queen's escutcheon. In the centre was a beautiful fountain 'and thereto a large gnomon which shows the hours in thirty different ways'. This intriguing sundial was a bait to tempt the unwary visitor to linger by the fountain. Paul Hentzner describes the trap; at a discreet distance a gardener, operating a wheel, could force up water through a number of small pipes which 'plentifully sprinkles those that are standing around' – a form of practical joking which was beginning to be common in England.

Around the sundial the garden was divided into several 'beautiful pleasant grassy walks', between which 'the plants are artistically set out in various ways, and surrounded by hedges trimmed in the form of seats.' Close by the gardens was an orchard 'beneath whose trees fragrant herbs are planted'.

The Privy Garden was bounded to the north by the Privy Gallery, a timber structure brought bodily from Esher at the time of Wolsey's disgrace and set up at Whitehall as one of the chief communications between the new buildings and the old. 'The taking away thereof before my Lord's face', wrote Cavendish, 'was to him a corrosive, which was invented by his enemies only to torment him.'

Mario Savorgnano, who visited Whitehall in 1531, was especially interested in the numerous galleries, describing them as 'long porticoes or halls, without chambers, with windows on each side looking on gardens or rivers, the ceilings being marvellously wrought in stone and gold, and the wainscot of carved wood representing a thousand beautiful figures; and round about there are chambers and very large halls, all hung with tapestries.'

On the other side of the Privy Gallery was the Sermon Court. Von Wedel describes this as a 'grass plot, surrounded by broad walks below and above, enabling many persons to promenade

HATFIELD   *above:* **THE OLD PALACE**
          below: **THE GATE HOUSE FROM THE OLD LONDON ROAD**

GREENWICH   *above:* GENERAL VIEW FROM THE EAST
              below: THE PALACE FROM THE SOUTH-EAST

there. In the middle of the place a pulpit is erected with a sounding board above. When the Queen commands preaching here, the walks are filled with auditors.' A print in Foxe's *Acts and Monuments* shows Latimer preaching before Edward VI from this pulpit. An immense concourse of people are present – 'four times so many', Howes informs us, 'as could have stood in the King's Chapel'.

It was often an exacting task to preach before Elizabeth. Bishop Aylmer once 'seemed to touch on the vanity of decking the body too finely'. Elizabeth was furious. 'Perchance the Bishop hath never sought Her Majesty's wardrobe,' suggested Harington, 'or he would have chosen another text.' Elizabeth did not lightly tolerate opinions which differed from her own, and if she disagreed with a preacher, she made it known at once. 'To your text, Master Dean! To your text!' she shouted at the unfortunate Dr Nowell, when he departed from his argument to inveigh against images in churches; 'leave that! We have had enough of that! To your subject!' To keep up a sermon for two or three hours under such conditions must have required stamina, and Thomas Platter observed that preachers at St Paul's fortified themselves with a bottle of wine and a loaf of bread within easy reach of the pulpit.

Between the Sermon Court and the river were the Queen's apartments. Elizabeth's bedroom was very dark, noted Gerschow, and had very little air. It had only one window, and the ceiling was entirely gilt. The bed itself was the most striking ornament to the room, being 'ingeniously composed of woods of different colours, with quilts of silk, velvet, gold and silver embroidery'. It was hung with 'Indian work of silk painted on one side'. There was also a table entirely covered with silver and a chair with no actual seat, but built up from the floor with cushions.

Next to this was a 'fine bathroom' for the Queen. Little is known of Elizabeth's personal hygiene, but at Windsor Paul Hentzner noticed 'two bathing rooms ceiled and wainscoted with looking-glass'. Evidently the provision of bathing facilities was normal.

The Queen's rooms had direct access to the river, and this was their greatest charm. There were times when she looked out upon a scene that could have rivalled the Grand Canal at Venice, when

5

the water was glittering with barges. On May Day in the first year of her reign, there was a mock battle between two pinnaces beneath her window, described in Machyn's *Diary*. Only oranges, eggs and squibs were used as ammunition, but things did not go according to plan, for a squib, falling into some gunpowder, 'set divers persons on fire', and one of the pinnaces capsized. 'But thanked be God', concludes Machyn, 'there was but one man drowned.'

Other aquatic occasions were more private and peaceful; on summer evenings, the Queen often sought the cool of the river in her barge, and the Thames at Whitehall became the rendezvous of the elite. In June of the same year, Baron Breuner, emissary of the Archduke Charles, took a boat on the Thames after supper to refresh his spirits. 'The Queen came there too,' he writes, 'recognized and summoned me. She spoke a long while with me, and invited me to leave my boat and take a seat in that of the Treasurer. She then had her boat laid alongside and played the lute.'

Of all the decorations in the palace, that of the Privy Chamber was the most remarkable, owing to 'that rare piece of Henry VIII ... done on the walls' by Holbein. This magnificent mural was painted in 1537 and occupied the entire wall of one end of the room. 'It has all the grandeur of style,' writes Roger Fry, 'all the lucidity and ease of arrangement of the greatest monumental design of Italy, together with a particularity and minuteness which would seem incompatible with those greater qualities of style had they not been thus wonderfully united.'

The same combination of bold forms and abundant detail was observable in the background. 'The scenery', wrote Carel van Mander, 'depicts a stately hall of variegated marble with richly embellished piers, niches and bold cornices, open at the top so that the blue sky shines in.' Against this backcloth of ornate Renaissance architecture, the house of Tudor was portrayed. To the right stood Elizabeth of York and Jane Seymour, to the left the two Henrys, grouped around the fire-place which formed the centre-piece to the mural.

Dominating the whole room was the figure of Henry VIII himself, standing in an attitude of aggressive self-assurance, his majesty and his manhood at once displayed in the gorgeous extravagance of his costume and in the robust virility of his capacious codpiece. 'The King as he stood there, majestic in his splendour, was so lifelike that the spectator felt abashed, annihilated in his presence.'

Holbein also gave his name to the gatehouse linking the Privy Gallery with the tiltyard. It is possible that he may have lived in it while he was working at Whitehall, but it is very unlikely that he designed it.

The two gatehouses added by Henry VIII (Plate 11) formed an odd contrast, and fortunately their appearance is accurately known. King Street Gate was an unhappy blend of Tudor and Italianate architecture. The tall cylinders of the towers, needlessly intersected by protruding cornices and pointlessly adorned with busts; the large mullion and transom windows cramped unnaturally into a framework of pilasters and entablature, and the squat, square aperture which served for a central archway showed that the ideas from Italy had been imperfectly understood and improperly applied. The classical style imposes rules which may not be broken. To indulge it without solecism required scholarship; to marry it with Tudor demanded considerable aesthetic imagination. The designer of King Street Gate appears to have been possessed of neither.

A very different building was Holbein Gate. By a happy contrast it was free, in all but a few trivial details, from the influence of Italy. In outline and modelling, it could hardly have been improved. The tall, clean-cut towers, the crenellated gables and projecting, embattled oriel gave it all the dignity and poise of a Tudor gatehouse. Near to, it had a richness of texture and moulding obtained by the chequered squares of brick and stone, the niches and roundels beneath the turret windows, and the four circular medallions which adorned the flat surfaces of the gable walls.

Besides these two gatehouses, the only features of any architectural merit were the hall and the chapel, but little is known of their appearance. The hall was clearly inadequate for the needs of a royal palace, for Elizabeth was obliged to supplement it with a temporary structure which was little more than a marquee but on a monumental scale.

In March 1581, Holinshed records, 'a Banqueting House was

begun ... on the south side of Her Majesty's Palace of Whitehall.'
It was three hundred and thirty-two feet in perimeter supported by
thirty 'great masts', each of them forty feet high. The walls were
only of canvas, painted on the outside 'with a work called rustic,
much like unto stone'. Around the walls, festooned with holly, ivy
and 'strange flowers garnished with spangles of gold', were ten
tiers of seats for spectators, and somehow or other the ingenious
deviser had fitted in two hundred and ninety windows. From the
ceiling 'most cunningly painted with suns and clouds and stars,
hung pendants of wicker work flounced about with all manner of
exotic fruit spangled with gold and most richly hung'. Von Wedel
very much admired this 'lofty, spacious house' with its elaborate
floral decoration. 'Up above in the bushes or the leafy trees', he
noted, 'there are many birds which sing magnificently.'

The whole building took twenty-four days to build and cost
£1,745. Three hundred and seventy-five men were employed on its
construction, two of whom, Holinshed informs us, 'had mischances;
one broke his leg, and so did the other'.

Elizabeth's Banqueting House was typical of the temporary extensions which the vast numbers at Court were continually necessi-
tating. This one, however, gradually became a permanent feature
of Whitehall. 'This house was builded very slightly,' noted Howes,
'and with much propping up it stood until the fourth year of King
James.' It was replaced immediately by another 'strongly builded
with brick and stone' whose destruction by fire later provided
Inigo Jones with the opportunity to give Whitehall Palace its most
important architectural feature.

Before the Banqueting House was built, plays and masques were
usually presented in the great chamber or in the hall. The seasons
most usually marked by this form of entertainment were Shrovetide and Candlemas, and, as usual, the accounts give a picture
of the problems of mounting a dramatic performance in a Tudor
palace.

At Candlemas in 1578 three plays were presented, *The Knight of
the Burning Rock*, *The History of Loyalty and Beauty* and *The History of
Murderous Michael*. The burning rock, an elaborate and realistic
scenic effect, was made at Bridewell, and a certain John Rose went

to great pains to see the job through. Payments are recorded to him for boat hire 'to the Court, to take the measure of the bigness of the rock, and back again'; sixpence had to be paid to the porter 'for late coming out the gate'; carriage had to be paid for bringing the rock from Bridewell to Whitehall, and workmen 'for making ready and setting up the frames, rocks and lights in the hall against Shrovesunday'. The burning had to be achieved somehow, and we read of 'aquavite to burn in the same rock' and 'rosewater to allay the smell thereof'. Finally there was trouble over one of the accessories, and payment had to be made for 'a hoop and blue linen to mend the cloud that was borrowed'.

The new year 1601 saw a more important theatrical occasion at Whitehall. During the previous December, Elizabeth had learnt that she was to be visited by Don Virginio Orsino, Duke of Bracciano. His visit would coincide with that of Grigori Ivanovitch Mikulin, ambassador from the Tsar, Boris Godunov. This was a great occasion, and Elizabeth was clearly out to impress. Whitehall was to be decked with all its most gaudy finery, and a memorandum was drawn up for Lord Hunsdon 'to give orders for the furnishing of four chambers very well and richly, and making clean the glass windows to give good light'. In the Council Chamber a 'carpet' was to be provided 'to cover the table that the oldness of the board be not seen'; the gentlemen of the Court were to be warned 'to be apparelled in the best sort they can'. Hunsdon was to speak to Sir William Knollys that 'the banquet be of better stuff, fit for men to eat and not of paper shows'; he was to appoint suitable music and to see that Robert Hales had occasion 'to show his own voice'; the Children of the Chapel were 'to come before the Queen at dinner with a Carol'. Most significant of all, Hunsdon was to make choice of a play 'that shall be best furnished with rich apparel, have great variety and change of music and dances, and of a subject that may be most pleasing to Her Majesty'. The play written for the occasion was *Twelfth Night*.

On January 6th, the Feast of the Epiphany, Mikulin was brought to Whitehall, and Elizabeth first bade him to the chapel to 'witness how in our religion we pray to God, and how in our country the Communion service is sung'. He noted the liturgical details of the ceremony; the Table covered with a damask cloth; the two un-lighted candles; the two books covered with gold 'which they call the Apostles [Epistles] and the Gospel'. The priests wore golden copes and the sub-deacons white surplices; the Queen made a symbolic offering of gold and frankincense and myrrh.

Orsino, who scandalized many Papists by attending the same service, has left some vivid details of the occasion – the massed officers of the Court 'all dressed in white – as was the whole court that day – but with so much gold and jewels that it was a marvellous thing'; the Queen, likewise in white, was so loaded with jewels that he was 'amazed how she could carry them'; the walls hung with golden tapestry and the cupboards charged with plate deeply im-pressed him – 'nor do I believe', he added, 'that I shall ever see a Court which, for order, surpasses this one.'

Unfortunately Orsino was writing to his wife and he saved his most graphic descriptions for when he should return. 'The Muscovy Ambassador (of whose ridiculous manners I shall give an account)' remains unridiculed; Elizabeth's Enchanted Palaces 'of which I shall tell you many things by word of mouth', are undescribed; and the première of *Twelfth Night* – 'and this too I am keeping to tell you' – is dismissed as a mingled comedy during which he stood next to Elizabeth, who continually conversed with him.

Elizabeth's patronage of theatricals and the elaborate ceremonial of the royal chapel aroused the fierce opposition of Puritans. In 1569 a savage little pamphlet entitled 'The Children of the Chapel Stripped and Whipped' put their case to the public. 'Plays will never be suppressed while Her Majesty's unfledged minions flaunt it in silks and satins ... they had as well be at their Popish services in the Devil's garments.' The advances of the Puritans annoyed Elizabeth, but the temper of the country was largely with them. Even statesmen such as Burghley were so preoccupied with the menace of Rome that they tended to underestimate the growing danger of the opposite extreme.

In the end, as is well known, it was the Papists who proved loyal to the monarchy and the Puritans who did away with it. Under Charles I the arts of peace had flourished as never before, 'but now Bellona thundered, and as a clear day is sometimes overstretched by a dismal cloud ... so was this serene peace by the Civil Wars'. Whitehall was destined to become the scene of the final tragedy.

During the war there appeared a pamphlet entitled 'A deep sigh breath'd through the Lodgings at White-Hall'. It shows the very picture of emptiness and desolation. No more was the rumble of coaches heard before the Court gates; the palace lay 'in a dumb silence ... as if it were the decayed buildings of ruined Troy'. The state rooms were deserted and stripped of their costly hangings; 'you may walk into the Presence Chamber with your hat, spurs and sword on, and if you will presume to be so unmannerly, you may sit down in the chair of state.' Across the street in the cockpit and revelling rooms dangled the pulleys and engines which had hoisted Inigo Jones's scenery, and, 'where at a play or a masque the darkest night was converted into the brightest day ... by the lustre of torches', you could wander freely and without a ticket.

Gone were the lewd crowds who had thronged the gates 'to ravish themselves with the sight of ladies' handsome legs and insteps as they took coach'; gone was the press about the wine-cellar door where beer and brandy had been dispensed to the household. In the great hall there were 'no strong smells out of the Kitchens to delight your nostrils', no 'greasy scullions to be seen head and ears in a kettle full of kidneys'. Nothing was left but bare walls and a cold hearth and 'the great Black Jacks set under the table, all full of cobwebs'.

A more official document, the House of Commons *Journal*, tells of the systematic wrecking of the decorations of the chapel. A committee was called to take resolutions 'for the demolishing of superstitious pictures at Whitehall', and in due course payments were made for two hundred and forty-one feet of white glass to replace the east window, and for 'colouring boards from which the carpenter had planed off the pictures'. At least two of these pictures were by Holbein.

It was this hatred of 'superstition' which placed Puritanism among the most formidable of the forces which combined to destroy the England of the Tudors, making the Civil War one of the Great Divides in English history. For superstition was held to cover not only such aspects of folklore as were perhaps more picturesque than profitable, but almost all the visual aids of medieval religion. One might not regret, with Aubrey, that 'the Divine art of printing and gunpowder have frighted away Robin Goodfellow and the Fairies'; one can be indifferent that shepherds, formerly dressed after the manner of Roman or Arcadian shepherds, should have grown 'so luxurious as to neglect their ancient, warm and useful fashion, and go à la mode'. These things must come and go. But the obliteration of priceless and irreplaceable works of art, in which the memory of a bygone age could have lived on, was another matter, and it is one of the ironies of history that the greatest destruction was wrought under one who styled himself 'Protector'.

Oliver Cromwell was less extreme in his views than many of his followers, and the survival of Whitehall and Hampton Court is probably due to the fact that he reserved them for his own use. At Whitehall, Dugdale informs us, the marriage of his daughter, Frances, was celebrated 'with much mirth and frolics, besides mixed dancing – a thing heretofore accounted profane'.

But the palace survived the Civil War only to fall a victim to the ravages of fire. In 1666, there was an outbreak in the Horse Guards, witnessed and graphically described by Pepys. He was dining in Dr Pierce's chambers when the news reached them – 'and so we run up to the garret, and find it so; a horrid great fire; and by and by we saw and heard part of it blown up with gunpowder.' As the news spread, panic seized the whole neighbourhood. 'The whole town is in an alarm ... drums beat, and trumpets, the King's Horse Guards everywhere spread running up and down the street.' Their efforts were on this occasion successful; 'by and by comes the news that the fire has slackened and so then we were a little cheered up, and to supper and pretty merry.'

In April 1691 was a more serious outbreak. 'This night', wrote Evelyn in his diary, 'a sudden and terrible fire burnt down all the buildings over the Stone Gallery at Whitehall to the waterside, beginning with the apartment of the late Duchess of Portsmouth (which had been pulled down and rebuilt no less than three times to please her) and consumed other lodgings of such lewd creatures, who debauched King Charles and others, and were his destruction.'

It burned violently for several hours, and gunpowder was again used to break the path of the flames.

Finally, in January 1698, almost the whole of the rest of the palace was consumed in one terrible conflagration. It all started with a Dutch woman, 'having a sudden occasion to dry some linen in an upper room' in Colonel Stanley's apartment. The linen took fire from the charcoal, and in a moment the building was ablaze. Despite the vigorous use of water and gunpowder 'it still increased with great fury and violence all night', so that by the morning all the main buildings between the Banqueting House and the river – all that remained of Wolsey's palace, Elizabeth's apartments and the beautiful Carolean additions, together with 'about one hundred and fifty houses, most of which were lodgings and habitations of the chief of the nobility' – had been reduced to rubble and ashes.

IV

RICHMOND

THE Queen's barge, when not in use, lay up on the south bank of the river near Paris Garden and was shown to visitors. 'It has two splendid cabins', wrote Paul Hentzner, 'beautifully ornamented with glass windows, painting and gilding.'

For Elizabeth, this was by far the pleasantest means of travel. Flowers were strewn upon the floor when she rode in it, reclining upon a cushion of cloth of gold with a crimson velvet rug about her feet. Twenty-one lusty watermen ensured that it was as swift as it was comfortable, and as the gilt prow parted the stream, she could enjoy at her ease the sweet prospect of the land she ruled. Perhaps, in all her progresses, there was no more enjoyable journey than by river to Richmond.

One can imagine the barge setting off from Whitehall Stairs, attended by a great concourse of swans, for immense numbers of these birds frequented the river, wandering up and down, so Hentzner tells us, 'in great security, nobody daring to molest, much less kill, any of them, under penalty of a considerable fine'. They owed their security to their feathers, which were plucked annually for the repairing of the upholstery in the royal household. In a few moments, the great unfinished-looking mass of Westminster Abbey and the high roofs of the palace and Parliament buildings had passed into the background; beyond was the country, and the barge made its way through scenes of rural beauty now long since banished to the upper reaches of the Thames. It was a land of rich meadows and silent backwaters, green and deserted, save where a heron, rising in lazy flight, or the blue flash of a kingfisher brought momentary animation to the scene. And so the delightful panorama of the Thames valley passed before the windows of the royal cabin, until the square towers of Syon House rose before it and cut their

74

crenellated outline against the sky. Here, where the river swings off to the left and the stream is divided by the narrow strip of Isleworth Eyot, the palace of Richmond (Plate 13) first came into sight, a cluster of slender towers and cupolas, better suited to command the prospect than to intimidate the countryside.

It is possible to recapture the appearance of this magnificent building only by linking it with something in one's own experience – the unforgettable first glimpse of Burghley House, or the more familiar view of Eton, whose happy blend of brick and stone makes it today the closest parallel we have to Richmond.

Along the riverside immediately before the palace lay the great orchard 'all planted with cherry trees and other fruits to the number of two hundred and twenty-three trees'. As with so many Tudor palaces, the towers and pinnacles of Richmond could be seen in springtime rising like some fairy castle out of a cloud of blossom. In the orchard was a large aviary called the 'Turtle Cage', and at the same season the air was filled with the voice of doves.

Behind the orchard a confused parcel of buildings, constructed mostly of brick and timber, grouped itself loosely around the tall conical roof of the livery kitchen. Here, under the shadow of the great hall, were flesh larders and fish larders, pastry and plummery, poultry house and scalding house, the woodyard, the coal house, and, at a discreet distance, 'a large House of office'.

The problem of sanitation was undoubtedly one of the reasons why the larger palaces clung to the waterside – a custom which not unnaturally rendered the rivers extremely unsavoury and made it imperative to get drinking water from uncontaminated sources. At Richmond, the cistern house, adjoining the livery kitchen, was supplied by two lines – one, known as the 'White Conduit', tapping the springs in New Park, the other, the 'Red Conduit', those in Richmond Town Fields. The water thus obtained served both for use and for ornament. In the inner quadrangle of the palace, overlooked by the tall lights of the hall and the chapel, stood a very large fountain, an elaborate piece of ornamental statuary which also served a utilitarian purpose. 'In the upper part', runs a contemporary description, 'there are lions and red dragons and other goodly beasts, and in the midst certain branches of red roses, out of which flowers and roses is evermore running and course of clear and most purest water into the cistern beneath. This conduit profitably serves the chambers with water for the hands, and all other offices as they need to resort.'

It is perhaps a little unexpected to find water laid on as early as 1498. It bears witness to the singular thoroughness and thoughtfulness with which this palace was conceived and built. This is the special interest of Richmond. Unlike Greenwich, Whitehall, Hampton Court or Newhall, which were built piecemeal by a succession of owners, Richmond was planned and constructed as a whole; it is, therefore, more closely linked than the others with the character of its founder, King Henry VII.

'He was a Prince', Sir Francis Bacon informs us, 'sad, serious and full of thoughts.' In figure comely, tall but slightly built; in countenance 'reverend, and a little like a Churchman', he showed in his undoubted piety the only steady ray that illuminated an otherwise deliberately inscrutable nature. While he was liberal in his endowment of religious foundations, 'yet he was a great almsgiver in secret, which showed that his works in public were dedicated to God's glory rather than his own'.

For Henry was in all things dispassionate. His sudden rise to power he took 'with such moderation and untransported discretion as it well appeared he had thoroughly conquered himself before he subdued the usurper his enemy'. None were admitted to his confidence or affection, and if any were seen frequently to consort with him, 'it was but as the instrument is much with the workman.' He was by nature covetous and his treasury was always full, yet 'he never spared charge which his affairs required, and in his building he was magnificent.'

No one who was privileged to see his palace could have doubted that. And yet it is probable that his interest in architecture was no deeper than the pleasure he took in the revels of his Court, at which he would 'come, and look a little upon them, and turn away'. It was the convention of Courts that their entertainments should be lavish and spectacular; he saw to it that they had their revels. His vast number of retainers required to be decently lodged; he built them a palace that covered ten acres of land. His royal rank demanded an imposing and opulent house; he built the Privy Lodgings with a magnificence 'much superior to anything that hath been seen here before'.

But, as with his religious foundations, Bacon assures us that his motives were disinterested. 'He had nothing in him of vainglory, but yet kept state and majesty to the height, being sensible that majesty maketh people bow, but vainglory boweth them.' It is, therefore, for state and majesty, rather than for vainglory and ostentation, that we must look in the house to which he gave his name.

It was from the north, from Richmond Green, that the most distinctive view of the palace (Plate 12) was to be obtained. The green itself, twenty acres of well-turfed and level land, planted with elms that formed 'a very handsome walk' on either side, opened the prospect to its best advantage. The length of the building lay upon the breadth of the green, and behind its curtain wall the palace spread a network of lodgings and courts and gardens and galleries over the entire plot contained today between Maids of Honour Row and the Thames.

This vast expanse, in all an area of just over ten acres, was partly taken up by gardens and base-courts surrounded by low brick buildings, turreted and embattled, above which the stone façades of the palace proper rose superbly – 'a splendid and magnificent house', as Aubrey called it, 'and after the most exquisite way of architecture of that age'. The rough, unfinished sketches of Wyngaerde (Plate 14) must be interpreted in the light of our own experience of the soaring elegance and fretted decorations of the perpendicular style. We must supply Richmond with the huge windows and elaborate fan vaulting of King's College and Christ Church.

Externally, the splendour and magnificence were chiefly concentrated upon the skyline, the prodigious number of towers, capped with their bulbous onion domes, making the most imposing show – 'and upon each of them a vane of the King's arms painted and gilt with rich gold and azure'. Nor did these ornaments merely crowd upon the eye, but in a high wind they became, as it were, the strings of an Aeolian harp and made strange music in the ear, which moved a contemporary writer to record his astonishment – 'as well the pleasant sight of them, as the hearing in a windy day was right marvellous to know and understand'. It was a medieval touch, for Chaucer had noticed the same effect:

> Alofte the toweres, and golden fanes goode
> Did with the wynde make full swete armony.

The first *coup d'oeil*, as with so many Tudor houses, created an impression of magnificent confusion. In fact, Richmond was the most orderly and most logical of buildings, and both in its plan and elevations was the perfect expression of the Tudor conception of a community household.

The symmetry of the building was based on the fact that the household assembled in force for only two purposes – to worship and to eat. This made the chapel and the hall the two largest units in the design, and at Richmond they stood, like stately twins, to east and west of the middle court. They were not, however, allowed in a palace the pride of place accorded them in a college. They projected forwards as the semi-detached wings of the royal lodgings, a three-storeyed structure cast round a single court and built throughout of the same freestone which distinguished these princely quarters from the homely brick and timber of which the inferior offices were constructed. This stone quadrangle contained the Privy Lodgings and galleries and was set about with fourteen towers 'which very much adorn and set forth the whole fabric and are a very graceful ornament to the whole house'.

There were thus two quite distinct architectural units at Richmond – an ornate perpendicular palace of stone, for the Royal Family, to which the chapel and hall were appended, and a simple but charming series of brick quadrangles for the household and offices.

A vivid picture of the domestic side of the palace is painted by Pedro Enriquez, who accompanied Philip II here on his nuptial visit to England. The unpopularity of the Spanish marriage had been brought home quickly and forcefully to the unfortunate hidalgos, who were robbed, insulted and assaulted on every side. Not unnaturally they formed an extremely unfavourable opinion of the English, but this in no way blinded their eyes to the beauties of England, and their most vituperative passages are often punctuated with praises of the landscape and buildings. 'We are in a pleasant land', complained Enriquez, 'but amongst the worst people in the world.'

Arrived at Richmond, his first impression was of the chaos caused by so great a concourse of retainers. 'Each officer', he noted, 'has a cook to look after his food in the Queen's Kitchens. There are eighteen kitchens, and there is such a hurly-burly in them that each one is a veritable hell. So that notwithstanding the greatness of these palaces – and the smallest of the four we have been in has more rooms and better than the Alcazar of Madrid – the crowds in them are so great as to be hardly contained.' Eighteen kitchens may seem a surprising number, even with so many mouths to feed, but Enriquez goes on to elaborate the detail of their prodigious output: 'The ordinary consumption of the Palace every day is from eighty to a hundred sheep, with a dozen fat oxen and a dozen and half of calves, besides vast quantities of game, poultry, venison, wild boar and rabbits, whilst in beer they drink more in summer than the river would hold at Valladolid.'

The numbers present on this occasion were clearly exceptional, but the normal establishment was very great. For Henry VII had been as pleased to surround himself with a small army of retainers as he was determined that his subjects should not, and wherever the person of the King was lodged, there would be also found the Cup-bearer, the Carver, the Sewer, the Grooms of the Privy Chamber, Spicery and Chandlery, the Confectioner, the Housekeeper, the Porter, the Chaplains and the Gentlemen of the Bedchamber – to mention only a few.

It was to house these when the King lay at Richmond that the outer quadrangle or wardrobe court was built, 'containing very many good rooms and lodgings both on the first and second storey'. This court, a plain but pleasing structure of homely brick, lay between the Privy Lodgings and the outer gate, and insulated the royal family from the world outside. In this respect, Henry was a prince of the Renaissance – instead of appearing before his subjects in the secure eminence of military superiority, he paraded the

gorgeous paraphernalia of royalty to isolate and elevate his person
above their level. For this reason, Richmond was a palace and not a
castle. Nevertheless, the outer gate – the only fragment of the
building to survive today – was equipped with strong gates 'of
double timber and heart of oak sticked full of nails right thick, and
crossed with bars of iron'. Tudor builders could never get right
away from the idea that some day their palaces might have to become strongholds – and events were to prove their misgivings to
be amply justified.

As in a college, the outer gate was kept by a porter and closed at
night, but, unlike college porters, he could be squared: there is
occasional mention of payments 'for late coming out the gate'. For
a large household had to be ruled with a firm hand, and the Tudors,
in their wisdom, saw that one of the central issues was the question
of feeding in. Having provided the Court with a great hall to eat in,
they found it necessary to forbid members to eat elsewhere.

In the Ordinances of Eltham, a set of household regulations
issued in 1526, Henry VIII complains of falling off in the standards
of attendance at Court 'by reason of their seldom keeping of the
King's Hall'. This not only led to ignorance and negligence of the
duties of the various officers, 'but also the household servants, put
to board wages, give themselves many times to idleness, evil rule
and conversation'. The remedy was sought in a reaffirmation of the
corporate life of the community. 'The King's pleasure, therefore, is,
that at all times when His Highness doth lie in his Castle of Windsor, his Manors of Beaulieu [Newhall], Richmond and Hampton
Court, Greenwich, Eltham and Woodstock, his Hall shall be ordinarily kept and continued.' Further, the solidarity of the household
was to be set upon spiritual foundations: 'at all such times of keeping the said Hall, the King's noble Chapel to be kept in the same
place.'

The hall and chapel thus played a significant role in keeping together the household and thereby maintaining the royal estate of
the sovereign. Appropriately, they were built with the utmost
magnificence and reflected in their mural decorations the glorifica-
tion of monarchy to which they were dedicated.

Between the windows of the hall were painted the kings of

GREENWICH   THE PALACE FROM THE SOUTH

GREENWICH   THE PA   CE FROM THE NORTH

England renowned in battle. Hengist, William the Conqueror, Richard I, and among them Henry himself, the victor of Bosworth, were depicted, all 'appearing like bold and valliant knights'. In the chapel were the figures of Edward the Confessor, Edmund and Cadwallader and other kings 'whose life and virtue was so abundant that it hath pleased Almighty God to show by them divers and many miracles, and to be reckoned as Saints'. Henry had the modesty not to include himself in this number.

The hall was a vast chamber, a hundred feet long by forty wide, with the traditional screens and gallery at the lower end, and the old arrangement of a charcoal fire placed in the centre, which necessitated a louvre or lantern above to let the smoke out. But the timbered ceiling was not, as in former days, 'beamed or braced', but was made up, like that of Henry VII's Chapel at Westminster, of hanging pendants and 'proper knots craftily carved ... after the most new invention'. Below the windows the walls were adorned with statues, and between the statues hung tapestries and cloth of arras so richly woven 'that this whole apartment was most glorious and joyful to behold'.

Across the middle court, and closely reflecting the architecture of the hall, was the chapel, a 'fair and large structure, covered with lead and battled'. The walls of the chapel were hung with cloth of gold and 'the altars set with many relics, jewels and full rich plate'. In the body of the church were 'handsome Cathedral pews, a removable pulpit, and a fair case of carved work for a pair of organs'.

Here, as everywhere, the music of the Chapel Royal had to be heard to be believed. Niccolo Sagudino, accompanying the ambassador Giustiniani on a mission to Henry VIII in 1515, was invited by the King to Mass, which was sung by choristers 'whose voices were more divine than human – and as to the counter-bass voices they probably have not their equals in the world'.

Henry had given the ambassadors a typical reception. They had come by barge from London and were first conducted to the great hall, where they were refreshed with bread and wine, and thence through the state apartments, lined with the King's Guard ('By my Faith,' exclaimed Sagudino, 'I never saw finer fellows!'). The King,

6

dressed in his Garter Robes and leaning elegantly against a gilt chair, was awaiting them in the Privy Chamber. 'Immediately on perceiving the ambassadors, His Majesty moved towards them and, after allowing his hands to be kissed, embraced them with the greatest possible demonstration of love and good will.' Gratified with this warm and friendly reception and impressed by the magnificence of all that he saw, Sagudino noted with evident satisfaction, 'I am very glad to have come on this mission.'

It is not possible to form more than a general picture of the state rooms in which these royal receptions took place, but, before entering the labyrinth of the Privy Lodgings, it is necessary to get the whole layout clearly in mind.

A bird's-eye view of the Moses Glover Estate map of Syon, although extremely crude, was evidently drawn by one who knew his way around Richmond. It shows clearly the main block with its girdle of towers, a three-storey building containing twelve rooms on each floor. These were cast round a small court, twenty-four by forty feet, 'which renders all the rooms which lie inwards to be very light and pleasant'. From this, the hall and chapel projected northwards, embracing another court, the middle court, in which the fountain stood. This court was closed to the north by the middle gate building, a much lower structure than the rest, devoted mainly to a small gatehouse and to the lodgings of the Lord Chamberlain.

The normal entrance to the palace was by this middle gate and thence, by a broad flight of stairs, up into the hall. The visitor was now level with the first floor of the Privy Lodgings, and passed through the lobby, Guard Room and Presence Chamber to the Privy Closet adjoining the chapel.

Next to this room, and 'opening by a fair window into the Chapel', were the royal closets in which the King and Queen attended divine service. They were 'richly hanged with silk and traverse, carpet and cushions for his noble Grace'.

A singular convenience at Richmond was the provision of covered communications, whereby members of the household could pass from one side of the building to the other without having to cross the courtyard. 'From the Chapel and Closets extended goodly passages and galleries, paved, glazed and painted, beset with badges of gold, as roses, portcullisses and such other.'

By means of these passages one gained access to the Privy Chamber, the King's bedchamber and the withdrawing room 'hanged with rich and costly cloth of Arras, ceiled, whitelimed and checkered ... with their goodly bay windows glazed and set out'.

The windows of the royal apartments looked out to the east over the Privy Gardens and orchard, 'kept and nourished with much diligence and labour'. They were bounded to the north by the tennis court, and to the east and south by an open loggia, built of brick and timber, two hundred yards in length. The orientation of these loggias enabled those walking in the gardens to enjoy the shade in the heat of the day and to catch the sun during the cool of the evening.

Although winters were certainly more severe, there seems to have been little change in the climate of England during the centuries. Fynes Moryson describes it as 'temperate, but thick, cloudy and misty ... for the sun draweth up the vapours of the sea which compasseth the Island, and distils them upon the earth in frequent showers of rain.' Henry VII judiciously provided for the vicissitudes of the weather and built above the loggias a closed gallery which was praised by the Commonwealth Commissioners as 'very pleasant and useful to the whole house'.

The gardens at Richmond appear to have been particularly well stocked for, during the latter years of Henry VIII, when the palace was occupied by Anne of Cleves, there is continual mention in the accounts of the carriage of fruit from here to Hampton Court. Peaches and pears, apples, filberts and damsons, salad herbs, flowers and rose-water were in constant demand, and payments for their carriage duly noted down.

They give an occasional insight, these rather forbidding accounts, into the life of the royal manor of Richmond. Presents of all kinds were for ever arriving from far and near, which meant a tip to the carrier and the sum entered in the registers. Rare animals from foreign parts figure side by side with homely gifts of apples from near neighbours, but fetched, of course, a proportionately higher gratuity.

A parrot was apparently more highly esteemed than the King of Beasts, for Richard Dekone gets £6.13.4 for a popinjay, while 'one that brought the King a lion' received only two pounds for his pains. A leopard, however, earned its carrier £13.6.8. The discovery of new continents brought a new harvest of gifts, and a present of 'wild cats and popinjays from the New Found Island' earned thirteen shillings and fourpence. From nearer home, Lady Neville's servant receives ten shillings for the carriage of a seal. This would have been for the table, for seals and porpoises often figured on the bill of fare, and were regarded as legitimate diet for Fridays and other fasts. The Archbishop of Canterbury's servant gets two shillings for a Llanthony cheese, and the Abbess of Syon the same sum for a delivery of rabbits and quails, while 'a poor woman who brought a present of apples from Hounslow to the Queen at Richmond' received one shilling and eightpence.

But perhaps the most frequent and revealing entries are those which tell of the constant use of the Thames waterway. 'To Louis Walter, bargeman, for conveying the Queen's Grace from Richmond to Greenwich ... in her barge with twenty-one rowers, every rower taking eightpence ... fourteen shillings.' The negotiation of London Bridge qualified the crew for additional 'danger money', as is implied by the entry 'the reward of a barge beneath the bridge, one shilling and fourpence'. The return journey was made for the same fare with 'a great boat the same day for conveying the ladies and gentlemen from Greenwich, with nine rowers at eightpence the rower'. Only occasionally did the waterway fail them, and we find, in 1578, entries for the hire of horses, 'the frost being so great that no boat could go and come back again'.

At Richmond Elizabeth spent much of her time, especially in winter. Perhaps the efficiency of her grandfather had made it warmer than the other palaces. The occasional glimpses of her life here are typical, showing her gracious and condescending before the public, gay and amicable before the Court and inclined to melancholy if left alone.

Thomas Platter saw her emerge from the Presence Chamber followed by all her lords, councillors, body-guard and retinue: 'As she looked down from a window in the Gallery on her people in the courtyard, they all knelt and she spoke to them in English, "God bless my people", and they all cried in unison "God save the Queen", and they remained kneeling until she made them a sign with her hand to rise, which they did with the greatest possible reverence.'

Having accompanied the Queen to divine service in the chapel, Platter and his friends made use of the tennis court. It is strange to notice the freedom which visitors to the royal palaces were allowed. Platter himself usually tried out the organ in any royal chapel he was shown, and became almost off-hand in his manner. 'They invited us to lunch at Court,' he writes of Richmond, 'but as we were afraid we should be kept too long ... we made our excuses and took our lunch in the village at an inn.'

After the death of Elizabeth, Richmond became for a time the private residence of Henry Frederick, Prince of Wales. A charming little sketch of him, done by Isaac Oliver, is now in the possession of the Duke of Buccleuch. It is a pale, grave little face that peeps out from the deep folds of a ruff, and we can appreciate the French ambassador's remark that 'none of his pleasures savour the least of a child.' His whole delight was in manly exercise, 'tossing the pike, or leaping or shooting with the bow', and he would display his accomplishments before visitors to his father's Court, thereby 'filling their hearts with love, and all their senses with delight'. He won the affection of Londoners also, and during his short life he was the centre of much colourful pageantry. When he removed from Richmond to Whitehall, the Thames was as gay as it had been in the days of Elizabeth.

On one occasion – it was the last day of May in 1610 – the citizens of London turned out in force in their barges to welcome him. The vast concourse of boats 'with their streamers and ensigns gloriously displayed' was supplemented by a monster whale and dolphin, each ridden by Tritons, to represent the Prince's two territories of Wales and Cornwall. The arrival of the Lord Mayor was the signal for the departure, and 'on they rowed with such a cheerful noise of harmony ... as made the beholders not meanly delighted.'

The colourful flotilla made its way as far as Chelsea, where it remained 'hovering on the water' until the Prince's barge appeared, and so accompanied him to Whitehall with great acclamations. At

Whitehall Stairs a final loyal address was given, and the company dismissed with these words: 'Home again then, fair fleet; you have brought a Royal freight to landing, and such a burden as hath made the river not meanly proud to bear. And since we needs must part, in our loudest voice of drums, trumpets and ordinance, be this our last accent. Long live our Prince of Wales, the Royal Henry!'

Alas, he had not two more years to live. Sir Charles Cornwallis, Treasurer of the Prince's household, who seems to have loved the boy as if he had been his own son, and followed his life to its tragic conclusion, has left the story of his untimely end.

It appears that 'the continual violence of his exercise or some settled melancholy' had long been undermining his health, and though he would make no change in his routine, 'yet did he grow more pale and thin from day to day ... so that sundry did speak suspiciously of his looks'. Then one day in October ('O Death, was there no remedy?') he was taken with a sudden sickness and faintness of heart, and for twelve days lingered, racked by convulsions pitiful to behold, and on the twelfth day 'quietly, gently and patiently yielded up his soul'.

The King, unable to bear the spectacle of such suffering, had retired to Theobalds 'more dead than alive' to await the inevitable news.

With the death of Prince Henry, the great days of Richmond were gone for ever, James and Charles making Theobalds their favourite seat and neglecting the palaces of their predecessors. The Commonwealth saw fit to destroy the house, but not before causing a detailed survey and description to be made. The process of demolition was stopped by the Restoration, but it was already almost complete. The great stone palace had gone, together with most of its offices; only the outer gateway remained of what had been the largest and most magnificent of Tudor palaces.

V

HAMPTON COURT

AT THE same time that Henry VIII acquired Whitehall from the See of York in 1529, he took over Wolsey's private residence of Hampton Court, thus obtaining for the Crown what were to be the two principal seats of the Tudors and Stuarts. But whereas Whitehall could be dismissed as 'a low, wretched building, only two stories high ... all built of brick without any curiosity or art of architecture', Hampton Court has always been, both in the nobility of its structure and in the magnificence of its decoration, the most beautiful residence of the English Royal Family.

Even in the latter part of the seventeenth century, when the term 'Gothic' was being introduced to express contempt for buildings not in the classical style, Hampton Court still continued to exact the respect and admiration of connoisseurs. The Italian Count Magalotti conceded that 'although the more elegant orders of architecture are not to be found in it, so as to make it a regular structure according to the rules of art, yet it is on the whole a beautiful object to the eye.' His visit to England was a considerable education to him, and the enlargement of his taste is shown in the unfeigned enthusiasm with which he describes Newhall, Hampton Court and Audley End, none of which were built according to his rules.

Tudor palaces did not conform to rules of art; their beauty was in the glorious expansive freedom with which they spread themselves across the land, an alternation of shady cloisters and sunny loggias, of green courts and brick façades, above which rose the high-pitched roof of the hall and the clustered towers, pinnacles, and chimney-stacks with which their builders delighted to adorn the skyline. Magalotti was quick to appreciate the proper character of Hampton Court. 'The numerous towers and cupolas', he wrote, 'judiciously disposed all over the vast pile of building, form a striking ornament to it, whether viewed near to or at a distance.' Balthasar de Monconys, visiting England at about the same time, made a similar observation. 'It is nothing but a quantity of towers, turrets and other baubles', he noted, 'which form a confusion which is not displeasing.'

Though more reluctant to praise, the Frenchman was more penetrating in his observation than the Italian; he noticed that whereas the inner courts of the palace, which contained the state rooms, were built without the least regard for symmetry, the outer court and west front presented a more or less uniform appearance.

This was typical of Tudor architecture. Annibale Litolfi, a Mantuan of Mary Tudor's time who shared the Spaniards' loathing of the English, explains the reason: 'As for the rooms, there is no imaginable order, as the English merely look to convenience.' The reception rooms were planned from the point of view of internal convenience, and seldom if ever made to conform to a preconceived façade. The outward beauty of the buildings was, therefore, something almost accidental, and owed as much to chance as it did to art. The east front of Hampton Court, when Henry VIII had added his royal apartments, was at once impressive and disorderly, in contrast to which the west front had an apparently deliberate balance of masses which was unusual for the times – the occasional lapses in symmetry being so far-flung as to escape detection if one is not looking for them.

In most respects the entrance front (Plate 15) is as Wolsey left it. The little spiny domes which capped the towers are a small detail which the imagination can easily supply, but the only big change is in the gatehouse. This used to be considerably taller, and dwarfed the architecture of the pendant wings, making it the most impressive and imposing entrance.

Through its archway, the visitor entered the base-court – a vast quadrangle one hundred and sixty-seven feet wide by one hundred and forty-two deep. Once more, the general disposition of features is regular, the size and spacing of the windows symmetrical. This sameness was due to the fact that nearly all the rooms contained in these buildings were guest rooms and very much alike. They were arranged in pairs, one large, one small, and had the unusual convenience of corridors running round three sides of the base-court. On account of the corridors, the windows of the guest rooms looked outwards – those on the north side over the roofs and gables of the Master Carpenter's Court, those on the west across the moat and on to the Green Court, while those of the south range enjoyed the delightful prospect across the pond garden and down to the River Thames.

The Thames, still high enough to be navigable, was sufficiently low to be 'a little pleasantly rapid', so that the waters were clean and clear, the bottom visible, 'the fish playing and in sight'. But the waters of the Thames were not adequate to Wolsey's sense of hygiene. He was wideawake to the dangers of plague and took every precaution to insulate his house from possible sources of contamination. To ensure a copious supply of the purest water, he determined to tap the springs at Coombe Hill, some three miles distant. The water was collected in several 'water houses' whence it was conveyed in leaden pipes through Surbiton, under the Hoggsmill River, under the Thames by Kingston Bridge, and so across the park to the site of the palace. It has been estimated that about two hundred and fifty tons of lead were required to bring water to Hampton.

In 1527, when a French embassy of exceptional distinction, headed by the Duc de Montmorency, Bishop du Bellay and a hundred of the 'richest and wealthiest gentlemen in all the Court of France', arrived in England, they were lodged at Hampton Court by Cardinal Wolsey. George Cavendish, who, in his capacity of Gentleman Usher, was responsible for many of the arrangements, describes the endless preparations for their reception. The whole place was alive with workmen, and as he went 'travelling daily from chamber to chamber', carpenters, masons, joiners and painters jostled in the corridors and crowded the courtyards. The Yeomen and Grooms of the Wardrobe were busy hanging the rooms with their gorgeous tapestries; the cooks 'wrought both day and night' in the confection of elaborate and ornamental dishes; there was coming and going of tradesmen, caterers and purveyors; 'there was carriage and recarriage of plate, stuff, and other rich implements', while in the guest rooms, two hundred and eighty beds were being prepared for the reception of the illustrious visitors.

It was arranged that the ambassadors should hunt at Hanworth, some two or three miles distant, after which they rode to Hampton Court, and each was conveyed to his chambers 'having in them great fires and wine ready to refresh them'. Here, in the comfortable relaxation bred of physical fatigue and luxurious surroundings, they awaited with pleasurable anticipation the summons to dinner. Meanwhile, the rooms set apart for the banquet were being brought to a state of richness almost unimaginable.

'Now were all things in a readiness', wrote Cavendish, 'and supper time at hand.' A fanfare of trumpets announced the banquet, and officers of the household went round the rooms to conduct the guests to their appointed places. The food appeared in the most elaborate shapes: there were castles and houses, a model of old St Paul's, animals, birds and human forms 'most lively made and counterfeit in dishes'. The table was no sooner cleared than it was laid again with the same diversity of invention; 'then went the cups merrily about, so that many of the Frenchmen were fain to be led up to their beds.'

Yet even this state of abundant repletion did not exhaust the Cardinal's hospitality; back in their rooms, the guests were served with 'liveries', the light refreshments for their nightly needs. 'Every chamber', noted Cavendish, 'had a basin and a ewer of silver, some gilt, some parcel gilt ... and one pot at the least with wine and beer ... and a fine manchet and a chet-loaf of bread.'

The state of magnificence to which Wolsey's Hampton Court attained is almost beyond belief. 'One has to traverse eight rooms', wrote Giustiniani, the Venetian ambassador, 'before one reaches his audience chamber, and they are all hung with tapestry which is changed once a week.' As might be expected, a considerable quantity of the tapestry depicted stories from the Bible, but, as if this source were not copious enough to supply the inspiration, classical and medieval mythology were brought in to swell the collection. Paris and Achilles, Hercules and Jason found places on the walls along with the *Romance of the Rose* or 'the Duke of Bry and the

Gyante Orrible' or such indeterminate subjects as 'a fountain and a lady, in her hair, standing by it'.

These woven pictures, however, were but a background to the richer hangings – canopies or cloths of state, traverses, which served to partition off some portion of a room, and 'window carpets' with cloth of gold paned in latticed diamonds with silver, which everywhere abounded. Wolsey's greed for carpets from the Levant became a diplomatic issue, and Giustiniani wrote anxiously to the Venetian senate that a present of that rare commodity 'might easily settle the affair of the wines of Candia'. He refers to duties levied on the import of sack by Venetian traders; 'but to discuss the matter further,' he added, 'until the Cardinal receives his hundred carpets, would be idle.'

On October 24th, 1521, Wolsey duly received a consignment of sixty carpets from the Signory of Venice.

The furniture of the rooms was answerable to the magnificence of the other appointments. The lengthy inventory tells of a great 'trussing bedstead of alabaster with my Lord's arms, and flowers gilt upon the sides'; of black velvet high-backed chairs embossed with the Cardinal's hat and a cross of crimson satin and Venice gold; of cushions upholstered in cloth of gold and violet satin, tasselled and fringed; of damask table-cloths 'paned lozengewise' – and these to be repeated throughout the hundreds of rooms in the palace. 'As for the furniture of the Chapel,' wrote Cavendish, 'it passeth my capacity to declare the number of costly ornaments and rich jewels that were used to be occupied in the same continually.'

Wolsey's ecclesiastical establishment was worthy of a cathedral. The chapel at Hampton had its dean – 'a great Divine and a man of excellent learning' – its sub-dean, precentor, Gospeller and Epistler, twelve singing priests, twelve singing children and sixteen singing laymen. As a choir, they were reckoned the finest in the land, and Henry, who delighted in church music, was known to complain that a new piece of music, produced on a sudden to be sung *ex improviso*, would be 'better and more surely handled' in the Cardinal's chapel than in his own.

It is hardly surprising that such a man as Henry should have come to resent being outshone by one of his own creatures, but

Wolsey was sufficiently conscious of the danger to tread warily. As early as 1521 he was addressing letters to Henry from 'your Grace's Manor of Hampton Court', while to other people, he continued to put 'from my Manor of Hampton Court'. He was still in residence as late as July 3rd, 1529, but, in the following year, Henry entered into full ownership, and the accounts show that he set up his arms and emblems all over the building to mark the fact. The dragons, greyhounds, leopards, lions and other beasts, painted and gilded and mounted on pedestals of white and green, brought a new and gaudy enrichment to the decoration of the palace, but they were only the forerunners of more radical alterations. For capacious and imposing as the Cardinal's palace had been, it was not sufficient to content its royal owner. Within a year, scaffolding was up, and sawyers, carpenters, tilers and labourers were set to work 'to take down the old Hall'. The two principal buildings, the hall and the chapel, were to be rebuilt and new lodgings for the King and Queen to be set up on the south and east sides of Cloister Green Court. 'Here there is space', noted Savorgnano, 'for the King to inhabit the centre floor, the Queen the one above, and the Princess the ground floor; in addition to which there are dwellings for the rest of the Court.'

The building of the King's new hall was pushed on at a great pace, for Henry was impatient to enjoy his ownership. Work progressed by day and by night, and among the accounts in the Record Office there figure payments for tallow candles 'spent by the workmen in the night times upon the paving of the Hall'.

Henry was at this time thirty-eight, and in the full flower of his manhood. Muscular, athletic and of a very forceful disposition, he was a tireless sportsman, and when he took up something, he made sure that he excelled in it. Hunting was a favourite pastime, and he hunted with tenacity and with vigour. 'He never took this diversion', wrote Giustiniani, 'without tiring eight or ten horses, which he caused to be stationed beforehand along the line of country he meant to take.' This could be a lengthy proceeding, and for quick exercise he had other amenities. 'He is extremely fond of tennis, at which game it is the prettiest thing in the world to see him play, his fair skin glowing through a shirt of the finest texture.'

Some of the same full-blooded vigour is to be seen in the prodigious scale of his building enterprises. During the first three years that he owned Hampton he was often spending as much as four hundred pounds a month on the rebuilding – a colossal sum for those days, which moved Sir Thomas Cromwell to suggest that 'if the King would only spare for one year, how profitable it would be to him.' The suggestion was ignored, and work was continued at high pressure.

It would be most interesting to know how far Henry played a creative role in the ordering of his buildings. The ample accounts, meticulously kept by Eustace Mascall, give the name of Henry Williams, priest, surveyor of the works at Hampton Court, and certainly the integration of the work of so great a multitude of artists, craftsmen and labourers was no mean contribution, but it may not have involved any original designing.

It is worth recording that almost all of the workmen were English, and most of them local; the same is true of the materials. Bricks came in their thousands from Taplow and Bronxham and from the kiln 'within the King's Park of Hampton Court'. Stone came by the ton from the quarries of Reigate, supplemented by a small order from Caen in Normandy.

That such a palace should have been built without drawing on wider resources for workmen or materials bears witness to a lively and flourishing tradition of craftsmanship. There is no evidence of any single creative mind behind the design – just Richard Ridge of London, John Wright of South Mimms, Reginald Ward of Dudley, John White of Winchester, the others of their like – and, in the background, Henry.

It was not long before the new apartments were ready to be occupied by the royal couple, and Anne Boleyn was the first mistress of the new palace. The ladies of the Court in those days contributed to the decoration of its rooms, and Anne and her ladies did some of the finest embroidery in the place. 'Those who have seen at Hampton Court the rich and exquisite works by herself,' wrote George Wyatt, 'for the greater part wrought by her own hand and needle ... esteem them amongst the most sumptuous that any Prince may be possessed of.' But their labours were not entirely devoted to the costly adornment of a royal home, and Wyatt knew where true values were to be found: 'Yet far more rich and precious were those works, in the sight of God, which she caused her maids ... to work in shirts and smocks for the poor.' Thus was the possession of treasures on earth combined with the laying up of treasure in Heaven.

It must have seemed unlikely to the occupants of the house that the little girl, Elizabeth, would one day be mistress of Hampton Court; there was so much that could go wrong.

In the troubled times of Edward VI, the household was called to action stations for a siege, but, although no attack came, the future remained dark and uncertain to all who were acquainted with the young King's health.

In Mary's reign, the prospect was bleaker still, with Philip's hated hidalgos fretting and grumbling in the ante-rooms and Elizabeth in danger of her life at Woodstock. Yet Mary herself would always have been a considerate mistress of the house. Her account books are full of little acts of charity and generosity.

One of the most sympathetic descriptions of Mary comes from the pen of the Venetian ambassador, Giacomo Soranzo. 'She is of very low stature,' he wrote, 'with a red and white complexion and very thin.' This is hardly surprising, since she rarely ate before two in the afternoon, and was accused of restricting her diet to 'fish, buttered eggs and oatmeal'. Soranzo's description accords with the pictures of her: 'Her eyes are pale and large, and her hair reddish; her face is round, with a nose rather low and wide, and were not her age on the decline, she might be called handsome.' She was only thirty-eight at the time Soranzo was writing, and the sufferings of her life had left their mark upon her countenance. But suffering is more destructive of beauty than of character, and it was a nature refined by suffering that looked out from behind her troubled features. 'Her Majesty's countenance indicates great benignity and clemency,' noted the ambassador, 'which are not belied by her conduct.' She was a woman with many enemies, and her reign saw many condemned to death, yet most would agree with Soranzo that 'had the executions depended solely on Her Majesty's will, not one of them, perhaps, would have been enforced', but 'deferring to her

Council in everything, she in this matter likewise complied with the wishes of others.'

There was, in fact, in her character some of that weakness that not infrequently goes with stubbornness, and one gets the impression of someone not big enough for her position and forcing herself to the utmost – and this in spite of recurrent ill-health. 'She is not of a strong constitution, and of late suffers from headache and a serious affection of the heart.' But in spite of this she was a prodigious worker. 'She rises at daybreak when, after saying her prayers and hearing Mass in private, she transacts business incessantly until after midnight, when she retires to rest; for she chooses to give audience not only to all members of her Privy Council, and to hear from them all details of public business, but also to all other persons who ask it of her.' There was some of the hopeless persistence of Philip II about her laborious life and apparent inability to delegate responsibility.

There was a great difference between her Court and that of her father, for, although audience was granted to all who asked it, entrance was refused to all others, and the gay throngs were banished from the courts and gardens of her palaces. 'The hall door within the court', noted Holinshed, 'was constantly shut, so that no man might enter unless his errand were first known, which seemed strange to Englishmen that had not been used thereto.'

But despite the lack of brilliance in her Court, Mary was not without a touch of her sister's vanity – a foible at once human and pathetic. 'She seemed to delight above all in arraying herself elegantly and magnificently', and she had an almost childish love of jewels. In two other respects, she was a Tudor. She was an accomplished scholar, 'more than moderately read in Latin literature', and she was a musician. 'Her Majesty takes pleasure in playing on the lute and spinet', noted Soranzo, 'and is a very good performer on both instruments.'

It was at Hampton Court that the most poignant episode of Mary's life occurred, for it was here that the elaborate and pitiful farce of her imaginary confinement was played out. So convinced of her pregnancy was she that she ordered processions and prayers that the infant 'might be a male child, well favoured and witty':

a little cradle 'very sumptuously and gorgeously trimmed' was prepared and inscribed with suitable verses; even the very dispatches that were to carry the joyous news to foreign countries were penned in readiness.

It was at this dramatic juncture, on April 25th, 1555, that Elizabeth set out from Woodstock in answer to a summons from her sister. She was still treated as a prisoner, and entered Hampton Court 'on the backside, the doors being shut upon her'. She was lodged in an outbuilding – possibly the Water Gallery – where she had a secret interview with Philip, who was clearly interested in the possibility of marrying her if Mary were to die. Later, she was summoned to the Queen's presence and a somewhat grudging reconciliation took place.

Two months later, the tragedy of Queen Mary's life reached its climax. The supposed pregnancy was diagnosed as dropsy. There is little at Hampton Court today to recall her sufferings, but a pathetic memento has survived – the book of private devotions used by this unhappy Queen. It is worn and fingered on the pages on which are to be found the prayers for the unity of the Church and for the safe delivery of a woman in childbirth.

In the year after her accession, Elizabeth made her first progress, starting from Greenwich in early July. She included in it a visitation of some of the palaces which were now her own. In August she was at Eltham, the great Plantagenet palace to which she had often been brought as a baby 'on account of the salubrity of the air'. From Eltham, she removed to Nonsuch, where Lord Arundel showed the most lavish hospitality. On August 10th, she left Nonsuch for Hampton Court and so returned as Queen to the palace whose doors had so recently been shut against her. Architecturally, it was one of the brightest jewels in her crown. 'All the apartments and rooms in this immensely large structure', wrote Rathgeb, 'are hung with rich tapestry of pure gold and fine silk, so exceedingly beautiful and royally ornamented that it would hardly be possible to find more magnificent things of the kind in any other place.'

Amid all the gorgeous apartments of the palace, one room stood out 'costly beyond everything', and the visitor was rare who failed

WHITEHALL   BIRD'S EYE VIEW FROM THE RIVER

to make special mention of the Paradise Chamber. Friedrich Gerschow, who considered Hampton Court to be the 'principal Royal residence in all England', describes his impressions of this room in some detail. 'At last we reached the Paradise Chamber,' he writes, 'the most magnificent and most splendid room in the whole mansion, perhaps even in the whole realm.' It appears, from the furniture, to have been the throne room, but it was also used for the display of a number of curious musical instruments and table games. 'The tapestry', continues Gerschow's account, 'was of Persian workmanship; on the table, which was twenty-eight foot long, lay a velvet coverlet reaching down to the ground, thickly set with pearls as large as peas. The throne was of brown velvet worked magnificently with gold and set with pearls and precious stones; especially brilliant were three large diamonds, worth a mighty sum of money; a table of Brazilian wood inlaid with silver, upon it lay a cushion with a mirror, and many turquoises thereon, a draught board of ebony, a chess board of ivory and then, on a little table, seven ivory fifes mounted with gold.'

According to Thomas Platter, these ivory pipes were for the imitation of 'all kinds of animal noises'. There was a backgammon table with the pieces 'perfumed and ornamented with crests and the dice of pure silver'. The ceiling, he tells us, was beautifully painted, and worked into the tapestry were the royal arms 'with an extremely large square diamond worth many thousands of crowns'. The focal point of the room was the throne and its lofty, jewel-studded canopy. 'Beneath this, the Queen is accustomed to sit in her magnificence, upon a very stately chair covered with cushions.'

Among the treasures of Hampton Court, one of the most interesting features was the collection of musical instruments. There was a perfumed virginal made all of glass, except for the strings, and inscribed in letters of gold upon the lid was the legend:

Cantabis moneo quisquis cantare rogans[1]
Vivat in aethernos Elizabetha dies.

---

[1] 'Rogans': presumably 'rogaris'. The couplet would then read, 'Whoever you are, who are asked to sing, I bid you sing: "Let Elizabeth live for ever." ' I am obliged to Mr T. Zinn for this translation and for pointing out the misprint in the original edition of Thomas Platter and in those derived from it.

7

There was another virginal 'whose strings were of pure gold and silver and they said the Queen often played this very charmingly'. In another room, there were organs, of which Elizabeth was a reputed connoisseur.

The exceptional richness of the Paradise Chamber was turned to financial advantage by those in charge. 'It is strange', remarked Justus Zinzerling, 'that the keeper of this room is so sordid that you must bargain beforehand about his fee; yet from his dress he appears to be a grand gentleman.' In all, three gratuities were necessary to make a complete tour of the palace, which was divided into the state apartments, the gardens, and then the royal apartments.

Thomas Platter made his tour just after the Queen had departed, but found the walls still 'hung with extremely costly tapestries worked in gold and silver and silk, so lifelike that one might take the people and plants for real'. He began his tour with the state rooms added by Henry VIII. 'First we were shown ... into a large and very long gallery hung all round with old woven tapestries. This led us to the dining or banqueting Hall, from which we entered the Church or Chapel containing a most excellent fine organ on which I played a while, then we inspected the gallery or loft from which the Queen listens to the sermon. On our descent and exit from the Church, the gardener presented himself, and after we had offered a gratuity to our first guide, the gardener conducted us into the Royal pleasure garden.'

These gardens, which lay to the south of the palace between the state rooms and the river, had been the creation of Henry VIII. A rough sketch of them has survived among the drawings of Wyngaerde. To the right of his picture, and occupying the south-east corner of the gardens, was the water gate – an impressive castellated building with an onion dome, into which the royal barge could be rowed. At the back of this stood the Great Round Arbour – a large gazebo bellying out into a succession of bow windows from which the most magnificent view of the palace and gardens could be obtained (Plate 16).

Long corridors, providing a covered approach to the numerous outbuildings, skirted the gardens, which were further enclosed by brick walls and a profusion of fruit trees. The accounts give details of these trees and their cost. Six hundred cherry trees at sixpence the hundred seem to be the cheapest and most used, but apples, pears, holly, cypress, juniper, bay and yew were also ordered.

The whole plot was divided up into squares, and the squares quartered into lawns and ponds, the dividing paths being lined with pillars bearing heraldic beasts. Thirty-eight of these, including dragons, lions, greyhounds, harts and unicorns, each painted in oils and bearing the royal arms upon a shield, mounted guard in the pond yard, while one hundred and eighty posts and nine hundred and sixty yards of railing, painted in the Tudor colours of white and green, outlined the King's new garden.

Flowers form a comparatively minor item in the bills. A hundred roses, at only fourpence the hundred, were supplemented by violets, sweet-williams, gilliver slips and primroses. No doubt there were other flowers, and certainly there were weeds. Women were employed at twopence a day on weeding the King's new garden.

On walking out into these gardens, the first thing to catch the attention of Platter was the arrangement of 'numerous patches where square cavities had been scooped, as for paving stones; some of these were filled with red brick dust, some with white sand and some with green lawn, very much resembling a chess board.' The general impression was one of an elaborate and artificial formality. 'There were all manner of shapes, men and women, half men and half horse, sirens, serving maids with baskets, French lilies and delicate crenellations all round ... all true to the life, and so cleverly and amusingly interwoven, mingled and grown together, trimmed and arranged picture-wise, that their equal would be difficult to find.'

In 1572, we find Elizabeth spending Christmas at Hampton Court, and she was there again at Shrovetide in the following year. These were the seasons for masques and plays, and, therefore, the busiest time for Sir Thomas Benger, Master of the Revels, and his staff. They were responsible for the 'apparelling, disguising, furnishing, fitting and garnishing and orderly setting forth of men, women and children, in sundry tragedies, plays, masques and sports for Her Majesty's regal disport and recreation'.

It was a very varied role. The tragedies, plays and masques were performed in the great hall, which needed adapting to such usage. It is not clear, from the accounts, whether any actual stage was erected, but considerable portions were 'boarded up'. The lighting had to be increased, and one bill for 'wire to strain across the hall and to hang the branches with the lights' shows how this was accomplished. It was in midwinter that these services were required, and one gets a glimpse of the difficulties under which they worked from the entry 'for hanging up tents to keep away the wind and snow from driving into the Hall'. Everything was piecework; nothing was ever done free of charge.

Then there were the properties – every one of them, from rafters and double rafters down to the smallest nails and staples, had to be accounted for. Long white beards at twenty pence the piece, 'bumbast' to make snowballs, rose-water to sweeten the snowballs presented to Her Majesty by Janus, wool to stuff counterfeit fishes, paste and paper for a dragon's head, knobs for a Senate House, carriage for trees and other effects for a wilderness – all were paid for and noted down by the Clerk Comptroller and signed with a flourish 'Edwardum Buggyn'.

Then there was the cast; sometimes it was 'Lord Leicester's Men', sometimes it was 'the Children of Paul's' or 'Mulcaster's Children'. The boys were lodged at a house called St John's 'whiles they learned their parts and gestures meet for the masque', and their board and lodging had to be found. Then there was Nicholas Newdigate to be paid 'for his pains in hearing and training the boys that should have spoken the speeches'. There were a barge and two wherries to be hired to bring 'the masking gear and children with their tutors and an Italian woman to dress their heads' from London to Hampton. They had to be warmed and fed 'while they waited to know whether Her Majesty would have the masque that night'. There was a barber to be paid for trimming their hair on the day and a shilling apiece for the actual performance. After it was all over, they were lodged at Mother Sparrow's across the river, and thence shipped back to London and landed 'sick, cold and hungry' to be treated to a final round of victuals.

There was always gaiety at the Court of Elizabeth, and, as her reign drew to its close, the tempo did not slacken. In September

1599 she was at Hampton Court for the last time, spending three or four days there sandwiched between two visits to Nonsuch, and annoying Lord Hunsdon by arriving 'more privily than is fitting for the time or becoming her estate'. She appears to have stayed more or less informally, using Lady Scudamore's lodging as her Presence Chamber and Mrs Ratcliffe's as her Privy Chamber in the vast palace which had so often been the scene of her gayest festivities. A last glimpse is caught of her 'dancing the Spanish Panic to a whistle and tabor, none being with her but my Lady Warwick'.

VI

NONSUCH

THE portraits of the Tudors are nothing if they are not lifelike. Thanks to the influence of Holbein and his school it is possible to visualize the personalities of their age in vivid detail. As they look down on us from the walls of our great houses and galleries, we can see them as blood relations; the men, resplendent in slashed silks, gleaming breastplates or sombre gowns, are solidly self-assured, and in their eyes we may discern the fire of the warrior, the gravity of the scholar or the subtlety of the lawyer. The women, starched and corseted, look tight-lipped and puritanical beneath the elaborate filigree of lace and jewellery that overlaid their ample upholstery; one can often see what Aubrey meant about children detesting the sight of their parents. Men and women alike are for the most part reserved and inscrutable; nevertheless, thanks to the intense realism with which they are depicted, to see their portraits is to meet them face to face.

The same is not true of the Tudor house, or of the Tudor scene in general. One tends to imagine it as tapestry rather than as landscape painting. The houses seem to lack the third dimension, and it is difficult to see them as solid, four-square buildings, raising their dome-capped towers high above the blossom of their orchards, the new-cut stonework of the windows gleaming white or honey-coloured against the leaded panes. Too often they are only known from quaint descriptions or from pictures that are crudely out of drawing.

Typical of this latter class is the royal palace of Nonsuch whose very name seems to enshrine this elusive quality. It has long been familiar from Speed's engraving (Plate 17) – an unconvincing likeness of a house, and wanting both perspective and proportion – or from Hoefnagel's sketch (Plate 17) with Elizabeth arriving before the improbable façade, looking more like a fairy godmother in 'Cinderella' than the Faerie Queene of Spenser's poem. The whole scene savours of pantomime rather than of reality.

Yet we know from von Wedel that Elizabeth had just such a coach, open on all sides beneath its plumed and bejewelled canopy; we know, too, that Hoefnagel was a careful and perceptive painter. His representation of the palace is not so much inaccurate as inadequate. For recent excavations have proved what Sir John Summerson had conjectured, that the dominant influence here was French. It is probably not too much to say that Nonsuch was Henry VIII's answer to Chambord, and it is particularly unfortunate that we should have no worthy record of the façade which rivalled, both in the elaboration of its skyline and in the abundance of its ornament, the magnificent front which Chambord presents to its gardens.

Somewhat ironically, the farther or entrance front of Nonsuch, in which the French influence is not to be discerned, has been accurately portrayed (Plate 18) by two competent artists, an unknown Flemish painter and Danckerts. Their paintings hang at the Fitzwilliam Museum and Berkeley Castle; either will serve our purpose.

Here at last it is: a portrait of a Tudor house. We can see it spreading its courtyards to right and left among the trees and raising its two gatehouses in a manner strongly suggestive of Knole. Thanks to the artist's use of light and shade, the whole building stands out in almost stereoscopic relief, and beneath the elevations we may discern the plan. The horizontal rows of roof, battlements and parapet, underlined here and there by a string course or the even perimeter of the encircling wall, enable the eye to travel easily over the vast expanse of masonry. Across these horizontal lines rise the vertical accents of towers, cupolas and chimneys, softened occasionally by a gable or the slope of a roof, as the whole group builds up to its climax in the central gatehouse and belfry – 'a very special ornament to Nonsuch House'.

These pictures leave little to be desired, but they are so unlike the façades of Speed and Hoefnagel that it is only in our day that they have been identified.

The two pairs of drawings emphasize the fact that there were two

distinct halves to Nonsuch: the inner court, decorated in the elaborate style of the French Renaissance, and the outer court, built
throughout in the plainest Tudor vernacular. At first sight the
history of the building would seem to explain this duality, for the
palace was begun in 1538 by Henry, but by the time of his death
nine years later only the inner court had been finished. Mary would
have pulled it down, had not the Earl of Arundel, 'perceiving a
sumptuous house to have been begun but not finished by his late
master', undertaken its completion. The change of patron, however,
does not explain the duality of style, for we are told that Arundel
achieved his task 'in so ample and perfect a sort as by the first
intent and meaning of the King the same should have been performed'. It seems that Henry planned the austere outer court as a
deliberate foil to offset the richness of the royal apartments.

It was not only this architectural *tour de force* that earned Nonsuch
its name; its varied charms were greatly enhanced by its situation
'on a small elevation in a rolling plain'. Dr Anthony Watson, rector
of Cheam from 1581 to 1590, has left a long and mostly tedious
catalogue of its delights. It is an uncritical eulogy in which one
scents the often obsequious relationship of parson to squire, but
parts of it are excellent. Here and there a vivid phrase will bring the
whole scene into focus.

From the north wind the palace was protected by pastures 'which
give way to a gently rising hill, clothed with woods and orchards,
and made most pleasant by the consort of birds'. From the south,
the same conformation of woods and slope repelled the rain, and
'the remorseless force of the winds, which always envies the glory
of art, and too often has shaken the memorials of the ages, is thrown
off by the pleasant brow of the hills, or tempered by the steadfast
patience of the trees.'

In this peaceful and sequestered spot Henry had begun the palace
of his old age. 'O ye Gods!' exclaimed Dr Watson, 'what labour,
what servants, what axes, what crowbars, what artists, what sums
of money were needed for so great a task!' The task was not made
easier by the fact that the site was already occupied by the village
of Cuddington with its church and manor house. Perhaps this
accounted for the axes and crowbars, for the village disappeared,

and in its place the palace walls began to rise from their foundations on a typically Tudor ground plan. In one respect, however, the traditional layout was departed from: there was no great hall. A possible explanation of this omission was that Henry built Nonsuch 'for his solace and retirement'. It was not intended to house the whole royal retinue, and when Elizabeth brought her Court here they had to lodge in tents.

'On our arrival,' wrote Thomas Platter in 1599, 'we saw a broad green meadow before the Palace on which were pitched a number of tents, round in shape or elongated like a Church, where many of the noble Lords in the train of the Royal Court had their quarters. For the Palace stands isolated, having neither township, village nor a single house in its vicinity, so that whoever is not accommodated in the Royal residence must manage under the tents.'

Towards the end of her reign, when Nonsuch became once more the property of the Crown, Elizabeth was frequently here, and Platter was able to see the palace full to overflowing with the colourful personalities of the English Court. 'We ordered our coachman to draw up on the meadow and alighted, and by way of a long grassy avenue enclosed by wooden palings, made our way to the Royal Palace, where the Queen was keeping her Court.'

Seen from the avenue, Nonsuch presented an exciting architectural ensemble; the two gatehouses, set on an alignment with the drive, rose one behind the other in majestic silhouette, and the gilded pinnacles of the palace peeped out from behind the severe castellation of the outer court. The immediate precincts of the house were enclosed by a brick wall, above which could be seen a profusion of trees, their green foliage setting off the blue slate of the roofs, the red brick of the chimneys and the grey stone of the walls to their best advantage. Most of them were fruit trees, and in blossom time the prospect must have been delightful.

Platter and his friends had an introduction from the Mayor of Dover to Lord Cobham, who appointed them a guide and gave instructions that they were to be taken to the Presence Chamber to see the Queen. With this to look forward to they started their tour of the building.

Let us imagine ourselves to be members of their party. We enter the first court, restraining our voices, for the echo will return across it as many as six times. We are now in a plain quadrangle; built of freestone throughout, rough-cobbled but with stone-flagged foot-paths radiating out from the gatehouse. It is of two storeys, the lower devoted to buttery, cellars and servants' quarters, the upper to the lodgings of the Court. We note, with Dr Watson, 'the ampli-tude of the rooms, the splendour of the windows, the manifestly Royal form of the building, the pinnacles aloft in the sky, which at the bottom are held up by little animals, and at the top bear dogs and griffins and lions resting on decorated shields'. To our left an archway opens to a smaller, darker court, 'which one would say was most suited to the removal of the dins of kitchens and the house-hold round of duties'. To the right, another archway leads to the stables.

Behind and before, the two gatehouses, rising 'with great no-bility through four floors', provide the most important architec-tural features. At this point we should remember Knole where the Green Court is thus dominated by its gateways.

With the middle gate, 'which outdoes the first by one tower, a clock, a symphony and six gilded horoscopes', began the transition from the severity of the first court to the exuberance of the second. Above the arch there bulged a triple oriel, so beautifully turned that it seemed as if 'the delicate hand of Praxiteles had hewn the mani-fold projection of the windows', and between the towers there rose a belfry from which there sounded twice an hour 'a musical con-course of bells'. An ascent of eight steps leading to its archway conducted the visitor to the inner court.

Already framed within the tunnel of the arch was the central feature of the court, a white marble fountain 'which raises water in abundance for the use of the mansion, and [is] remarkable for the exquisite ornament of the statues round about it'. So Braun de-scribed it; Watson elaborates upon the statues. A white horse poised 'as if leaping up a slope' dominated the fountain; below him the three Graces, their arms entwined, poured streams of water into a marble basin, 'the pleasant burden of two golden griffins'. The pattering fountain, the gleam of wet marble and of burnished brass provided a little overture to the piece of architectural virtuosity which was to come. Advancing a few paces more, the visitor found himself within the court. 'When you have greeted its threshold,' exclaimed Dr Watson, 'and seen with eyes dazzled the shining lustre of the stone, glittering with purest gold, it is not surprising if it should hold you senseless.'

It was indeed a breath-taking sight, for the whole façade shone white and gold in the rich profusion of its decoration. The white panels, mistaken by Platter for 'great blocks of white stone', were in fact modelled in a kind of stucco. 'From the powdered ashes of stone, skilfully moistened,' Watson informs us, 'a material was formed most apt for any impression, which, having followed a natural course of drying is seen to be harder than adamant. Industry mastered this medium, and all places are full of Kings, Caesars, Sciences, Gods.'

The modelling was in deep relief, being in some places as much as five inches thick, and the panels must have been extremely weighty. To fix them to the façade they were secured with frames of slate, richly carved and brightly gilded. A hundred and twenty-five years after they were put up, John Evelyn came to Nonsuch 'and took an exact view of the plaster statues and bass-relievos'. He much admired the way they had lasted and lamented that they were not preserved in some dry place – 'a gallery would become them.' His most interesting comment was on their supposed origin; it was no doubt a tribute to their excellence that he decided they 'must needs have been the work of some celebrated Italian'. In fact, the Italian influence was mediated to Nonsuch through the French. The slate was from France, and of French workmanship. The most important Italian to work here, Nicholas Bellin of Modena, was borrowed from Fontainebleau.

Across the courtyard from the fountain, and looking back towards the gatehouse, was a figure of Henry VIII enthroned in splendour, presiding over the multitudes of gods and heroes with which he had peopled his quadrangle. To the east, at his right hand, were his own apartments. Upon their walls the whole of Mt Olympus was portrayed, and the Labours of Hercules depicted in full. To the west were the Queen's rooms, their walls adorned with appropriately feminine graces, ranging from those of classic mythology to the theological virtues. To give unity to the whole scheme, the entire upper floor was devoted to the Roman emperors, thirty-one of them 'from Julius Caesar to Aemilianus, all flow together in most pleasing concord.' On the eastern side of the court, a bronze statue of Scipio marked the entrance to the King's apartment. Through this gate Platter and his friends now entered the palace.

They came on a Sunday, and the Court being then in residence, it was not possible to see over all the apartments, but they were brought straight into the Presence Chamber and 'placed well to the fore, so as better to behold the Queen'.

As they waited they had time to take in some of the details of the Presence Chamber. The tapestries commanded first attention, then the floor, 'strewn with straw or hay, only where the Queen was to come out and up to her seat were carpets laid down worked in Turkish knot'. The throne, of red damask embroidered with gold, was 'so low ... that the cushions almost lay on the ground', and overhead was a great canopy 'fixed very ornately to the ceiling'.

Between twelve and one o'clock men began to appear from an inner chamber holding white staffs in their hands, and then a number of lords entered, and finally the eagerly awaited Queen herself, 'alone without escort, very straight and erect'. For Thomas Platter this was the great moment of his visit to England. Elizabeth was by now an almost legendary figure, and the sight of her would be one of the most treasured possessions in the storehouse of his memory.

'She was most lavishly attired in a gown of pure white satin, gold-embroidered, with a whole bird of Paradise for panache, set forward on her head studded with costly jewels; she wore a string of huge pearls about her neck and elegant gloves over which were drawn costly rings. In short she was most gorgeously apparelled, and although she was already seventy-four,[1] she was very youthful still in appearance, seeming no more than twenty years of age. She had a dignified and regal bearing.' There is something suspicious about the number of foreigners who mistook the age of Elizabeth for twenty.

[1] She was in fact only sixty-six.

In the Presence Chamber the Queen listened to a sermon delivered by 'a preacher in a white surplice, merely standing on the
floor facing the Queen'. But 'since it was very warm and late'
Elizabeth was not disposed to listen for long, and she sent word to
the preacher to finish, upon which she at once withdrew.

Trestle tables were now set before the royal throne, and a solemn
procession of guards and gentlemen, advancing into the room with
triple obeisance, set cloth, knives, salt and manchet upon it, 'with
honours performed as if the Queen herself had sat there'. The table
laid, another procession entered of some forty of the guard in red
tabards; 'they are all very tall, fine young men,' wrote Platter, 'and
all similarly attired, so that I never in my life saw their like.' Each
of them bore a dish, 'and I observed amongst them some very large
joints of beef, and all kinds of game, pastries and tarts.' A lady-in-
waiting did the carving, and the portions were carried into the
adjoining chamber to Elizabeth, 'and she ate of what she fancied,
privily however, for she very seldom partakes before strangers.'
After the third course had come and gone 'the Queen's musicians
appeared in the Presence Chamber with their trumpets and shawms,
and after they had performed their music, everyone withdrew, bow-
ing themselves out just as they had come in, and the tables were
carried away again.'

Platter was deeply impressed by the personnel of the Court of
Elizabeth; the grandeur of the lords and esquires; the fine build and
comely features of their retainers; the stateliness of the ceremonial,
and above all the habit of kneeling to address the Queen. 'I am told
that they even play cards with the Queen in kneeling posture.'

Having seen the Queen served, Platter and his friends were taken
back to one of the tents and given dinner, after which they started
once more to look round, this time being taken to the gardens.

Like Chambord, Nonsuch was dedicated to the Chase, and the
grove of Diana occupied a place of honour in the gardens. In the
middle of the grove was a fountain, and in the midst of the fountain a group of statuary portrayed, 'with great art and lifelike
execution', the story of Actaeon turned into a stag as he was
sprinkled by the goddess.

Nearer the palace walls, all was formality. There were the usual knots, in which 'all kinds of plants and shrubs are mingled in intricate circles as though by the needle of Semiramis'; there were the usual statues 'which seemed to rival the perfection of Roman Antiquity'; there was the usual orchard, there was the usual maze. But in the remoter corners of the ten-acre plot were two particular attractions. One was a tall and shady wood, and the other a man-made wilderness.

The wood was pierced with long, dark alleys, some of them lined with boards for tennis and other ball games, others left plain for gentler forms of recreation. What most delighted Platter was 'the delicious song of the birds in the tall trees, densely planted along the sides in ordered array', for the little bosquet formed a natural aviary.

In the south-west corner was planted a wilderness, which could be overlooked from the shade of a noble plane-tree. 'There many people sit down,' wrote Dr Watson, 'and, dressed in the gayest of clothes, converse on various topics, listen to the calls of the animals and the song of the birds ... and unless I am very much mistaken, are captivated by the pleasure of this leafy wilderness.' In Lord Lumley's time the wilderness appears to have housed an impressive menagerie – but one can never be quite sure that anything at Nonsuch was real. Platter mentions no livestock apart from the birds, but he notes that 'in the pleasure gardens are charming terraces and all kinds of animals ... most artfully set out, so that from a distance one would take them for real ones.'

At the western extremity of the gardens, 'pleasantly situated upon the highest part of Nonsuch Park', was the banqueting house, one of the first of its kind in England, and unusually capacious, its architecture reflecting that of the palace. Its top storey was provided with balconies at each corner, which were no doubt intended for spectators when the Court was hunting.

Returning to the Privy Gardens, the visitor would have had the most spectacular view of Nonsuch; 'direct your gaze toward the lofty towers, the turreted walls, the projecting windows, the plaster work, the exquisite statues.'

The great towers, five storeys high, were the most conspicuous features, 'the chief ornament of the whole house of Nonsuch'. The

higher they rose, the more elaborate they became. The fourth floor
formed a projecting drum with a continuous band of window for
all-round visibility. Above this were the battlements of light timber
and lead construction, supporting a ring of heraldic beasts. From
within the parapet there rose a second drum, fenestrated like the
first, and crowned with a cupola on which the lions and griffins
clustered with their crowns and pennants. These towers were in the
direct tradition of Richmond and Oatlands, built to command a
magnificent view over the countryside.

Between the towers ran the gallery, breaking forward into a great
bay window in the centre of the façade. The gallery, of course, was
one of the most important rooms, and formed the connection between the King's apartments and those of the Queen. For want of
accurate information it must be left with Dr Watson's inadequate
phrase, 'magnificent with every device and the most sumptuous
appointment'. The imagination can supply a little more, for it is
certain that the gallery owed something of its decoration to that at
Fontainebleau. In the autumn of 1540, Henry VIII was corresponding with his ambassador to France, Sir John Wallop, about a certain 'Modon' – Nicholas Bellin of Modena. He was wanted for
debt in France, but Henry was not anxious to let him go. He was
making himself far too useful at St James's and Nonsuch.

In another letter from Wallop the relative architecture of France
and England is discussed. Francis I was particularly interested in
Hampton Court. 'He heard say', relates Wallop, 'that your Majesty
did use much gilding in your said houses, and especially in the
roofs, and that in his buildings he used little or none, but made the
roofs of timber finely wrought with divers colours of wood natural.'
Francis was going to show Wallop his latest building at Fontainebleau, and especially the gallery which bears his name. Later, this
promised visit is described. 'I went into his bedchamber, which I do
assure Your Majesty is very singular as well with antical borders as
costly ceilings, and a chimney right well made.' Of the proportions
of the gallery 'no man can better show Your Majesty than Modon,
who wrought there in the beginning of the same.' Here, then, is the
link between the buildings of Henry VIII and Fontainebleau. A
further reference is also significant: 'a fourth part is all antique of

such stuff as the said Modon maketh Your Majesty's chimneys.'
Nicholas Bellin was working at Nonsuch from 1541 to 1544; there
can be little doubt that the gallery there had affinities with his work
at Fontainebleau.

As a style of decoration, the work at Nonsuch was linked with
Fontainebleau; as a type of residence it had more in common with
Chambord. Both were country houses rather than palaces, provided
with every facility for hunting and for watching the hunt. Both were
remote from any town or village which might have accommodated
an overflow, so neither were places to which 'any great resort'
might be made. Both had a special place in the affections of their
owners. Of Francis I we have the picture of him setting out for
Chambord with a gay 'allons chez-moi.' Of Elizabeth we have the
letter of Roland White: 'Her Majesty is returned again to Nonsuch,
which of all places she likes best.'

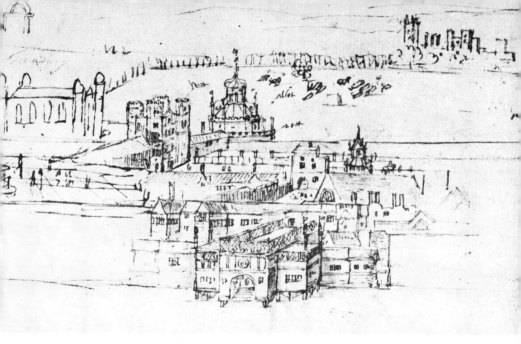

BIRD'S EYE VIEW FROM THE RIVER   *By courtesy of the Ashmolean Museum*

WHITEHALL

THE 'HOLBEIN' GATE   THE KING STREET GATE

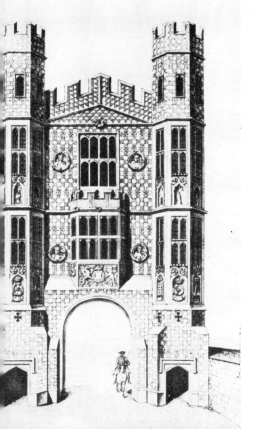

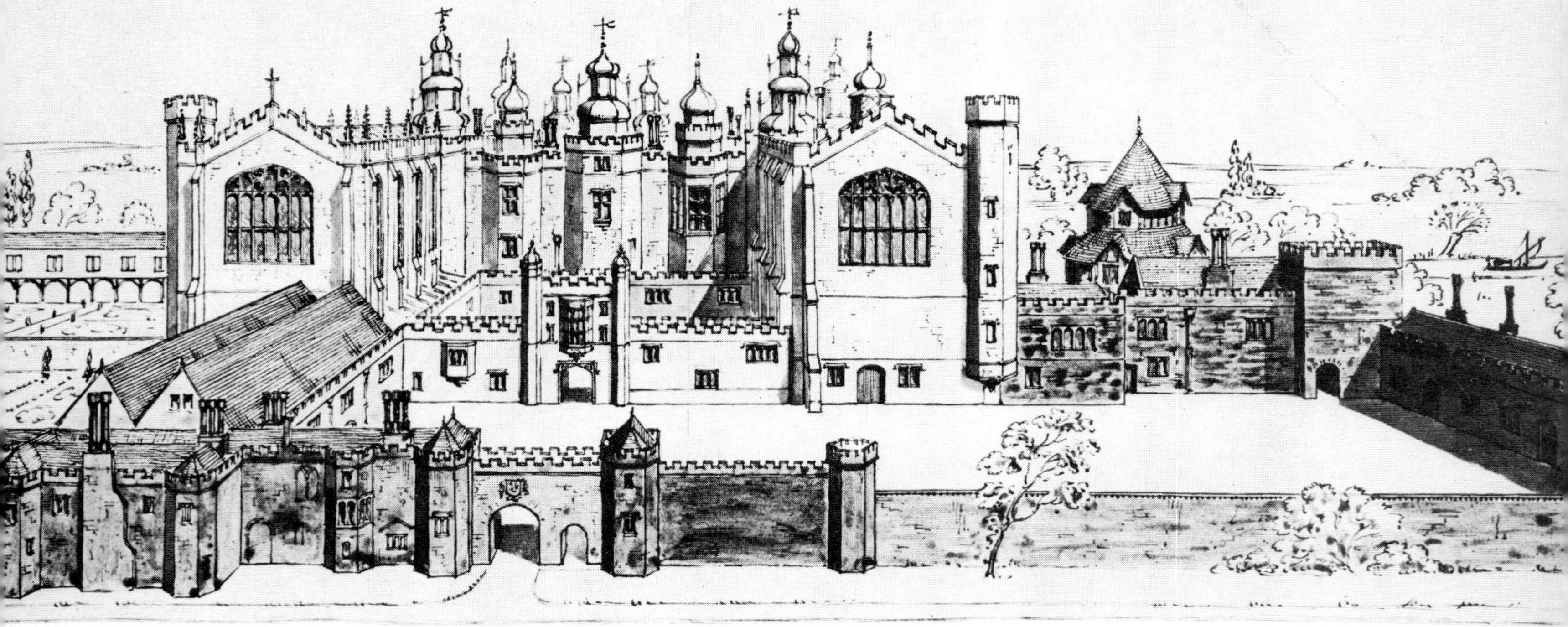

RICHMOND THE PALACE FROM RICHMOND GREEN, TO THE NORTH-EAST

PART TWO

THE PROGRESSES

VII

THE QUEEN IN PROGRESS

When it pleaseth her in the summer season to recreate herself abroad, and view the estate of the country, every nobleman's house is her palace.

WILLIAM HARRISON

I F ANY single circumstance distinguished the Tudors and early Stuarts from their successors it was the restless persistence with which they moved from place to place, maintaining an astonishing number of royal houses, but availing themselves also of the lavish hospitality of their richer subjects. It was sometimes a little difficult to discover the whereabouts of Henry VIII. 'I sent one of my men to Hampton Court', wrote Chapuys, 'but he was already gone to Windsor and other places to amuse himself ... for the last fortnight he has done little else but go from place to place.' Caspar Breuner found the same difficulty with Elizabeth. 'The Queen has not been here since the 21st of June', he wrote from London, 'and does not return until October; she moves from one summer residence to another for change of air, it being very unhealthy here at this time of year.'

These moves may well have been imposed by sanitary necessity. One can imagine the effect, at Hampton Court, of having 'a great house of easement over the moat'. At Greenwich there is mention in the accounts of the jakes on the King's side and on the Queen's side, of the Lords' jakes and the Common jakes. These had to be cleaned out regularly by the gong-farmers or night-soil men. The application of water to sanitary arrangements in fact dates from 1596, when Sir John Harington constructed the first water closet in his house near Bath. A friend, writing under the name of 'Philostilpnos', urged him to make known his invention, claiming that he would thereby 'not only pleasure many great persons, but also do Her

Majesty great service in her palace of Greenwich and other stately houses, that are oft annoyed with such savours as where many mouths are fed, can hardly be avoided'. It is possible that the workings of his ingenious mind bore some fruit in royal circles, for, among the verses with which he prefaced his book, *The Metamorphosis of Ajax*,[1] was one 'to the Ladies of the Queen's Privy Chamber, at the making of their perfumed Privy at Richmond'.

Another cause for the repeated moves of the Court was the danger of plague. At the end of September 1563, Elizabeth was at Windsor. People were dying in the vicinity of Reading and Newbury, and the Marquis of Winchester wrote to Cecil, urging that the Queen should remain where she was; 'and if her Highness shall be forced to move, as God forbid, I think then best the Household shall be put on board wages ... and herself repair to Oatlands, where Her Majesty may remain well if no great resort be made to the house.'

The first emergency measure was to separate the Queen from her household; the second to ensure an easy line of retreat. 'There is at hand Hampton Court, Richmond and Eltham, large houses for room, and good air. And now cold weather and frosts will bring health, with God's help.' It is easy to see why they were continually on the move.

Henry VII had bequeathed two thousand pounds for 'new making and repairing' of the highways and bridges that connected his principal houses with London and Canterbury. The former were to be 'well and substantially ditched on both sides ... well and nicely gravelled and raised upon a good height, with such a largeness as two carts may pass one by the other'.

No greater blessing could have been left to the Tudor dynasty. At all times in the year, there might be observed the procession of struggling pack-horses, lumbering wagons and breathless outriders that inevitably preceded the royal equipage. The amount of luggage taken by Elizabeth on her progresses was staggering. 'When the Queen breaks up her Court with the intention of visiting another place,' wrote Rathgeb, 'there commonly follow more than three hundred carts laden with bag and baggage.' Harrison puts the

[1] A pun on the words 'a jakes'.

number of carts at four hundred and adds the total of two thousand four hundred horses.

Von Wedel describes the arrival of a progress at Westminster: 'Riding ahead were her servants, then followed two of her guard, then came her equerries and behind these her chamberlains, of whom there were about twenty. Then came the Privy Councillors.' With them rode the Archbishop of Canterbury with fifty of his own horsemen. Elizabeth herself, in a gold coach, was preceded by Burghley and Walsingham. 'The Queen, sitting all alone in her splendid coach, appeared like a Goddess such as painters are wont to depict.' Behind her rode Leicester, as Master of the Horse, and more of the Privy Council; then the maids of honour, twenty-four of them, bravely mounted and beautifully attired, followed by some fifty more of the Queen's guard. Two empty coaches, presumably held in reserve in case of emergency, brought up the rear.

Von Wedel had the opportunity of inspecting some of the Queen's coaches when he was at Greenwich. One was 'so small that only two persons can sit in it; but so contrived that both the fore and hind wheels are attached far from the body'; a second was of red leather studded all over with silver gilt nails. The third is a little difficult to picture – it had twelve wheels somehow 'placed under the axle in a way that I cannot describe'. It is possible that these coaches were the first to be seen in England. Edmund Howes, in his continuation of Stow's *Chronicle*, mentions that, in 1564, 'William Boonen, a Dutchman (the first who brought the use of coaches into England) became the Queen's coachman, and after a while divers great ladies ... made them coaches and rid in them up and down the country to the great admiration of all beholders.' Previously to this, ladies of quality had been content to use wagons.

A pleasant accompaniment to the pageantry of a royal progress was the ringing of church bells – a form of exercise to which the English were much addicted – and the bells of St Margaret's always announced the removal of the Queen as she passed from Whitehall to Greenwich, from Greenwich to Richmond, from there to Oat-lands for a few days hunting, or down to Nonsuch, her favourite of all her palaces.

None of Elizabeth's palaces was of her own building. Thanks to the activities of her father and grandfather, she had inherited a considerable number, and she contented herself with their upkeep. But, although she cannot be described as a patron of the art, she did exercise a formative influence on the architecture of the Home Counties by her habit of making these progresses. During the course of the summer, she descended with a considerable retinue upon a succession of houses, expecting to be decently lodged and expensively entertained.

Expensively entertained she was. The wealth of Elizabethan England made a deep impression on foreigners. Von Wedel observed that many a yeoman kept greater state and a more opulent table than the nobles of Pomerania; 'he must be an unskilful farmer who does not possess gilt silver salt cellars and silver cups and spoons.' An average gentleman, in England, would keep at least twenty domestics, while the really rich kept over a hundred. 'The Gentry and Nobility here have more retainers than I have seen in any country in all my life.' Unless their business kept them at Court they resided not in the cities but in their country mansions. 'They keep up very grand establishments,' wrote Giacomo Soranzo in 1554, 'both with regard to the abundance of eatables consumed by them, as also by reason of their numerous attendants, so that the Earl of Pembroke has upward of one thousand clad in his livery.'

The economic background to this was simple. Owing to the size and fertility of the land there was abundance of food in England. 'For this reason', noted another Italian, 'the expenditure of the gentlemen's houses does not reach a very high figure, although they keep many servants. For goods such as meat, bread and beer are cheap, and with these they supply the household.' It was quite easy so long as one owned land. 'Live not in the country without corn and cattle about thee,' Lord Burghley advised his son, 'for he that putteth his hand to his purse for every expense of household is like him that keepeth water in a sieve.'

This wealth was drawn directly from the land, and the enormous number of domestics which it supported made the palaces of nobility what they were – great rambling structures which spread their multiplicity of courtyards and patchwork of gardens over many acres of land. This sprawling irregularity often resulted from piecemeal construction, lodgings and outbuildings being added as circumstances seemed to require, until the original mansion became lost amid the jumble of towers, gables and chimney-stacks which provided the most striking features of the Tudor skyline.

Royal visits not infrequently provided the occasion for such extensions, and in this manner the country seats of Sir William Cecil and Sir Nicholas Bacon, 'begun with a mean measure', swelled into palaces to meet the demands of a frequently visiting sovereign.

A letter from Sir Anthony Wingfield to William More of Loseley in 1576 shows that Elizabeth could be exacting about her accommodation. 'After I had advertised my Lord Chamberlain', he wrote, 'what few small rooms, and how unmeet your house was for the Queen's Majesty ... she determined to go to the Manor House.' It appears, however, that, in the following year, she did stay at Loseley.

The first warning usually came from the royal Harbingers, Ushers of the Queen's Bedchamber, who visited the house to acquaint the owner of Her Majesty's purpose to come there, to see how conveniently she might be lodged, and to ensure that the neighbouring villages were free from the plague. Then, as the pair rode off to return their report, or to warn the occupants of some near-by mansion next to be visited, the household would quicken into a hive of unwonted activity. Lord Hertford, 'fully expecting Her Majesty's coming to Elvetham, drew all his servants into the chief thicket of the park where, in a few words, he put them in mind what quietness and what diligence they were to use'.

Competition to entertain the Queen was often great. Lord Buckhurst, receiving her at Wythiam, was 'fain to send to Flanders to supply him, the others having drawn the country dry'; he bemoaned that her visit could not be delayed a year, so that he could have got his house 'more fitted for her entertainment'. Meanwhile, Lord Hertford, nothing daunted by the prospect of this royal visitation, 'with all expedition set artificers to work, to the number of three hundred, to enlarge his house with new rooms and offices'.

The Queen's influence was not only reflected in the size of the houses; she was known to turn her attention to aesthetic questions as well. During a visit to Sir Thomas Gresham at Osterley, Fuller informs us, 'Her Majesty found fault with the court of this house, as too great, affirming that it would appear more handsome if divided by a wall in the middle.' She awoke the next morning to find the court partitioned as she had suggested, for Gresham had sent at once to London for workmen who speedily but silently erected the wall during the hours of darkness. The English, Michael Soriano noted in his dispatches, 'attempt to do everything that comes into their heads, just as if all that the imagination suggests could be easily executed'.

Some such presupposition certainly seems to have underlain the entertainments offered to the Queen as she went on her progresses. Ambitious transformation scenes, often entailing extensive excavations, were no sooner conceived than put into execution. At Elvetham a crescent-shaped lake was constructed, across which Tritons, wading waist-high in the water, towed a fully rigged pinnace in which 'three virgins with their cornets played Scottish gigs.' At Mount Surrey, a great pit was dug and covered with green canvas from which nymphs emerged, and 'in the same cave was a noble noise of music of all kinds of instruments severally to be sounded.' At Beddington, Sir Francis Carew covered a cherry tree with a great tent to enlarge and retard the ripening of the fruit, and long after the cherry season was over, 'when he was assured of Her Majesty's coming, he removed the tent, and a few sunny days brought them to their full maturity.'

Wherever she went, Elizabeth was obliged to listen to intricate and interminable orations or to witness by the wayside the enaction of masques and pageants, decked with all that wealth could procure or ingenuity contrive. These entertainments had one thing in common: they were studded with laboured compliments to her person. Often the speaker, feigning ignorance of her estate, pretended to discern her quality from her natural graces. Tactful allusion was also made to her spinsterhood. 'Chastity suddenly, in view of the Queen, sets upon Cupid and spoils him of his coach.' Poor Cupid, he was frequently chastised in deferred compliment to a Virgin Queen!

Compliments, however, were by no means always allegorical. Elizabeth was accustomed to receive gifts of considerable value at any house in which she stayed, and by way of further honouring her host, she often helped herself. 'To grace his Lordship more, she, of herself, took from him a salt, and a spoon and fork of fair agate.' It was all enormously expensive. 'Tuesday, September 12th [1590],' noted Sir Julius Caesar, 'the Queen visited my house at Mitcham, and supped and lodged there, and dined there the next day. I presented her with a gown of cloth of silver richly embroidered; a black network mantle with pure gold, a taffeta hat, white with several flowers, and a jewel of gold set therein with rubies and diamonds. Her Majesty removed from my house after dinner the 13th of September to Nonsuch with exceeding good contentment; which entertainment of Her Majesty ... amounted to £700 besides my own provisions and what was sent unto me by my friends.'

That was for one night. Some of the entertainments at Theobalds cost Burghley between two and three thousand pounds – that is to say, as much as the whole cost of building a house on the scale of Gorhambury or Loseley. Nevertheless, owners usually considered the money well spent. Lord Burghley, comparing his own Theobalds with Sir Christopher Hatton's Holdenby, said 'God send us long to enjoy her, for whom we both meant to exceed our purses in these.'

The two houses were very similar; the plan of Holdenby was in all important respects the same as that of Theobalds. It had the same arrangement of the hall dividing the two main quadrangles; the same arcaded entrance front between staircase towers, and the same impressive silhouette – 'at every corner of the inward square, four magnificent towers or turrets'.

In August 1579, Burghley visited this new house, and Hatton, who was absent, wrote to ask for his criticisms. 'I humbly beseech you for your opinion to the Surveyor', he wrote, 'of such lacks and faults as shall appear to you in this rude building.' Since it was based on Burghley's own house, no better critic could be desired; 'as the same is done hitherto in direct observation of your house and plot at Tyballs [his spelling of Theobalds] so I earnestly pray your lordship that by your good corrections at this time it may prove as like to the same as it hath ever meant to be.' The next day Burghley made his way to the mansion, and was clearly impressed. 'Approaching to the house,' he wrote, 'being led by a large, long, straight, fair way, I found great magnificence in the front, or front pieces, and so every part answerable to allure liking.' Within he was no less pleased: 'I found no one thing of greater grace than your stately ascent from your Hall to your Great Chamber; and your chambers answerable with largeness and lightsomeness that truly a Momus could find no fault.'

It is clear from the account of Burghley's visit that the building of Holdenby was well advanced by 1579. Two years later it seems to have been in full use. In 1581 it was visited by a certain Barnaby Rich. He found that the house 'for the bravery of the buildings, for the stateliness of the chambers, for the rich furniture of the lodgings ... and for all other necessaries appertinent to a palace of pleasure, is thought by those who have judgment to be incomparable and to have no fellow in England that is out of Her Majesty's hands'.

Architecturally, Holdenby might have held its own beside Greenwich or Nonsuch, but there was a significant difference between a house and a palace which its own history was to show. For royal residences were kept empty and unfurnished in the absence of the Court, and special arrangements had to be made to rehang the tapestries if visitors of distinction were expected. In 1610, three years after Holdenby had been purchased by the Crown, it was standing bleak and deserted and payments were made for wood and coal 'to air the great house', so little was it used, 'by reason whereof the rooms grow musty, the walls decay and the chimneys fall down.' It had not been thus in the days of Hatton. Barnaby Rich had found the place teeming with life. 'Though the owner himself useth not to come thence once in two years,' he wrote, 'yet I dare undertake there is daily provision to be found convenient to entertain any nobleman with his whole train that should hap to call in of a sudden. And how many gentlemen and strangers that come but to see the house are there daily welcomed, feasted and lodged.' The impression is almost that of a free hotel for the socially respectable.

This open hospitality was a feature of the Tudor house that does not seem to have far outlived the century. In 1632, Donald Lupton was bemoaning its decay: 'It is thought that pride, puritanism, coaches and covetousness hath caused him [Hospitality] to leave our land; there are six upstart tricks come up in great houses of late which he cannot brook. Peeping windows for the ladies to view what doings there are in the Hall, a Buttery Hatch that is kept locked, clean tables, a French cook in the Kitchens, a Porter that locks the gates at dinner time, the decay of black jacks in the cellar and blue coats in the Hall.'

Hatton had spared no cost on the building of Holdenby, 'the last and greatest monument of his youth'. It lay round two main courts, a large and regular structure, reminiscent of Longleat in its use of the Roman orders, but true to the Tudor plan. But whereas Longleat nestled in a valley bottom, Holdenby was mounted upon a hill and set about with pastures and fish-pools and gardens and orchards, terraced with 'many ascendings and descendings', so that where Sir Christopher had found a craggy and unprofitable land, there was now formed 'a most pleasant, sweet and princely place'.

Fuller, who regarded it as the finest house in Northamptonshire, made the interesting suggestion that 'whoso seriously compareth the state of Holdenby with Burghley will dispute with himself whether the offices of Lord Chancellor or Treasurer of England be of greater revenues; seeing that Holdenby may be said to show the Seal and Burghley the Purse in their respective magnificence.'

It would have been more apt to have compared Holdenby with Theobalds, the principal residence of Lord Burghley, which was situated between Cheshunt and Waltham Cross and 'reckoned one of the most beautiful houses in England'. Burghley had intended the original mansion for a modest private residence destined for his younger son, but answering to the repeated visits of the Queen the mansion grew to a prodigious size. By the time that Burghley had finished with it, Theobalds presented three courts on an alignment with the drive, offering the most impressive perspective to the visitor (Frontispiece). In addition to these an important wing projected southwards and further offices rambled away to the north. There were five open loggias on the ground floor and as many galleries above, and when, in 1585, the 'old house' was rebuilt as the Fountain Court, there was added a magnificent new suite of apartments.

It is strange how the destinies of Theobalds and Holdenby were linked. Both were built by chief officers of Elizabeth; both appealed so much to James I that he acquired them, with the result that both were sold up during the Commonwealth and fell into ruins. It is perhaps not surprising that houses designed for the entertainment of royalty should have been thought worthy of royal ownership. Nonsuch and Newhall, Hatfield and Knole alternated between royal and noble owners. The fact is that the richer members of the aristocracy kept what amounted to a small court; when Sir Francis Bacon was at Gorhambury 'it seemed as if the Court were there, so nobly did he live.'

Some interesting details of the life of a large household are given by Holinshed in a note on Sir Thomas Cheyne: 'The number of his servants to whom he gave liveries were two hundred and five, whereof in household were six score, besides strangers that were daily coming and going. And his servants had no just cause – either for lack of great wages truly paid them every quarter, and board wages every Sunday, or plenty of meat and drink, and lodging in good feather beds – to live out of order.' Sir Thomas was so concerned that after his death they should not 'run at random' that he left to some annuities, to some a year's wages and to others keep for three years until his son's coming of age.

There is a remarkable improvement in the standard of living revealed in this. 'The times could still be remembered', wrote William Harrison, 'when the goodman of the house made his fire against the reredos of his hall' and lay upon straw with a log for a bolster, covered only in 'dogswain and hopharlots'. As for servants, it was seldom they had any sheet beneath them 'to keep them from the pricking of the straws that ran oft through the canvas and razed their hardened hides.'

It is here, and not in any consideration of styles or of architects, that the true significance of the Tudor house is to be found. The outstanding feature of the period is not the advent of the cornice and pilaster, but the extraordinary improvement in domestic comfort. The period begins with the laying on of water at Richmond; it ends with the invention of the water closet.

The huge households brought a distinctive element into the architecture of Tudor mansions. Outwardly they were still often castles; inwardly they were palaces, but essentially – and this is the best guide to the imagination – they were colleges. When the Duke of Stettin visited our universities he noticed that the colleges were 'all built round quadrangles, and each of them like a lordly mansion.'

Outside the context of the royal visits, the great houses of Tudor England were built to contain communities of complex structure. At Gorhambury three members of the household kept their coaches, and one Hunt, 'a notable thrifty man', left an estate of a thousand a year in Somerset. At Theobalds as many as twenty gentlemen with four-figure incomes were numbered among Burghley's attendants. At Cowdray the hierarchy was carefully tabulated and the duties of each rank specified by Lord Montague in his household book; it shows clearly the collegiate nature of his establishment. When social distinctions were more readily accepted through being more clearly defined, it was possible for a real communal life to exist, and for this purpose the structural layout of a college lent itself admirably. The basic elements, the chapel and the great hall, representing the spiritual and material needs of the community, were exactly as we know them at Oxford or Cambridge. The most perfect architectural expression of this was at Richmond, where hall and chapel stood detached and answered each other on opposite sides of the inner quadrangle.

Next to the requirements of the community came the needs of the individual, and the senior members of the household were provided with rooms (usually two in number) which were ranged after the fashion of a college round the sides of the courtyards. This accounts for the many external doorways, as may be seen today at Kirky, and for the absence of passages or other internal communications. It may have been this arrangement which led to the abandoning of many Tudor houses during the seventeenth and eighteenth centuries, when the whole conception of a domestic household had altered.

Like the college, the Tudor country house was in some ways the successor of the monastery, as, according to the charitable instincts of its owner, it became the centre of poor relief in the district. There was provision in the household book of Lord Montague for the feeding of strangers and the finding of work for the poor. At

Audley End the old abbey hospital was rebuilt by Lord Suffolk and turned into alms-houses – a delightful group of buildings which happily survives. Lord Burghley was particularly noted for the extent of his charity. Some twenty or thirty poor were relieved daily at Theobalds gate, while a weekly sum of ten pounds was set aside for providing others with work. Even some of the buildings had their origin in Burghley's desire to give employment to idle hands, and across the London road he built an alms-house for 'decayed and overworn captains'. For all this the houses were less reliable as charitable institutions than the monasteries which they replaced.

As the cultural centres of England they were more effective. They were nurseries of art, and by constantly calling upon local talent to produce masons, carpenters, joiners and other craftsmen they kept alive a national and popular tradition. Representing in themselves workmanship of the highest quality, they set a standard which affected the houses of humble farmers. William Harrison noted with pride that 'many farmers ... have for the most part learnt to garnish their cupboards with plate and their joined beds with tapestry and rich hangings ... whereby the wealth of our country doth infinitely appear.'

The wealth was not all lavished upon the entertainment of the Queen. The brilliant receptions at Gorhambury must be offset with the picture of Bacon enjoying, amid the splendour of his surroundings, 'a philosophic retirement', pacing up and down the oak plantations with Mr Bushell in unobtrusive attendance, ready with pen and ink-horn 'to set down his present notions'. Many of the nobility and gentry entertained scholars and amassed libraries, among which Lord Lumley's at Nonsuch was accounted 'right worthy of remembrance'. Others, as Aubrey puts it, 'espoused not learning, but were addicted to field sports and hospitality'. Too many had shared the fate of Sir Richard Sackville, of whom Roger Ascham relates that 'a fond schoolmaster, before he was fully fifteen years old, drove him with fear of beating from all love of learning.'

In both types of household Elizabeth was perfectly at home. She could ride with the huntsman and talk with the scholar, and it was

her willingness to meet her subjects on their own ground which
gave that personal touch to her reign that so often lends charm to
its study. Her progresses, making a virtue of necessity, were instrumental in keeping her close to her people.

In the beginning of July, when the woods had lost the bright,
kaleidoscopic tones of spring and settled into the dark, unvaried
green of summer; when the red and gold and umber of willows and
poplars had given place to the green and grey and silver of their
mature foliage; when the heavy shimmer of a summer's day hung
across the landscape and the city streets became hot and unhealthy,
the Queen shut up her London palaces and set out on progress to
show herself to the surrounding counties and to win the hearts of
her people in her own inimitable manner.

VIII

A PROGRESS INTO EAST ANGLIA

IN 1578, Elizabeth's progress was to East Anglia, and it proved to be one of the most memorable that she ever made. 'I did never see Her Majesty better received by two counties in one journey than Suffolk and Norfolk now', wrote Richard Topclyffe to the Earl of Shrewsbury.

In spite of the fact that the administrative problems behind a progress must have been prodigious, Elizabeth's moves were often so sudden as to appear unpremeditated. Of her arrival at Audley End, the Vice Chancellor of Cambridge had precisely one day's notice, and the gentry of Suffolk 'had but small warning certainly to build upon'. They had not, however, left things to chance, and there had been a rush on rich materials. 'All the velvets and silks were taken up that might be laid hands on and bought for money, and soon converted into such garments and suits of robes that shew thereof might have beautified the greatest Triumph that was in England.' Thus it was that the Sheriff, Sir William Spring, was able to meet the Queen and escort her through Suffolk with 'two hundred young gentlemen, clad all in white velvet, and three hundred of the graver sort apparelled in black velvet and fair chains ... with fifteen hundred serving men more on horseback, well and bravely mounted ... which surely was a comely troop, and a noble sight to behold'.

The first to entertain the Queen was Sir William Cordell (or Cordall) of Long Melford Hall, and the standard he set 'did light such a candle to the rest of the Shire' that the gentry vied with one another in the offering of sumptuous and elaborate entertainments.

Sir William was a man who had risen, like so many of the Elizabethans, through the legal profession. At the end of Henry VIII's reign, his father is still referred to as 'Yeoman'. Twenty years later,

RICHMOND
GENERAL VIEW FROM THE SOUTH

RICHMOND

By courtesy of the Ashmolean

above: THE CENTRAL BLOCK (the sketch at top is of Oatlands)   *below:* BIRD'S EYE VIEW

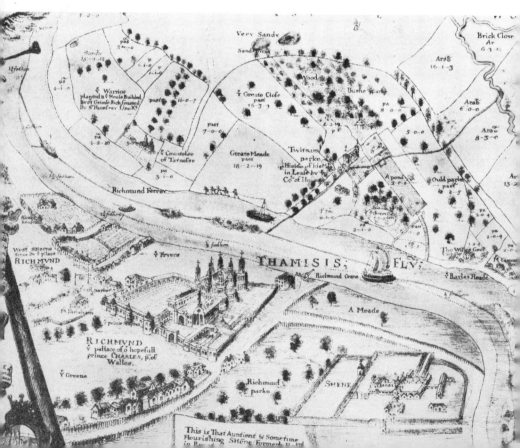

William is Knight, Master of the Rolls and Privy Councillor, and in the following year, Speaker of the House of Commons. Himself a scholar, he became a patron of learning and was concerned with the founding of St John's College, Oxford, to which he was Visitor.

It is interesting to note that, although Cordell was enriched with monastic lands – the manor of Melford having belonged to the Abbey of Bury St Edmunds – the grant of the lands dates from the reign of Philip and Mary.

Like most of those who had risen suddenly to position and property, Sir William Cordell built himself a country house, and he proved as successful at building as he had been at law. 'Truly this house of Long Melford', wrote James Howell to Daniel Caldwell, 'though it be not so great, yet it is so well compacted and contrived with such dainty conveniences every way, that if you saw the land-skip of it you would be mightily taken with it.'

Situated on 'a cheerful rising ground', the house commanded an excellent view of the deer park round about it, and its most singular feature was devised for the watching of sport. 'Between the two eastern towers on each side of the entrance front,' Sir William Parker informs us, 'high up, about level with the parapet of the roof, there was a suspended bridge, from which spectators could see the hunting and hawking.' With such a house, Elizabeth could not fail to be delighted, and her visit marked the highest point of Cordell's career, for three years later he was laid to rest in Long Melford Church.

The next day she rode to Lawshall, a few miles distant, and the event was recorded with pride in the parish register. 'It is to be remembered that the Queen's Highness, in her Progress, riding from Melford to Bury ... dined at Lawshall Hall to the great rejoicing of the said Parish, and the country thereabouts.' Her host was here Sir William Drury, who made her 'a costly and delicate dinner' and thence accompanied her to Hawstead, his principal residence.

Hawstead was a house in many ways typical of its age. 'Its situation,' wrote Sir John Cullum, 'as of many old seats in this neighbourhood, is on an eminence, gently sloping toward the South'. A base-court consisting of barns, stables, slaughter-house and smithy was separated from the mansion house by a moat. Round the moat lay a handsome terrace, and from the terrace, one enjoyed an excellent view over the surrounding country. Thus the siting of the house gave it naturally an outlook which was often secured artificially by the raising of a mount 'which in many old gardens was to be clambered up for the sake of prospect'.

Both the moat and the eminence gave Hawstead something of the atmosphere of a stronghold. This impression was increased by the fact that ordinary access was by means of a small wicket only, set in 'the great, well timbered gate that rarely grated on its hinges'. The narrow entrance brought one suddenly face to face with a strange memorial of Elizabeth's visit. 'Immediately upon your peeping through the wicket', continues Sir John, 'the first object that unavoidably struck you was the stone figure of Hercules'; he stood beneath an elegant Renaissance canopy in the centre of a stone fountain which he supplied with water in an extremely indecorous manner. The pedestal bore the date 1578, from which it is to be inferred that the statue was specially erected for the Queen's visit.

The outward appearance of the house was not less interesting. It was of timber and plaster, the first storey heavily overhanging the ground floor, and the tiles projecting over the first, so that the wall surfaces were seldom wet, and lasted extremely well. From a constructional point of view, the plaster, which contained much hair and pebbles 'as big as horse beans', was extremely tough. From an aesthetic point of view, it was astonishing. 'The plaster in the front', says Sir John, 'was thickly stuck with fragments of glass which made a brilliant appearance when the sun shone, and even by moonlight.'

In 1590 Sir William Drury was killed in a duel with Sir John Burroughs in a foolish quarrel about precedence. 'Be well ware, my Besse,' wrote Elizabeth to his widow, 'you strive not with Divine ordinance, nor grudge at irremediable harms.' Her husband she had lost, but she still had a Queen 'who leaves not now to protect you when your case requires care, and minds not to omit whatever may be best for you and yours. Your most loving careful sovereign.' Elizabeth was capable of entering into a truly pastoral relationship with those who were closest to her.

Not all of the Queen's visits, however, were of such a friendly nature. On Sunday, August 10th, she came to Thetford and lodged with Mr Rookwood, 'Master of Euston Hall'. Since Rookwood was a Roman Catholic, it is perhaps unfortunate that we chiefly know of him only through the pen of Richard Topclyffe, the implacable hater and hunter of Papists. It is not probable that his opinion is unbiased. 'Her Majesty,' he wrote to Lord Shrewsbury, 'by some means I know not, was lodged at his house, Euston, far unmeet for Her Highness, but fitter for the blackguard. Nevertheless, her excellent Majesty gave Rookwood ordinary thanks for his bad house, and her fair hand to kiss.'

The Lord Chamberlain, however, knowing of Rookwood's religion, summoned him and, after examining him, 'commanded him out of Court' – which, at that moment, meant out of his own house. But the matter did not end there. A piece of plate having been reported missing, a search was instigated, and, during the search, 'in the hayrick such an image of Our Lady was found as for greatness, for gayness and workmanship I did never see a match.' At the time of this discovery, the Queen was watching a country-dance, and, at a dramatic moment, the incriminating figure was brought in and held up 'like a beast raised upon a sudden from Hell by conjuring'. Elizabeth ordered it to be burnt, which was done then and there by the country folks 'to her content and to the unspeakable joy of everyone – but some one or two who had sucked of the idol's poisoned milk'.

Rookwood was committed to Norwich jail and, soon afterwards, forfeited to the Crown the estate on which he had so lately entertained his sovereign. He died, twenty years later, still in prison at Bury St Edmunds. A relative of his, Ambrose, was executed for his share in the Gunpowder Plot.

From Euston, the Queen crossed the county boundary into Norfolk, where the gentry, not to be outdone by their neighbours of Suffolk, turned out with a troop of two thousand five hundred horsemen, 'which goodly company waited on their Sheriff a long season'.

At Kenninghall, 'the Earl of Surrey[1] did shew most sumptuous

[1] Though the Earldom of Surrey was forfeited on the attainder and execution of the Duke

cheer', and the banquets and pageants began afresh as the Queen made her leisurely approach to Norwich, 'her most dutiful City'. On Saturday, August 16th, she was dining with Lady Style at Bracon Ash, about five miles from the city. At one o'clock the people of Norwich turned out in hundreds and set off down the road for Hartford Bridge to welcome their sovereign. They waited for nearly an hour before the royal equipage appeared, and then 'the cries of the people to Almighty God for the preservation of Her Majesty rattled so loud as hardly for a great time could anything be heard; but at last, as everything hath an end, the noise appeased' and the Mayor offered the sword of the City, together with a silver gilt cup containing a hundred pounds in gold. In accepting it, Elizabeth made the surprising statement that 'Princes have no need of money.' It was in the hearts and true allegiance of her subjects, she said, that the real Treasury of the Prince was to be found. Nevertheless, she accepted the hundred pounds.

The royal procession now resumed its journey and came to a place called the Town Close, 'within a flight shot or two of the City, where the Castle of Blanche Flower was in most beautiful prospect'. It was one of the attractions of a compact and under-populated age that a city such as Norwich could be viewed as a whole by those approaching it, and the fabric of the city spoke of its history.

In the days of Elizabeth, Norwich was still a city of weavers, and this had the odd effect of making it seem deserted, the majority of the inhabitants being 'so employed with their manufactures within doors that this appears a melancholy place, except on Sundays and public days, when the streets swarm with them'. But whatever the turn-out on Sundays may have been, the town was in fact very thinly inhabited, for most of the houses and even many of the churches were roofed with thatch, as the result of which fires were common, so that, in the words of an eighteenth-century historian, 'there is void enough in it for another colony; and from the inter-mixture of its houses and trees, it is called a City in an orchard.' But if the houses were ravaged by fire, the inhabitants were afflicted no

of Norfolk in 1572, his eldest son Philip, later Earl of Arundel, continued to be known by the courtesy title of Earl of Surrey.

less by plague, and it was on the consequent depopulation that the picturesque effect depended, so that in a sense the beauty of the city reflected the suffering of its people.

From the south, the two most prominent features were the castle and the cathedral, representing the twin claims of Church and State upon the inhabitants. The castle, with the romantic name of Blanche Flower, served the unromantic function of common gaol, but the cathedral, whose spire was second only to that of Salisbury, preserved its medieval beauty almost untouched until the Civil War.

The city was protected on its east side by the River Wensum, and to the westward by its wall – a girdle of flint and stone pierced by eleven gateways and guarded by forty towers. On the extreme right, as Elizabeth viewed it, the Bishop's Bridge and gatehouse provided the only access to the town from the river side. There were grim memories associated with this spot, for it was here in 1531, in the ditch known as the Lollard's Pit, that 'little' Bilney, the Cambridge Reformer, had been burnt to death before a great concourse of people. Nine more victims, both men and women, had shared his fate on the same place during the reign of Mary.

The memory of Ket's rebellion, too, was still young, and many of those who now acclaimed the Queen had gathered with the malcontents on Mousehold Heath, received their pardon from Dudley, and seen their leader hang in chains from the castle. Both Church and State, in fact, were in need of peace and it was her promise of this that made Elizabeth doubly welcome to the city of Norwich. In her honour, the walls about St Stephen's Gate were 'gallantly and strongly repaired', the gatehouse itself 'most richly and beautifully set forth' with a blaze of heraldic decorations, and the significant verses displayed:

> Division kindled strife;
> Blest Union quenched the flame:
> Thence sprang our noble Phoenix dear,
> The peerless Prince of Fame.

At her first entrance through the gate, Elizabeth was greeted with a burst of song 'which was marvellously sweet and good', as

Churchyard noted, 'albeit the rudeness of some ringer of bells did somewhat hinder the noise and harmony'.

Today a royal visitor would be taken to the chief industry of a town and shown over the factory. For Elizabeth, there was no such centralized industry, so a show was put on to inform her of the chief occupations of the citizens, and the industries of the city provided the pageants for her reception.

The first pageant represented weaving. The stage was decorated with paintings of the various types of loom in use, and, on the scaffold, were girls spinning worsted yarn. In the middle stood 'a pretty boy richly apparelled, which represented the Commonwealth of the City'. It was his task to recite the explanatory verses. He began:

> 'Most gracious Prince, undoubted sovereign Queen,
> Our only joy, next God, and sure defence;
> In this small show our whole estate is seen,
> The wealth we have we find proceed from thence ... '

Elizabeth was delighted. She 'particularly viewed the knitting and spinning of the children, perused the looms, and noted the several works and commodities which were made by these means'.

Leaving the weavers, she continued towards the market where a second pageant thwarted the street. This pageant, far from depicting the realities of industry, dealt with the more legendary aspects of history. Ladies representing Norwich, Deborah, Judith and Esther, and Marcia Queen of England, all complimented the Queen in verses which sometimes had the lilt, but seldom the humour, of the Gollywog rhymes.

> 'Penelope did never thirst
> Ulysses more to see,
> Than I, poor Norwich, hungered have
> To gain the sight of thee.'

Much of it must have been extremely boring to one of Elizabeth's intelligence, but they were her people, and this was their way of expressing their loyalty and devotion. Her mind was never far from them, and their offering was accepted uncritically.

One day, when passing the hospital door, the Queen found Stephen Limbert, master of the grammar school, ready with an oration. 'Her Majesty drew near unto him', writes Churchyard, 'and thinking him fearful, said graciously unto him "be not afraid". She then summoned the French ambassador and certain English lords to hearken, and herself listened attentively throughout the oration.' It was a pompous and pedantic performance. 'It is the best that ever I heard,' declared Elizabeth, 'you shall have my hand.' Nor did she only give him her hand to kiss, but further complimented him by sending after him to know his name. That moment must have burned for ever in his memory.

Thomas Churchyard was at the back of most of the entertainments. 'I was the first that was called and came to Norwich about that business,' he writes, 'and remained there three long weeks before the Court came thither, devising and studying the best I could for the City.' He has secured the immortality of his devices by being his own reviewer.

The civic authorities, however, do not seem to have been very cooperative – Churchyard hints darkly at some 'crossing causes in the City' – and fixed no definite times and places for him 'to venture the hazard of a Show'. He was left to take his opportunities as best he could, contriving, when possible, to be 'full in the way where Her Highness should pass towards her dinner'. On one occasion she was heading for Gossie Park to hunt, and people were not lacking to discourage Churchyard from interrupting her. But the opportunity was not to be missed. 'I hastily prepared my boys and men,' he writes, 'with all their furnitures, and so set forwards with two coaches, handsomely trimmed.' The masque was a morality play, or so the names of the characters suggest. They were curiously 'public school' virtues – Modesty, Temperance, Good Exercise and Shamefastness, who attended Chastity in her inevitable triumph over Cupid.

The next day he was less successful. The Queen was dining at Mount Surrey, and Churchyard bundled all his paraphernalia down and took up his position between the back door and the Queen's barge. But the place proved too narrow, 'whereupon we took boats and conveyed our people down the water towards a landing place that we hoped the Queen would come unto. And there, having all things in readiness, hovered on the water three long hours.' But darkness overtook them before the Queen emerged, and they were obliged to retire, trusting for better luck the next day. This they had, for Elizabeth heard about their disappointment, and caused the Lord Chamberlain to inform Mr Churchyard when and where she might be intercepted on the morrow.

Dearer to the heart of Elizabeth than these laboured speeches and extravagantly wrought productions was the spontaneous expression of loyalty and affection by the people. Churchyard, who might well have been too preoccupied to notice, was deeply impressed by this 'new kind of reverence' shown by those who were unaccustomed to royalty which, he said, 'makes the old haughtiness and stiff-necked behaviour of some places to blush and become odious'.

The time passed pleasantly and therefore quickly, and 'frowning Friday' came all too soon. The people of Norwich rallied themselves for a final farewell, and the streets were hung with herbs and flowers, wrought into garlands and coronets, as far as St Benet's Gates. 'The doleful hour of her departure came', writes Churchyard, 'and she passed from the Court to those gates with such countenances, both of Her Majesty's part and her subjects, now dolorous, now cheerful, as plainly showed the loving hearts of both sides.' There were still verses to be recited and there was music in the air.

Elizabeth now doubled back on her tracks, staying at Kimberley, Wood Rising and Thetford, and so bringing her progress into Cambridgeshire, where she continued to 'make the crooked paths straight where she cometh, and draw the hearts of the people after her wheresoever she travels'.

At Kirtling, Lord North seems to have been particularly lavish in his hospitality. Churchyard's claim that he was 'no wit behind any of the best for a frank house, a noble heart and well-ordered entertainment' is supported by his household accounts 'at the Queen's Majesty's coming thither on Monday the first of September to supper and tarrying there until Wednesday after dinner'. They add up to a total of £762. 4. 2.

Apart from one hundred and twenty pounds spent on a jewel for the Queen, almost all of it went on food and drink. The greatest expenditure was on poultry and game which reached a total of one hundred and fifty-eight pounds. Besides chickens and pigeons there are twenty-three different species of bird on the menu, of which quails, dotterels and peewits were in highest demand. Eighty-eight pounds went on meat, not counting sixteen buck from the park which provided one hundred and twenty-eight pasties. A cartload and two horseloads of oysters cost only five pounds, but gulls were six shillings apiece. Four hundred and thirty pounds of butter were accounted for, and 2,522 eggs. Lord North had special cooks down from London as Sir Nicholas Bacon had at Gorhambury, and like Sir Nicholas, he lost a certain amount of pewter and other vessel in the course of the festivities.

But if there was a lordly disregard for cost in the provision of food and drink, there was a remarkable economy observed with regard to buildings. The banqueting house, new kitchens and 'trimming-up chambers' cost Lord North only thirty-two pounds, and 'making a standing for the Queen in the Park' a mere twenty-five shillings. The most plausible explanation would be that Kirtling was already a house capable of receiving the Queen and her train, and needed no special embellishment.

Situated in 'the woody part of the county of Cambridge' about five miles from Newmarket, it was built of brick with stone trimmings, 'raised on a platform, and nearly surrounded with a deep and broad moat filled with water'. It was one of the many Tudor houses to have an outer gatehouse standing free in front of the mansion (Plate 19) instead of being incorporated in one side of a quadrangle. The gatehouse, together with the moat, gave Kirtling a militant aspect which agreed well with the pugnacious spirit of its owner.

Roger North was a personal friend of Leicester's and followed him in 1585 to Holland, where he distinguished himself by his bravery at Zutphen. Although wounded in the leg on the previous day, he rushed into battle 'with one boot on and one boot off, and went to the matter very lustily'. In later years, when he was leading a peaceable country life at Kirtling, he was 'violently attacked with dullness of hearing'. Elizabeth sent him the following recipe: 'Bake a little loaf of bean flower, and being hot, rive it in halves, and into each half pour in three or four spoonfuls of bitter almonds; then clap both halves to both ears at going to bed, keep them close, and keep your head warm.' It was typical of the maternal care extended by Elizabeth to the chief officers of her realm that she should have sent this, but history does not relate what effect, if any, the recipe produced.

When the Queen left Kirtling, North went with her, and they finished the progress with an appropriate flourish at Lord Leicester's manor of Wanstead. 'To knit up all', wrote Thomas Church-yard, 'the good cheer was revived, not only with making a great feast for the Queen and the French Ambassador, but also in feasting solemnly the whole guard ... using such courtesy unto them for the space of two days as was and is worthy of perpetual memory.'

It would be pleasant to end on that note. But Churchyard did not see what he was not meant to see, and even the watchful eyes of Elizabeth could be deceived for a time. It was here at Wanstead on September 21st, 1578 – less than a month after the Queen's visit – that Leicester was secretly married to Lettice, Countess of Essex. It was nearly a year before Elizabeth heard of the match, and she was furious at the news. Leicester, after a period of house arrest, was of course forgiven, but for Lettice a special hatred was reserved in the heart of the Queen, who ever after referred to her as 'that she-wolf'.

IX

KENILWORTH CASTLE

IT WAS a curious feature of the Elizabethan age that while most of its leading families were upstart, pedigrees were still accorded an almost exaggerated respect. Self-made men took historic titles and put out claims to ancient lineage that were more remarkable for their ingenuity than for their regard to truth. The most preposterous of all was Elizabeth's own genealogical tree in which her ancestry was traced to Adam.

It was an upstart age because of the boundless opportunity which it offered to any who had the vision to grasp it, and these were not a few; but of all who stepped neatly but firmly into the shoes of the ancient nobility, none aimed higher or held on with more tenacity than the house of Dudley, whose three generations coincided almost exactly with those of the Tudor dynasty.

The first, Edmund, was a creature of Henry VII's, the instrument of his rather shady financial programme. Henry VIII made the popular gesture of having Edmund executed, but not before his three sons had acquired, through their mother, the historic quarterings of Beauchamp, Neville and Talbot.

The second, John, rose to be dictator of England and the first man unconnected with royalty to be a duke, taking the resounding title of Northumberland. His fall was the heavier, and nothing in his life became him less than the leaving it. At the beginning of Mary's reign his wife and five sons were all in the Tower, mostly on charges of treason. At the end of her reign, only Ambrose and Robert survived, but already the tide of their fortunes was beginning to turn.

Although the first of the Dudleys had risen through his adroitness at law, it was upon the more medieval virtue of military prowess that his sons and grandsons relied for their advancement, and in this they showed great courage and undisputed ability. It is, there-fore, not altogether incongruous that when they had risen to the foremost positions in the realm, Ambrose and Robert should have taken the historic earldoms of Warwick and Leicester and occupied the castles traditionally joined to them. Warwick and Kenilworth were more suited to the pretensions of the Dudleys than the flashy palaces of the Tudor nouveaux riches.

The castle of Kenilworth, situated 'as it were in the navel of England', combined the military advantage of a tactical position with the natural attractions of a fertile and well-forested country. To these endowments of nature had been added the enrichments of a succession of owners. First, there was the Mere – an artificial but ample lake, 'nourished with many lively springs' – embracing the castle walls upon two sides and stretching away a mile or more to westward, a vivary for fish and waterfowl. Then to the north of this was planted the 'goodly Chase – vast, wide, large and full of red deer and other stately game for hunting'.

With the passing of centuries the attractions of sport outweighed the advantages of war, and the building that had begun as a strong-hold under the Normans became a palace of the Plantagenets. The keep, built at the end of the twelfth century by Geoffrey de Clinton, was supplemented by the large and beautiful additions of John of Gaunt. These additions – the great hall and state apartments – filled two sides of the inner court with their geometrical tracery and bulging oriels, while presenting towards the west the majestic sym-metry of the Strong and Sainteowe Towers. Henry V had taken the buildings right outside the fortifications and made the 'Plaisance en Marais', a summer lodge on the far side of the Mere.

It was in continuation of these more domestic and vulnerable edifices that Robert Dudley made his additions in about 1571. Leicester's Buildings, a tall, compact block at the south-east angle of the inner court, were placed in audacious apposition to the keep, daring to answer it across the entrance to the court, and contrasting its ponderous magnificence with the airy lightness of their enormous windows.

Across the base-court to the east, he built the fine, half-timbered barn for stables, and north of this an elegant gatehouse, providing access to the seven acres encircled by the curtain wall. In this spacious and imposing ensemble (Plate 21), Leicester was ready to receive his Queen in 1575.

The story of the Queen's reception is told by Robert Laneham, a man of apparently humble origin, who owed his advancement to the rank of Gentleman Usher to Lord Leicester's favour, 'whereby I now go in my silks, that else might ruffle in my cut canvas'.

In the course of a long and unusually informative letter to his good friend Humphrey Martin, Laneham includes in parentheses some interesting details of the life of a Gentleman Usher. 'A-mornings I rise ordinarily at seven o'clock: then ready, I go to the Chapel; soon after eight I get me commonly to my Lord's chamber.' Here he made his breakfast on the livery – the loaf of manchet and the bowl of ale left by the Earl's bedside in case he was hungry or thirsty in the night. Of course, a proper breakfast was available for Laneham below stairs, but he had his reasons for preferring the leavings of a rich man's table, for the livery was usually left untouched. 'I drink me up a good bowl of ale', he assured his friend; 'when in a sweet pot it is defecated by all night's standing, the drink is the better, take that of me.'

His particular office was to wait upon the Council and to see that due order was observed in their chamber. 'If any make babbling, "Peace," say I, "wot ye where ye are?" If I take a listener, or a pryer in at the chinks or at the lock hole, I am by and by in the bones of him.' Laneham was strict in the care of his office, and it is obvious that the household had learnt to respect him. He found his own level in the community, and led a richer and more interesting life through his attachment to Leicester than would otherwise have been open to him.

Nevertheless, his natural qualities must have been instrumental to his rise, for though of lowly birth, Laneham was an educated man. He had been to St Paul's and to 'St Antoniez' (Antony's or Antholin's?) and could boast the academic distinction of having 'in the fifth form passed Aesop's fables'. Later, he had travelled as a merchant, and so got his languages. These came in useful at the Council Room, for it sometimes chanced that an ambassador called for his lackey or inquired the time. This was Laneham's cue to answer him in his own tongue, so that they 'marvelled to see such a fellow there: then laugh I and say nothing.'

His accomplishments made him a welcome guest at meals and many who kept their tables were glad of his company: 'Dinner and supper I have twenty places to go to, and heartily prayed to.' Then the evenings were spent with the ladies. Sometimes he would 'foot it with dancing'; sometimes he would play to them – 'now with my gittern, now with my cittern, then at the virginals'. Like so many Elizabethans, Laneham was a talented musician, and when he was done with his instruments, he would give them a song, until the ladies flocked round him 'like bees to honey, crying "another, good Laneham, another".'

The secret of his accomplishment was the fact that his employment left him ample time in which to improve himself, and he was a great reader. 'I have leisure sometimes, when I tend not the council, whereby now look I on one book, now on another. Stories I delight in; the more ancient and rare, the more delightsome to me.' Doubtless, it was his delight in history that made him an historian, and prompted him to leave not only an invaluable account of Elizabeth's visit, but a momentary flood of light upon the obscure history of Kenilworth.

Laneham, in fact, was a typical by-product of an Elizabethan house. By taking advantage of the new schools, by the happy chance of a nobleman's favour, by rubbing shoulders with the great and the learned, he had taught himself to appreciate the good things of life, and the beautiful surroundings in which he was called to live made a deep impression on him. Especially he learned to love the 'rare beauty of building' displayed by Kenilworth Castle – 'every room so spacious, so well belighted and so high roofed within, so seemly to sight by due proportion without'. The lofty grandeur of the buildings was only equalled by the airy lightness of the apartments, 'in day-time on every side so glittering by glass, at nights by continual brightness of candle, fire and torchlight'.

For a brief moment, as we turn his pages, the crumbling ruin, restored to wholeness by the labours of an antiquary, springs to life; the courts and chambers are filled with the colourful paraphernalia

of an Elizabethan household and the chase re-echoes to the huntsman's horn.

Leicester's hospitality began at Long Itchington, some seven
miles from Kenilworth, where he 'gave the Queen a glorious
entertainment, erecting a tent of extraordinary largeness for that
purpose'. When dismantled, it required seven carts to take it away,
'by which the magnificence thereof may be guessed'.

Elizabeth approached the castle by the tiltyard, an embattled
compound lying between two gatehouses – the Gallery Tower and
Mortimer's Tower. The whole structure occupied the ridge of the
dam which separated the Mere from the Lower Pool. Here the
porter, after a little buffoonery, 'caused his Trumpeters, that stood
upon the wall ... to sound up a tune of welcome'. They were, in
fact, pasteboard figures of gigantic stature with 'huge and monstrous trumpets counterfeited, wherein they seemed to sound; and
behind them', noted Gascoigne, 'were certain trumpeters that
sounded in deed.' These gargantuan figures were an allusion to the
tradition that Kenilworth had been one of King Arthur's castles.
In pursuance of this theme, many of the mythical personalities who
figured in the pageants came from the Arthurian legend.

At the Queen's first entrance, there was a floating island upon the
Mere 'bright blazing with torches'; upon the island was the Lady
of the Lake, who addressed Elizabeth upon the history and antiquity of the castle.

There was much to be said on this subject. The early history was
concerned with Caesar's Tower, the great Norman keep whose
cavernous window recesses had been filled by Leicester with Elizabethan mullions and transoms. Its walls, twenty feet thick at ground
level, had made it immensely strong, and it had been the scene of a
famous siege after the death of Simon de Montfort at the Battle of
Evesham. For six months it had held out against the King, until at
length 'the garrison being in great want of provisions and attacked
by a pestilential disease, and seeing no probability of young Montfort's being able to bring them any assistance, were obliged to
capitulate.' Here, too, Edward II, taken off the coast of Wales, was
first imprisoned, being afterwards taken to Berkeley Castle where
he was atrociously murdered.

With the coming of John of Gaunt the castle had seen more peaceful and prosperous times, and these were reflected in the domestic and decorative nature of the additions which he made to the Norman stronghold. He left the inner court surrounded by buildings 'with great high bay windows on every side, well proportioned'. Behind them lay the state apartments, and in particular the great hall, a vast double cube ninety feet in length. Much of its beautiful perpendicular decoration survives today in the deep-set, traceried windows. To this the imagination should add an elaborate hammer-beam roof with the broad span of forty-five feet, which made the hall here second only to that at Westminster.

One of the finest views of Kenilworth was from Bull Hill (Plate 20), about half a mile to the north-east. From here the whole castle could be seen 'raised on an easily mounted hill', the long curtain wall following the undulations of the ground, and the natural contours accentuated by the grouping of masonry – so disposed that the tallest buildings occupied the highest ground. To the extreme left the Gallery Tower and the long wall of the tiltyard are reflected in the waters of the Lower Pool. Nearer to, and partly hidden behind the cottages of Bull Hill, is Mortimer's Tower, once the main entrance, from which the roof ridge of Leicester's Barn, the castle stables, leads the eye along to the first important mass – the new block of Leicester's Buildings. In front and below, the curtain wall bellies out into the rotund bastion known as Lunn's Tower; to the right and above rises the square-cut, rough-hewn block of the keep, newly embellished with clock and belfry. The clock had two faces painted with 'blue byse[1] for ground and gold for letters, whereby they glitter conspicuous a great way off'. Against the massive bulk of the keep the four turrets of the new gatehouse stand out by contrast of their lighter frame. From this point the buildings tail away into a further stretch of wall, punctuated here and there by a tower or buttress, that loses itself amid the roofs and chimney-pots of Clinton End.

The night was far spent by the time that Elizabeth entered under Mortimer's Gate, crossed the dry moat which separated the inner from the outer court, and went to her chamber. Her arrival was

---

[1] A blue paint much used by the Tudors.

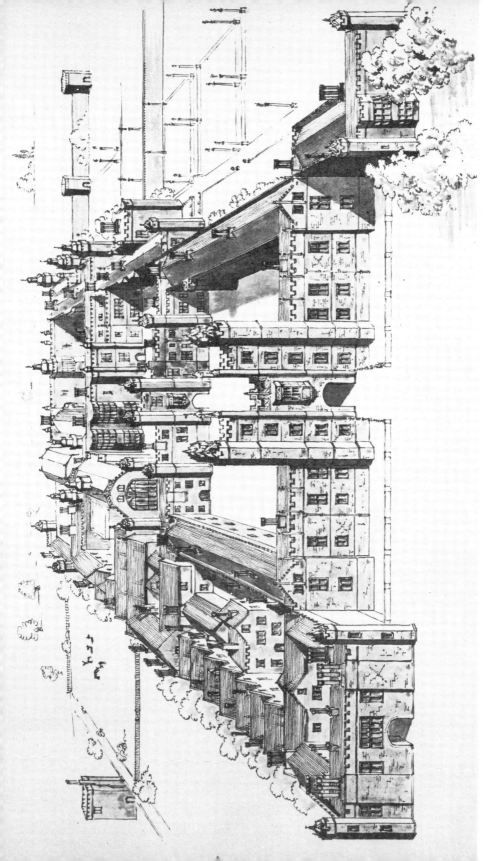

HAMPTON COURT   BIRD'S EYE VIEW

above: THE PALACE FROM THE SOUTH, SHOWING THE WATER GATE AT EXTREME RIGHT

HAMPTON COURT

below: THE PALACE FROM THE NORTH, SHOWING THE TILTYARD IN THE FOREGROUND

announced by 'so great a peal of guns and such lightening by fire-
work ... the noise and flame were seen and heard twenty miles off'.

The following day was Sunday, and spent as the Lord's Day
should be spent, 'in quiet and vacation from work, and in Divine
service and preaching in the Parish Church'. There was one corner
of the castle consecrated to such peace and recreation, and that was
the enclosed garden, lying to the north of the inner court beneath
the shadow of the Norman keep. Its seclusion was apparently well
guarded, for even Laneham, who enjoyed the freedom of so much
at Kenilworth, considered himself fortunate to obtain admission:
one day, 'as the garden door was open and Her Highness hunting,
by license of my good friend Adrian, I came in at a beckon.'

One can imagine with what feelings of privilege and pleasure he
entered this inaccessible sanctuary and shared the delights which it
offered to his Queen; to walk 'aloft upon sweet shadowed walk of
terrace, in heat of summer, to feel the pleasant whisking wind above,
or delectable coolness of the fountain spring beneath'. All the
senses could be gratified at once – the song of birds in the ears, the
scent of herbs and flowers in the nostrils and the taste of strawberries and cherries upon the lips. Everywhere was beauty to rejoice the eye, and beauty that was in constant and pleasing motion –
'the birds fluttering, the fish swimming, the fountain streaming' –
so that Laneham accounted himself lucky 'to have so full a fruition
of so many of God's blessings'.

Within the compass of the curtain wall a single acre sufficed for
the whole layout, and advantage was taken of the fortifications to
provide the most striking feature of the gardens – the terrace walk,
from which their varied beauties could best be appreciated. 'Hard
along the Castle wall is reared a pleasant terrace', wrote Laneham.
Here, from an altitude of some ten feet, one could survey the garden, spreading out beneath one like a patterned carpet, studded with
obelisks, spheres and 'white bears all of stone upon their curious
bases'.

A classic temple abutted the terrace, with columns and cornice
and round arched windows, the entablature encrusted with diamonds, emeralds, sapphires and rubies 'garnished with their gold'.
It was used as an aviary and filled with birds from many lands,

selected as much for the brilliance of their plumage as for the melody of their song.

In the centre of the garden was raised a marble fountain with great intricacy and elaboration of statues and bas-reliefs – 'whales, whirlpools, sturgeons, tunnies, conches and whelks, all engraven with exquisite device and skill' – and in its basin, continually replenished with the same fresh falling water, there swam a multitude of fish. There was so much in this fountain to delight the eye and engage the attention that it was easy to stand for some time in contemplation of its detail; but he who gazed too long upon its varied wonders 'was sure of a cooler'. Somewhere in the background someone turned a cock, and the unadvised visitor was squirted from all sides with water 'spurting upwards with such vehemency as they should by and by be moistened from top to toe'. There were many such instances of practical joking in Tudor gardens. Perhaps the most elaborate ensemble to survive today are the gardens of Hellbrun near Salzburg.

Here, and in the cool stone chambers of the castle, Elizabeth would pass the heat of the day, and enjoy such respite as was left her by the elaborate and extravagant entertainment with which Leicester had planned to divert her.

In the evening, there was hunting. 'The swiftness of the deer, the running of the footmen, the galloping of horses, the blasting of horns, the hallooing and shouting of the huntsmen with excellent echoes … from the woods and waters in valleys resounding' all excited Laneham to a pitch of enthusiasm in which he rated hunting above all other pastimes and declared 'there can be none in any way comparable to this, and specially in this place, that of nature is formed so fit for the purpose.'

These sylvan pleasures, however, were quickly superseded by entertainments of a more sophisticated nature. 'The game was gotten', writes Laneham of the eighth day's hunt, 'and Her Highness returning came there upon a swimming mermaid (that from top to tail was eighteen foot long).' Beside her in the water was Triton, 'Neptune's Blaster', who brought an embassy from that 'Prince of Profundities, the Great God of the Swelling Seas'. Lastly came Arion, riding upon a dolphin large enough to contain within its capacious paunch a six-voice choir and a small orchestra, and there, 'in the evening of the day, resounding from the calm waters', was performed a concert 'incomparably melodious' from within the monster's belly. Laneham was transported with delight. 'Grace of God,' he exclaimed, 'music is a noble art!'

But every form of entertainment described by Laneham received his superlative admiration. On Thursday, July 14th, there was a bear-baiting in the outer ward of the Castle. The Gentleman Usher was there, and found it great sport 'to see the bear with his pink eyes leering after his enemies' approach, the nimbleness and wait of the dog to take his advantage, and the force and experience of the bear again to avoid the assault'. It was a blood-thirsty sport, and Laneham frankly admits that to see how the bear 'with biting, with clawing, with roaring, tossing and tumbling, would work himself free ... was a matter of a goodly relief'. No matter that it was done 'at such expense of blood and leather ... as a month's licking, I ween, will not recover'. Nothing makes one feel more remote from the Elizabethan age than their capacity for taking pleasure in the sufferings of men and beasts.

It did not, however, pass altogether unrebuked. Philip Stubbes, writing his *Anatomy of Abuses* in 1583, has the credit of seeing far beyond the limitations of his age. 'What Christian heart can take pleasure to see one poor beast to rend, tear and kill another, and all for his foolish pleasure?' he asks; 'it is a common saying ... love me, love my dog; so love God, love his creatures.'

Another diversion, which derived from the maxim that nothing is so amusing as the misfortunes of other people, was the quintain, 'where the speciality of the sport was to see how some for their slackness had a good bob with the bag, and some for their haste, too, would topple downright and come tumbling down to the post.' The quintain might be described as the poor man's joust. Lusty village lads, mounted on farm horses and armed with alder poles for lances, charged at the dummy, which swung round on receiving a hit, with a heavy bag of flour. Only a clean blow with a dexterous follow-through enabled the contestant to avoid being knocked from his mount. If he were unfortunate enough to miss altogether he probably hit the board full tilt with his face. There was certainly nothing barbarous about the quintain, but its appeal was strictly to the coarser grain of humour. ' 'Twas a lively pastime', concludes Laneham; 'I believe it would have moved a man to a right merry mood, though it had been told him that his wife lay dying.'

Another evening they were entertained by an Italian contortionist, who tumbled before them 'with sundry windings, gyrings and circumflexions; all so lightly and with such ease as by me, in a few words, it is not expressible by pen or speech ... I blessed me, by my faith, to behold him, and began to doubt whether it was a man or a spirit.' He finally decided that the fellow must have had a back 'metalled like a lamprey, that has no bone, but a line like a lute string.'

It was a packed programme with which Leicester entertained the Queen during the seventeen days of her visit. The only respite she seems to have enjoyed was when, on the hotter days, she 'kept the Castle for coolness'.

The pagan gods had each contributed their proper blessing on her stay. Jupiter, by granting 'due season and fair weather' save for a few showers granted to his sister Ceres; Luna, the 'silver moonshine that nightly shone'; Aeolus, by 'holding up his winds and staying of tempests'. Flora gave her flowers in the greatest diversity and abundance; Ceres, the malt for beer of which, in three days, 'seventy-two tons were piped up quite'; Bacchus, 'full cups everywhere'. From Mercury proceeded poets, painters, carvers, players and their craft; from Phoebus, his 'continual and most delicious music'. Seldom can an English house have seen seventeen days to match the Kenilworth entertainment. It was the brightest era of that castle's history; the highest, too, to which the star of the Dudleys ascended. For if Robert equalled his father by occupying the most prominent position of any subject in the realm, he surpassed both him and his grandfather by dying in his bed. It was left to his stepson, Essex, to pay the traditional price of overweening ambition upon the block.

With the death of Leicester, the fortunes of Kenilworth declined. Reverting to the property of the Crown, it played no important role in the Civil War, in spite of which it was decided, in 1649, to destroy the fortress. Colonel Hawkesworth, who superintended the slighting, breached the dam half-way across the tiltyard, and so drained the Mere; the whole of the north side of the keep was blown out, and some of the outer fortifications dismantled. Hawkesworth himself retained the gatehouse as a private residence, which it still remains; a colony of weavers was established for a short time in Leicester's Buildings, and the holes made by their apparatus may still be seen in the walls. But neglect accomplished what Hawkesworth had begun, and for want of repair the whole castle rapidly fell into decay.

In 1716, when the memory of the Civil War was fading and military architecture beginning to savour of antiquity, a visit was paid to Kenilworth by Dr Richard Hurd, sometime Bishop of Worcester, and a few companions. Their description is a fitting epilogue to its story.

'When we alighted from the coach,' he writes, 'the first object that presented itself was the principal gateway of the Castle.' It was by now a farm-house, and the only part of the vast ruins to be inhabited. 'On our entrance to the Inner Court, we were struck with the sight of so many mouldering towers, which preserved a sort of magnificence even in their ruins.' There is a pale foreshadowing of the Romantic Movement in their unfeigned appreciation of this venerable and picturesque antiquity.

By the aid of Dugdale they were able to identify and reconstruct in the imagination the several parts of the fortress, and so they amused themselves until they came at last to a broken tower from which a flight of steps enabled them to gain the parapet walk. This walk unfolded to their gaze the magnificent panorama 'of the gardens on the north side; of the winding meadow that encompassed the walls of the Castle (Plate 21) on the west and south; and had besides the command of the country round about them for many miles'. Here the full impact of the historic ruin could be felt; 'there was something so august in the mingled prospect of so many antique towers falling into rubbish, and in the various beauties of the landscape that we were all of us, as it were, suspended in admiration and continued silent for some time.'

Confronted by the strange power of an ancient building to throw back across the centuries the lingering echo of a bygone age, their reverent and pensive silence was the most impressive tribute that could be paid.

X

COWDRAY

ON THE fifteenth of August, 1591, 'the Queen, having dined at Farnham, came with a great train to the Right Honourable the Lord Montague's ... about eight o'clock at night.'

It is difficult in these days of swift and easy travel to imagine the mingled pleasure and discomfort of a progress or to recapture the emotion with which a traveller greeted the first sight of his destination. This part of Sussex was particularly inhospitable; it was notorious for mud. The roads, right into the eighteenth century, were 'bad beyond all badness', and Defoe records having seen a lady of quality 'drawn to Church in her coach by six oxen; nor was it done in frolic or humour, but from sheer necessity'.

Even when the physical obstacles to travel could be overcome, it was a forlorn, infertile country through which the traveller had to pass. Edward VI, coming from Petworth to Cowdray, had to dismiss all but a hundred and fifty of his train – it had numbered four thousand – 'which were enough', he wrote, 'to eat up the country, for there was little meadow or hay all the way I went'. The passing of two centuries made little impact on Sussex, and when Horace Walpole visited it, it was still desolate and inhospitable. 'The whole country has a saxon air', he wrote, 'and the inhabitants are savages'. Only to the mind of an eighteenth-century landscape gardener did it occur that this 'most sterile soil and dreary region was capable of embellishment'.

In such a context, the arrival at Cowdray, whose park had long been an oasis of beauty and civilization amid this sorry scene of desolation, must have been a most thankful experience.

The house was approached from Midhurst by a long causeway lined by a double avenue of trees. To the right, across Town

Meadow, could be seen the little conical mound of St Anne's Hill on
which had stood the ancient castle of the Bohuns. To the left lay the
park, 'having great variety of ground in it and well wooded with
pines, firs and other evergreen trees'. There were also some of the
finest Spanish chestnuts in England. The avenue opened into a grass
forecourt, always trim and neatly swept, for it was among the duties
of the porter, with assistance from the poor of the parish, 'to keep
the long alleys without the gate, and the Green before it'. The green
was separated from the alleys by the River Rother, but the banks
were so precipitous that, until one was on the very bridge, one
might remain unaware of its existence.

From the bridge, the whole entrance front of Cowdray was in
view (Plate 22). The first impression was of a great stone façade,
regular and symmetrical, in the centre of which rose a very noble
gatehouse, its inward turrets capped with cupolas between which
appeared the spiky lantern of the great hall. To either side a short,
battlemented wing ended abruptly in a massive square tower with
tall bay windows. Behind the battlements, a number of red brick
chimney-stacks broke the skyline, bringing a touch of homely colour
to the cold grey walls. Despite the large and regularly spaced windows, the overall effect was one of immense strength; in times of
emergency, Cowdray was to rank as a castle.

Upon the first appearance of the Queen in the avenue, loud
music sounded, which continued until she reached the bridge, when
it suddenly stopped. This was the signal for the first oration to
begin. It was the porter, dressed in armour and standing between
two carved wooden janitors 'more like Posts than Porters' who
spoke. 'The walls of Thebes were raised by music,' he began; 'by
music these are kept from falling.' According to prophecy, the
foundations of Cowdray would be insecure until steadied by the
arrival of 'the wisest, the fairest and most fortunate of all creatures'.
This was the burden of his speech, but, in case there was any doubt
as to its application, the fact that *She* had arrived was rammed home
with the usual reduplication of epithets – 'O Miracle of Time!
Nature's Glory! Fortune's Empress! The World's Wonder!' –
until the speaker, happily remembering that he was a porter and not
a poet, discharged his business by presenting Her Majesty with a

golden key. The Queen then alighted, embraced Lady Montague
and her daughter, and passed through the gatehouse into the
quadrangle. Over the arch was the blazon of the Browne family
with the motto 'Suivez Raison'.

In 1543, Sir Anthony Browne had inherited Cowdray from his
half-brother, William FitzWilliam, Earl of Southampton. Sir
Anthony had been one of the most favoured of Henry VIII's subjects, and had received considerable grants of Church land. Besides
Easebourne and Waverley, which he inherited along with Cowdray,
he was given the manors of Send and Godstow, St Mary Overy's,
which became his town house, and Battle Abbey, where he made
the site of the Minster Church his garden, marking the pillars of the
nave with a double row of yew trees.

Among other appointments, he had been entrusted with the
delicate task of being Henry's proxy at the marriage of Anne of
Cleves, where he expressed himself 'never more dismayed in all his
life ... to see the lady so far unlike what was reported'. A painting
of him at Cowdray showed him in the white and blue costume which
he had worn at the wedding – his right leg, noted Walpole, 'entirely white, which was robed for the act of putting into bed with
her. But when the King came to marry her, he only put his leg into
bed to kick her out.'

There is no doubt that Henry's champion could cut a superb
figure, 'his neck and shoulders bare and very brown; a monstrous
sword; the breeches straight and slashed ... a hat and feather, with
a Gillyflower in the hand, and the George round his neck'. Thus
portrayed in another picture at Cowdray, he seemed to personify
the vigorous first cross between medieval manhood and Renaissance culture that was typical of Tudor England.

His character, too, had something of the oak and something of the
willow in its make-up. Lloyd has left for posterity a suggestive
sketch: 'The times were dark, his carriage so too; the waves were
boisterous, but he the solid rock or the well-guided ship that could
go with the tide. He mastered his own passions and other's too, and
both by time and opportunity; therefore he died with that peace the
State wanted, and with that universal repute the statesmen of those
troublesome times enjoyed not.' Perhaps it was not for nothing

that his motto hung over the gates of Cowdray; 'Suivez Raison'.

Across the quadrangle were the principal lodgings (Plate 22). Two imposing bay windows distinguished the withdrawing-room, great chamber and parlour, while a tall, many-lighted oriel and three high-set traceried windows punctuated the façade of the hall. The front was all of freestone, and although asymmetrical, was nicely balanced in the disposition of its parts. Over the battlemented parapet rose the gables and chimney-shafts of the lord's lodgings and the high-pitched roof of the hall crowned with a magnificent louvre or lantern – a little army of heraldic standard-bearers mounted on pinnacles piling up towards the cupola in which the whole mass of the building reached its climax. Two outpost sentinels marked the extremities of the hall roof, and as it were presented arms towards this inmost group. The louvre, placed towards one end of the hall, was so situated as to occupy the centre of the whole façade, and rising directly behind the fountain, provided a focus around which the architectural composition was balanced.

To the right, and partly obscuring one of the windows of the hall, was the entrance porch, roofed with a fan vault which incorporated in its elaborate tracery the trefoil and anchor of Lord Southampton.

This nobleman, of whom a fine full-length portrait used to hang in the drawing-room, was the principal builder of Cowdray. It is certain, however, that Sir David Owen, from whom he purchased the manor, had already begun the reconstruction. The house may safely be said to have been built between 1520 and 1543.

Southampton is remembered by Walpole and Cobbett chiefly as the gaoler of Margaret, Countess of Salisbury, his cousin, though the tradition that she ever owned Cowdray is completely erroneous. This lady was the daughter of the unfortunate Duke of Clarence and mother of Cardinal Pole. Lord Southampton was given the difficult task of arresting her in her home near Havant and conveying her, by way of Cowdray, to the Tower. She was a staunch Romanist, and accused of complicity in the Pilgrimage of Grace. Her cousin tried to reason with her 'in both sorts, sometimes doulx and mild, and now rough and asperly', but he admitted himself baffled by her obstinacy.

Incriminating evidence, however, had been found at Warbling-
ton, and she was beheaded on May 27th, 1541. Undaunted to the
end, she refused to lay her head upon the block, bidding the execu-
tioner 'if he would have her head, get it as he would, so that he was
constrained to fetch it off slovenly.' Her father, her brother and one
son had all perished in the Tower before her, and with her death
'the very name of Plantagenet became extinct.'

The Southampton cognizance was the silver trefoil, and he left it
'sprinkled all over the leaden pipes of his mansion house'. Through
his porch the Queen entered, and Cowdray once more opened its
doors to a royal visitor.

'That night Her Majesty took her rest, and so in a like manner the
next day, being Sunday, being most royally feasted.' Details of her
fare are few, but of that Sunday morning's menu an eloquent picture is given in words of the most powerful simplicity: 'the proportion at breakfast was three oxen and one hundred and forty geese.'

It was often noted by foreigners that the Englishman was a prodigious eater, and it was no easy task in barren Sussex to provide
for a royal retinue. Nevertheless, on the visit of Edward VI, Sir
Anthony had so contrived things that his young sovereign was
'marvellously, yea, rather excessively, banqueted'. It is no wonder if
the courtier sometimes paid for his love of wine and trenchering
with 'an aching head and grumbling guts'.

On Monday, at eight o'clock in the morning, Her Majesty took
horse with all her train, and rode into the park. There was a delicate
bower prepared, 'under the which were Her Highness's musicians
placed'. To their musical accompaniment a nymph sang, offering a
crossbow to the Queen, with which she killed four deer in the pad-
dock. The Countess of Kildare had the tact to kill only one. 'Then
rode Her Grace to Cowdray to dinner.'

Seen from the parks, Cowdray lost its shape. In place of the regular towers and windows of the entrance front, the symmetry dis-
solved into a disorderly mass of brown roofs and grey walls,
bulging out towards the east into the apse of the chapel, and losing
itself in the low line of stable and office buildings south of the
kitchens. Along the skyline towers, battlements, gables and chimneys grouped themselves about the hall lantern much as the houses

of a village might group themselves round the spire of the church.

The appearance had altered but little in 1781, when Grimm made his water-colour sketches. The tall sash windows of the great stair-case and state apartments were an attempt to make the east front more in keeping with the redecorations ordered by the sixth Lord Montague, and two similar lights in the south gallery had done something to modify the severity of that part of the house. But the greatest change revealed by Grimm's paintings was in the imme-diate surroundings of the mansion. To the south and east, he shows pastures and hay fields reaching right up to the walls. This had the effect of making Cowdray look more like a castle than was intended. It was doubtless the work of an eighteenth-century landscape gar-dener, for a map made by Thomas Heather in 1712 reveals a very different context to the buildings. The double avenue still lined the causeway; to the left of the green, when one had just crossed the bridge, was a plantation – in all probability an orchard – while a large rectangular plot surrounding the house on three sides is marked with the single word 'Gardens'. Details are not given here or elsewhere, but the want must be supplied by an imagination in-formed by the existing accounts of other Tudor gardens. The set-ting of trim walks and parterres, with the same homely profusion of fruit trees noticed at Nonsuch, would have done much to soften the military appearance suggested by Grimm's water-colours. Although it was built with an eye to the possible need for defence, Cowdray is better considered as a college than a domesticated castle.

This is an important consideration in Tudor architecture; the great houses owed their size and the disposition of their members, not to the creative genius of an architect, but to the domestic needs of the household, which constituted a little college or Court. In times of insecurity and change, men tended to gravitate towards the rich and the great, seeking the security of their powerful protection. This had long been a recognized practice, but with the emergence of a new land-owning aristocracy – a process greatly accelerated by the distribution of monastic estates – a new and merely domestic form of commendation began to replace the legal and military basis of feudalism.

A great house attracted to itself both gentlemen and yeomen, who were given positions ranging between those of courtier and servant according to their birth and ability. Thus was formed what was significantly called the 'family'. With their common worship in the chapel, their common meals in the hall, and their own elaborate hierarchy of rank, they formed a self-contained social unit largely supported by the produce of the estate, which thus became a self-contained financial unit.

There were many customs at Cowdray which closely resembled those of a college, not the least obvious being the wearing of black gowns by the senior officials of the household.

Anthony Browne, second Viscount Montague, who succeeded in 1592, left a detailed record of the duties expected of the members of his family, and of the etiquette observed. 'It is a ridiculous piece of mimicry of Royal grandeur,' wrote Horace Walpole, on seeing it, 'an instance of ancient pride, the more remarkable as the peer who drew it up was then barely twenty-four years of age.' This is a little unfair; young Montague was doing no more than to tabulate the customs observed in his father's and grandfather's day and by all other noblemen of his degree. The household book of the Percys is very similar to his own.

A household book gave the exact function of each member of the family and many interesting details on their way of life. Most important of all was the Steward of the Household. To him fell the provisioning of the larders with 'beeves, muttons, grain, wines' and other such commodities, besides liveries, badges, coals and wood. He paid the servants their wages quarterly and settled the accounts with the 'purveyors of beeves' and other tradesmen. He was responsible for the upkeep of the fabric of the house, and was expected frequently to ride into the 'parks, pastures, marshes and other grounds to see that they be not abused by the bailiffs or keepers'.

His position, in fact, was one of considerable trust and confidence. He was charged to give 'sound advice in matters of most importance' and was let in on most of his master's secrets. He was to be obeyed in anything 'except it be dishonest in itself, or undutiful to the Prince or State'. In his hands was the discipline of the household, but all 'incorrigible persons and wilful maintainers of their outrageous misgovernment and intolerable disorders' received the wrath of their employer unmediated through the offices of the Steward.

The lord of the mansion ruled his family – his wife, children, relatives and domestics – as a warden governed a college, and part of his task was to build up a sense of community among them. 'I exhort, admonish and require them', wrote Lord Montague, 'that they studiously embrace unity, peace and good agreement among themselves.' He knew the danger of faction and backbiting to which small communities are subject and he appointed a hierarchy to deal with complaints, allowing, nevertheless, that any member might 'boldly repair' to himself if satisfaction were not forthcoming. 'Not my best affected officer or dearest child', he boasted, 'shall be able to abuse the meanest in my house, but shall be reproved by me to the full contentment of the party injured.'

Notwithstanding the premium which he put on the corporate life, Lord Montague himself tended to withdraw from it. His 'place of diet' never appears to have been in the great hall where the rest of the household ate, but was in one of the rooms on the private side. In later houses this separation of the master from the family led to the disappearance of the great hall from the ground plan and its replacement by the servants' hall, which seldom had any architectural merit, and here, though the rigid hierarchy of rank was maintained until Edwardian days, there was little social difference between the Steward and the pantry boy. In Tudor families, this was not the case. Some of the servants ranked as gentlemen and some as yeomen, and differences of rank were as much respected as those of sex, for it was not infrequently that the servants were required to share beds. It was among the duties of the Gentleman Usher to appoint rooms 'so as two go to a bed, always provided that a gentleman be matched with a gentleman, and a yeoman with a yeoman'. There is nothing to indicate whether the gentlemen stood a greater chance of having the bed to themselves.

A typical example of this class of gentleman servant was Richard Lambe. Though 'descended of a good house in the North Country' he had been reduced by the wars of York and Lancaster to the condition of poor relation. Lord Montague, who was his wife's uncle, received him into his household, where he was 'his gentleman' for many years. Another member of the Cowdray household worth naming was Guy Fawkes.

His embarrassing presence was due to the fact that, although they had been greatly enriched by Church lands, the Brownes were Roman Catholics. It is evidence of Elizabeth's policy of demanding loyalty rather than orthodoxy that the Brownes remained in favour with both Queen and Pope. When called upon to subscribe to the Act of Supremacy, Montague boldly replied that he had taken his oath to the Holy See and could 'by no means dispense with it'. The attempted invasion of England by Spain, however, was another matter, and one of the first to bring his troops to the Queen at Tilbury was Viscount Montague. As Camden said, the Queen, 'having experienced his loyalty, had a great esteem for him, tho' a stiff Romanist'.

Nevertheless, he had to tread warily and was at pains to prove his loyalty to the Queen. Her presence at Cowdray was an opportunity not to be missed. On the Wednesday, he conducted Her Majesty 'to take the pleasure of the walks' and steered her towards one of the fish-ponds where an angler was seated at his nets. Without even looking at the Queen, the angler delivered a soliloquy on the subject of treason. 'There be some so muddy-minded that they cannot live in a clear river,' he meditated, 'as camels will not drink till they have troubled the water with their feet, so they cannot stanch their thirst till they have disturbed the State with their treacheries.'

William Browne, the youngest of Lord Montague's sons, was more extreme in his loyalty to Rome. Although brought up to all the pomp and abundance of Cowdray, at the age of thirty-one he found his vocation and was 'content to spend his life in the humble duties of a Jesuit lay brother'. After a lifetime of menial and arduous labour, he could say with humility, 'I do not remember for twenty years to have needed any other spur than the love of God.'

It is not possible to reconstruct the appearance of the chapel at Cowdray in Elizabeth's reign, for it received an extensive redecoration during the 1730s, but structurally it remained unaltered since Lord Southampton's time. It was large for a private chapel – fifty feet long by twenty wide – and furnished with a gallery over the

west end for the Browne family. Evidently it was intended that the
entire household should worship there. It is known from confes-
sions extracted by Topclyffe that Cowdray was one of the rallying
points of Roman Catholics during difficult times, and even served
as a conversion centre. It is possible that the chapel of the house
continued to serve its purpose in the life of the community under
Elizabeth, but a discreet silence was observed on the subject.

The great hall ranked next in importance to the chapel in the life
of the family. At Cowdray, the Buck Hall took its name from the
eleven carved oak bucks which formed its most conspicuous ornament. It was a room of unusual magnificence (Plate 23), and since
Lord Montague ate in private, devoted to the use of servants and
strangers. They could hardly have been more sumptuously lodged.
Their hall was fifty-five feet long by twenty-eight across, and at its
highest point reached sixty feet. This was to accommodate the lofty
hammer-beam roof – shown in all its elaborate perpendicular
tracery in Grimm's water-colour – which was the particular glory
of Cowdray.

Grimm shows the walls below the level of the windows painted
in classical architecture – the work of Pellegrini, dating from the
early eighteenth century. They were probably originally panelled
in the fine linen-fold pattern shown on the screens in his picture.
But the eleven bucks formed the chief decorative motif of the hall.
One stood erect at the dais end, supporting the royal arms and the
blazon of the Browne family. 'There were ten others', noted
Richard Gough, 'large as life, standing, lying or sitting.' The two
sitting bucks, over the entrance screen, held heraldic banners, and
apparently the bow and arrows used by Elizabeth during her visit
to Cowdray were slung round their necks.

Here, in the Buck Hall, was the centre of domestic ritual, pre-
sided over by the Gentleman Usher as Master of Ceremonies.

The office of Gentleman Usher had particular reference to the
lord's quality as a viscount. It was his business to precede his master
when travelling, and among other things, to ensure that due respect
was paid to him. These outriders were sometimes known as Harbingers. Archbishop Laud's equipage was preceded by two such
men who rode before him crying 'Room for my Lord's Grace!

Gentlemen, I pray you be uncovered for my Lord's Grace.' The Lord Mayor's Harbingers were less courteous, noted von Buchenbach, but squirted water upon the crowds to make them give way.

At home, the Gentleman Usher had to ensure that a solemnity was observed appropriate to a viscount's household. To this end he had charge of all the inventories and oversight of all the apartments; he had authority 'in civil and kind manner' to give orders to other servants and used it to see that his master's table was duly and reverently served.

The ritual of 'covering time' was performed at ten. The Gentleman Usher called the Yeoman Usher who summoned the service – that is to say, the Yeomen of the Ewry, Pantry, Buttery and Cellar; he saw that the Carver and Sewer (wine-pourer) washed, and then delegated the ordering of the ceremony to the Yeoman Usher.

On entering, each servant made two 'curtesies', one in the middle of the room and another at the table. Then the Yeoman Usher, kissing his hand, placed it on the centre of the table where the Yeoman of the Ewry were to lay the cloth, which was then spread. Next the pantry contingent were brought in and laid the knives, spoons, salts and trenchers and a small loaf or manchet for each place. Every article was laid with a small obeisance, and every servant before retiring made his 'solemn curtesy'.

The table having been laid and His Lordship informed, the Gentleman Usher now returned to the hall and called out: 'Gentlemen and Yeomen, wait upon the Sewer for my Lord', whereupon some half-dozen at the least went to receive the dishes from the kitchen. As the procession passed back through the hall, the Usher, who had waited by the screens, called out: 'By your leave, my masters', and everyone stood and uncovered as the dinner passed through.

During the meal, the Usher was to stand by and keep 'a vigilant eye on the meat, to the intent that it be not imbezzled', and afterwards superintended the clearing away. Now it was the turn for the household to have their dinner, each at his appointed place in the Buck Hall. Strangers were fed, conditional upon their seemly behaviour, and a modified form of the same ritual accompanied the serving of the Steward's table.

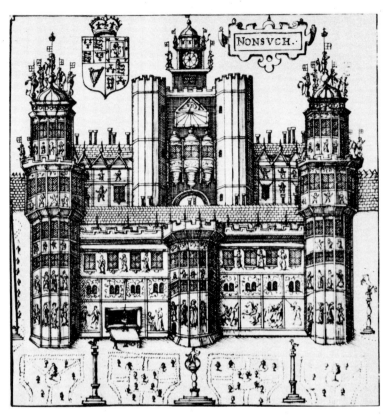

NONSUCH

above: THE SOUTH FRONT, FROM JOHN SPEED'S MAP OF SURREY (1611)

below: THE SOUTH FRONT FROM HOEFNAGEL'S DRAWING (1568)

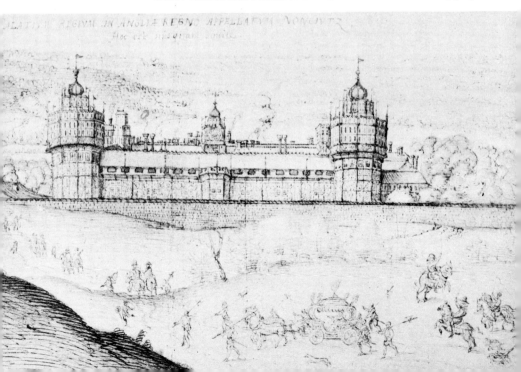

above: **THE ENTRANCE FRONT FROM THE NORTH-EAST**

NONSUCH

below: **THE ENTRANCE FRONT FROM THE NORTH-WEST**

Several details of the ways of the household are revealed in the duties expected of the Yeoman of the Chamber. He looked after the state rooms, seeing that they were swept and kept 'clean and sweet with flowers and boughs'. First thing in the morning, he had to remove the pallets on which servants had been sleeping from the drawing-room, for it was the custom in even the greatest houses, as, indeed, it was later the custom even at Versailles, for servants to lay down their beds in the state rooms. Later houses, such as Theobalds, provided a large number of pallet chambers, but it is doubtful whether all the servants would have been so accommodated.

The kitchen, after the medieval manner, was in a separate block, joined to the mansion by the buttery building. It formed a massive, many-sided tower, with tall, turret-like chimney-shafts, which gave it a striking and militant aspect. The windows, deeply recessed between these shafts, were enlarged in the seventeenth century; it is probable that the original lights were smaller and would thereby have enhanced the impression that this was the keep of a fortress rather than the kitchen of a country house.

This part of the mansion survives almost intact, but for an idea of the furniture, we must turn to Grimm. He has exaggerated the height of the building, but he shows clearly the tall facets each with its deep-set window right at the top, and its wide Tudor arch at the base containing oven or cooking range. High up in the wall, a tiny oriel whose delicacy contrasts with the plainness of the rest, bulges out from a little mural chamber. There is no record of its purpose. Perhaps it enabled the lady of the house to keep an eye on what went on below, but there is no evidence of her taking any interest in these affairs. The preparation of food was man's work, and the kitchen staff was organized into its own little hierarchy which, in no way, suggests such supervision.

This was, in fact, the concern of the Clerk of the Kitchen who was responsible to the Steward for all purchases concerning his department. He had oversight of the Baker and Brewer, and had to ensure that their output was in proportion to their supply. He furnished the cooks with the raw materials for their dishes and with the appropriate concomitants – cheese curds for wildfowl and 'rye for the baking of red deer'.

Next to the Clerk came the Chief Cook and the Second Cook. Here Lord Montague trod lightly with respect to grades and ranks lest 'thereupon should grow any heartburning or disdain', and, though they were distinct members, yet he reminded them that it was all of one office; so he expects that they 'concur well and seek the mutual credit either of other'. It was in their interests that they should get on together, for, in the Buck Hall, they were to sit next to each other at the Clerk of the Kitchen's table.

The kitchen, in fact, formed a sub-division of the household, with its own unity and its own lesser loyalties. Lest their remoteness from the sight of the lord of the mansion should lessen their sense of personal respect for him, some of the deference which was due to his person was accorded to his food. 'I will that he [the Clerk of the Kitchen] suffer none to stand unseemly with his back to my meat while it is at the range', directed Lord Montague. It was not unusual for reverence to be shown to inanimate objects in the absence of the person whom they, in some way, represented. An anonymous Italian visitor to the Court of Queen Mary noticed a chair covered with brocade in the ante-room, before which the gentlemen uncovered; 'because this chair represents the King,' he noted, 'they never pass it without doing reverence.' There may well have been a practical advantage, however, in persons not turning their backs on a roasting joint.

The Kitchen Boys, who are not enumerated, formed a separate division of the household. They did not eat in hall but had their diet with the Sculleryman in his office.

The title 'Sculleryman' may have a ring of inferiority to modern ears, but, at Cowdray, he seems to have performed the duties expected of a butler today, and to have enjoyed a position of some responsibility. It was his special charge to see that the silver and pewter 'be neither imbezzled nor abused', and its cleaning was his daily work, unless he was called upon by the Chief Cook to fulfil his other obligation, which was to 'have singular regard to the tempering and making of mustard'.

And so, throughout all the thirty-seven different offices of the household, the duties and responsibilities are noted and enumerated. This was the organization that lay behind the running of a great house in Elizabeth's day; this was the ideal of community living which it sought to express. It is a fascinating peep behind the scenes left by the methodical mind of Lord Montague.

On the stage, the pageantry of Court life went forward with all its elaborate paraphernalia. On Tuesday, August 18th, the Queen was taken to dine at Easebourne Priory. Wednesday was picnic weather, and the company 'dined in the walks, feasted most sumptuously at a table four and twenty yards long' with a background accompaniment of 'most delicate music'. At odd intervals, odd individuals delivered loyal and verbose addresses. On Thursday, they dined again in the Privy Walks of the garden, this time at a table forty-eight yards long, and the country people came in to dance with pipe and tabor; Lord and Lady Montague stood up to dance with them 'to the great pleasure of all beholders and the gentle applause of Her Majesty'. The following day, the Queen departed, and the household settled down once more to its daily routine existence.

The later history of Cowdray is not without interest. During the seventeenth century, the Brownes suffered heavy loss for their loyalty to Rome; during the eighteenth, their fortunes seem to have recovered, for the sixth Viscount could afford some extensive landscape gardening – with not altogether felicitous results – and at least a partial redecoration of the house. But the attempt to 'improve' was merely decorative and involved no structural alterations except to some of the windows. In 1782, Dr Johnson visited 'the venerable seat of the Lords Montacute' and was more impressed by its historic form than by its attempt at a contemporary décor. 'Sir,' he said, 'I should like to stay here for twenty-four hours. We see here how our ancestors lived.' This was already the chief interest of Cowdray.

In the autumn of 1793, both Cowdray and the Montague succession came to an abrupt and catastrophic end. The interior of the house was being prepared for the reception of its new master, George Samuel, the eighth Viscount; he had just left Winchester and was travelling on the continent with his friend, Charles Burdett. He was about to marry. Everywhere in the house there were workmen, and most of the art treasures had been stored in the north gallery, at the west end of which, 'by the strangest inadvertence', the carpenters and glaziers had been allowed to set up a workshop.

'On the night of Tuesday, September 24th,' wrote Richard Gough to the Society of Antiquaries, 'Mrs Chambers, the house-keeper, who with the porter and one or two more servants were the only occupants of the spacious mansion, had retired to bed at her usual hour of eleven, in the full confidence that all was safe … She had scarcely slept an hour when she was alarmed by the watchman with the cry, "Fire in the North Gallery!" – and immediately saw it in flames with all its valuable contents, without a possibility of saving a single article.' Among other things William the Con-queror's Sword and Coronation Robe and the Roll of Battle Abbey were destroyed.

'The inhabitants of Midhurst', continued Gough, 'were soon ready to assist in large numbers, and no help was wanting to remove the furniture, pictures and library from the three other sides of the quadrangle. But the firmness of the material rendered it absolutely impossible to break down any part so as to stop the progress of the flames; they quickly spread to the east side of the Court, in which was the great hall, chapel and dining parlour.' Thus the strength of Cowdray became its final downfall. By morning, the great house which had been one of the monuments of English architecture, which 'no traveller of taste ever neglected to view', had been reduced to a blackened and smouldering ruin.

Old Lady Montague was stunned by the blow. 'I cannot express what I feel', she wrote to the Countess of Newburgh, 'but must leave it to the feelings of your own heart.' Beneath her grief for her house was a sense of bitterness against her staff, whom she could not but blame for their carelessness – 'how else could such a house have been so destroyed?' In the end, her Christian virtues got the better of her: ' … but I shall feel angry, and that is sinful, so I will only return to the fact of your kindness.' Lady Newburgh had offered hospitality to herself and her daughter.

Poor Lady Montague! She little knew that a far heavier blow was about to fall. The day after the fire, the Steward wrote to young George Samuel to inform him of the disaster, but he mistook the address, putting 'Lausanne' where he should have put 'Lucerne'.

Had his letter arrived when it was due, it would have brought the young man hurrying back to England. As it was, before the letter could catch up with him, he had lost his life in a foolhardy attempt to shoot the rapids of the Rhine near Laufenburg. An old tradition, which claimed to originate from the last Steward of Cowdray, suggests a sinister interpretation of this double tragedy. Cowdray was under a curse – the curse of fire and water pronounced against the despoilers of the monasteries. Montague's old servant, Dickinson, who was with him to the last, is said to have tried to restrain him by force, saying, 'O my Lord, it's the curse of water! For God's sake give up the trial.'

Whatever may be the historic value of the 'Curse of Cowdray', it is certainly true that the house was destroyed by fire and the heir by water. Nor did the coincidence end there. Lord Montague's sister, Mrs Poynz, who continued to live in a lodge in the park, lost both her boys in a sailing accident off Bognor.

An attempt was made to revive the succession by releasing the monk, Mark Anthony Browne, from his vows of celibacy. But the effort of readjustment appears to have been too great for him, and he died within a few months of matrimony.

No attempt was made to restore Cowdray. The house was completely ruined. In the kitchen, the solitary survivor of the disaster, confused heaps of furniture, some of it in the last stages of decomposition, lay about for years, and the contents of the library, saved from the flames, were left to perish from damp and neglect. 'The floor was strewn with parchments and papers', wrote Sir Sibbald Scott; 'some had been thrust by handfuls into the cupboards, and many were gathered in little heaps in corners where gusts of wind had driven them, and where the damp had caused them to adhere in masses, rendering many of them illegible.' A few, more favoured, were 'set apart for the vacant gaze and rude treatment of those who cannot read them'.

As for the ruins, they were left to the multitudes of jackdaws and starlings. Bramble and elder invaded the courtyard, and ivy enveloped the blackened walls and staring window-holes with its treacherous mantle. High overhead, the hands of the clock still pointed to the hour at which the glories of Cowdray had been lost for ever.

XI

THEOBALDS

Two circumstances combined to make the reign of Elizabeth the first Golden Age of domestic architecture in England. One was economic: the concentration of riches and land into the hands of a few families – many of them only a generation removed from obscurity – which provided the essential condition for the building of large and imposing houses. The second was a new interest in architecture as such, the diffused impact of the Italian Renaissance.

The first cross between the Italianate and the vernacular issued in a vigorous and original style, producing houses of great variety and of varying greatness. There were massive stone palaces such as Longleat and Burghley; there were audacious erections such as Harwick and Wollaton; there were quiet and dignified homesteads such as Loseley and Gorhambury. Modern critics may differ as to the respective merit which they allow to each, but to the Elizabethan, there could be no doubt: Lord Burghley's palace at Theobalds was considered the finest house in England, and, if Sir Christopher Hatton's Holdenby was a distinguished second, it only reflected more glory on Theobalds, from which it was avowedly copied. James I endorsed contemporary opinion on his accession by adding both to the property of the Crown.

Begun by Sir William Cecil in 1564, finished in 1585 and wantonly destroyed as the result of the Civil War, Theobalds was at once the most historic and the most interesting house of its age; the most historic because it was the most visited by Elizabeth herself, and her chief Minister's chief house; the most interesting because it was built over a period of many years, at leisure and with deliberation. Initial mistakes and inadequacies were corrected, and, in the many revisions, little can have survived that was not consistent with Burghley's idea of what a great house should be. In the

166

fragmentary material preserved at Hatfield, one can see Burghley almost feeling his way towards the masterpiece which was so admired by his contemporaries.

For Theobalds was not the work of an architect, but the product of a highly accomplished team of craftsmen working under the guidance of a highly intelligent and cultured mind. It is, therefore, tragic that Theobalds, of all Elizabethan houses, should have disappeared so completely. Not only is there nothing standing from which any idea of its appearance can be formed – there is not so much as a sketch of the house as it stood. Two plans by Thorpe, two partial elevations in the library at Hatfield and two tiny corners of brick and stone that remain upon the site today, are the only visual aids available. To these may be added a number of descriptions, some long, some short, some vague and some particular, which the house attracted during the eighty odd years of its existence. For three centuries these confused and scattered evidences have perplexed and baffled topographers.

In recent years, however, Sir John Summerson has managed, by a collation of all the material at once painstaking and imaginative, to summon up the ghost of Theobalds. It is now possible to make sense of the descriptions and even to draw the palace itself with some confidence.

The view which was most familiar to Englishmen was that obtained from Theobalds Gate. It was on the road from Waltham Cross to Cheshunt – where now a suburban station greets the eye – that the glorious prospect burst into view. From the archway stretched an avenue, 'a most stately walk', carried upon a raised causeway and shaded by alternate elm and ash, at the end of which the palace stood back about a furlong from the highway. From here, the regular procession of the courts, the receding blocks of towers and lodgings, the regiment of slate-hung cupolas and weather-vanes, the forest of chimney-stacks, pinnacles and other ornaments, all crowding upon the eye at once, built up that impression of immense size so dear to the Tudor builder, while through the several archways the vista penetrated to the Fountain Court, where the marble figures of Venus and Cupid could be distinguished from the high road. 'The like walk, for length, pleasantness and delight', wrote the Commonwealth Commissioners, 'is rare to be seen in England.'

If this was the likeness of the greatest of Elizabethan houses, it was not achieved at a single sitting. Sir William Cecil had three main residences – 'one in London for necessity'; one at Burghley for his mother; and, lastly, one at Theobalds, intended for the younger son, Robert, 'which at the first', wrote a contemporary biographer, 'he meant for a little pile, as I have heard him say, but, after he came to entertain the Queen so often there, he was enforced to enlarge it rather for the Queen and her great train, and to set the poor in order, than for pomp and glory'.

Pomp or no pomp, it is clear that Burghley was accused of extravagance in building from a letter of his dated August 14th, 1585 – the year of the final enlargement of Theobalds. 'I confess my folly in the expenses', he wrote, 'because some of my houses are to come, if God so please, to them that have not land to match them; I mean my house at Theobalds, which was begun by me with a mean measure, but increased by occasion of Her Majesty's often coming, whom to please I never would omit to strain myself to more charges than building it.'

This is the keynote for the understanding of Theobalds; it was not, like some Italian house, conceived in a studio and superimposed upon a landscape. It grew, little by little, out of the domestic necessities of a great statesman, obliged by custom to maintain an enormous household and by royal command to accommodate an even more numerous Court.

The original building consisted of a single courtyard, with the entrance on the north and the hall on the south, and another irregular office court to the east. Perhaps even before this project was completed, another – more ambitious – had succeeded to it. The main approach was swung to the east, the old office buildings replaced by a spacious entrance court, and as part of the general reorientation, the hall was moved to the block which separated the two quadrangles.

In September 1571, Elizabeth came to visit Theobalds. The hall block was by then completed, but it is probable that the outer court was still under scaffolding. In the following year, when she came again, this court also was finished and ready for her reception. One can imagine with what pride and care Lord Burghley – for he had just received the title – allocated the rooms for the royal visit. His list survives in the archives of Hatfield.

The outer court he called 'the Great House'. On the south side, overlooking the gardens, were to be the Queen's rooms. The chapel, occupying the two lower storeys at one end, left only the Vine Chamber above it, which was her withdrawing-room. Her bedroom and a small gallery occupied the rest of the second floor. Above the Queen's bedroom, in a 'tower chamber', slept Lady Carew. This tower, of which the ground plan gives no hint, must have been the central feature of this façade, and was answered by a corresponding one on the north wing. Below the Queen's rooms were those of Lady Stafford and the Marchioness of Winchester, and, on the ground floor, east of the Chapel, were rooms allocated to service – 'the robes, the grooms of the Privy Chamber, and the waiter's dining room' amongst them.

On the north side, the Suitor's Gallery on the top floor was reserved for 'the Queen's Majesty to dine in', and the rooms below to various members of the household. In the base-court, servants were lodged in garrets over the bakehouse and brewhouse, and directions were given that the Queen's chests, which were doubtless numerous, should be carried into the gallery by way of these.

The west side, or hall block, was devoted to state rooms: the hall itself became the 'Great Chamber', the great parlour the 'Presence Chamber', and the dining-room the 'Privy Chamber'. The parlour over the kitchen was to receive Lord Leicester, and the 'tower chamber over that', Mr Christopher Hatton.

Hatton, it will be remembered, was the builder of Holdenby. Although Theobalds and Holdenby were regarded as the finest houses in England, they did not receive the attention they deserved from artists. On the occasion of Elizabeth's second visit to Theobalds she was presented with a 'portrait' of the house – probably the Tudor equivalent of an 'Academy Perspective', showing what the finished mansion would look like. Unfortunately the portrait has not survived.

It is a pity that Theobalds was never painted by one of those ingenious artists who acquired such skill in imagining from the air
what could only be seen from the ground. Such a bird's-eye view is,
indeed, just scribbled on Thorpe's survey. It is crude and inaccurate, but enough to afford a glimpse of how the subject might have
been handled by Kniff or one of his school.

Such a viewpoint would have shown at once the arrangement of
the five courts of the finished palace (Frontispiece), built in the
form of a T with its cross towards the main approach. In the middle,
and common to both axes, was the base-court. It was entered from
the avenue by an ornate gateway and flanked to the left by the brewhouse, bakehouse and laundry, and to the right by the stables. To
either side of the base-court was a further courtyard containing
offices; the buttery court behind the stables, in which grew 'a great
Holly Tree', and the dove-house court behind the brewhouse. In
the vicinity of the dove-house court was the orchard – without which
no Tudor house would have been complete – well stocked with
'divers sorts of special fruit curious for taste and variety', with a
moat 'reasonably well stocked with fish ... going almost round the
said orchard'.

Behind the base-court, and forming the stem of the T, were the
two quadrangles of the original house. The 'outer court', in which
the Queen had her lodgings, has become the 'middle court', and the
'Old House' west of it has been rebuilt with great magnificence and
renamed the 'Fountain Court'.

Seen from the air, the central feature would have been the hall.
Though smaller in scale than the towers by which it was surrounded,
it was richer in treatment, having an elaborate Renaissance porch
surmounted by a lofty and highly decorated bell tower. The feature
was probably similar in important respects to the south entrance at
Hatfield. Around it, the palace deployed its courts and gardens. To
the west, the noble buildings of the Fountain Court, containing the
state apartments on the first floor, combined the variety of a Tudor
façade with the symmetry of an Italian plan. It was this plan which
introduced the dominant theme of Theobalds – the four massive
pavilions at each corner of the Fountain Court, carried up to a third
storey and crowned each with four dome-capped cupolas. Some

idea of the effect may be obtained from the remains of Audley End today.

In the time of its pristine grandeur, Audley End was probably the finest house in England, and like Holdenby, it was a development of the theme announced at Theobalds. It is perhaps a significant coincidence that all three houses should have become, for a time, royal palaces. Evelyn, visiting Audley End in 1654, describes the effect of its most distinctive feature; 'it shows forth like a diadem', he wrote, 'by the decoration of the cupolas and other ornaments to the pavilions.' Another description of Audley End which could largely be applied to Theobalds comes from the pen of Neumayr von Ramssla: 'Because of its beautiful architecture it is to be preferred above all the royal houses, for it has three *Palatia*, one behind the other, each higher than the other.' This fashion, French in origin, of making the front range of buildings low in order to reveal a second behind it, was first introduced to England at Theobalds. Here the two sides of the middle court ended in high pavilions. On the inward angles of these two pavilions were tall staircase towers, and between the towers, a low, two-storeyed building. This range, presenting an open loggia towards the Middle Court and carrying a closed gallery above, was built low so that much of the detail of the hall porch and belfry could be seen from the high road. A central archway, pierced through this and flanked with projecting bay windows, provided the principal means of access.

The house stood in a pleasure garden so large that one could go for two miles without coming to an end of the walks. It had the additional attraction that the outer perimeter could be explored by boat, the entire garden being encompassed with water. From this side the full majesty of the architecture could best be appreciated, for like so many houses that are imposing and even forbidding on the entrance side, Theobalds reserved its fairest face for its most intimate friends.

The effect was produced by the combination of dramatic skyline with contrasting colours. The spectacular array of twenty cupolas, the bold relief of the tall pavilions and projecting bays, the slender, pinnacled belfry riding over the hall roof and the countless groups of elegant chimney-shafts made the silhouette of Theobalds its most impressive feature. Pink brick façades trimmed with white stone and glittering with enormous windows, blue slate-hung turrets with gilded weather-vanes and open loggias painted with classical frescoes built up a colour scheme to dazzle and delight the eye. We would see Theobalds as Sir Christopher Wren saw Versailles in 1664: 'The mixture of brick and stone, blue tile and gold, makes it look like a rich livery.'

Here Burghley was to live, surrounded by a throng of servants and suitors, for his reputation for impartiality in justice 'drew upon him such a multitude of suits', his biographer states, 'as was incredible but to us that saw it'. Here Elizabeth was to stay not less than twelve times, 'in as great royalty and served as bountifully and magnificently as at any other place'. Even in her absence, there was something of a Court at Theobalds. Many of the first noblemen in the land, anxious to apprentice their sons at the best school of statesmanship, put them into Burghley's service. He was thus served by men of quality and ability, and it was not unusual for as many as twenty gentlemen of a thousand a year to attend his table.

But it was Burghley's distinction, at the height of his power and fame, to preserve the virtue of simplicity. Unlike many Elizabethan parents, he was devoted to his family, and 'if he could get his table set round with his little children, he was then in his Kingdom.' But it was seldom that he had occasion to taste of these plain and homely joys. He was a man with a prodigious capacity for work and a nervous energy that kept him 'in a continual agitation both of body and mind', so that he was never less idle than when he had most leisure. Only at mealtimes could he put business out of his mind, and, in the company of old friends 'it was notable what merry stories he would tell.'

His relaxations were few and simple. He was a great reader, and had a passion for pedigrees, which he would jot down in his almost illegible hand, and which formed an important motif in the decorations of his house. Apart from these diversions, 'if he might ride privately in his garden upon his little mule, or lie a day or two at his little lodge at Theobalds, retired from business and too much company, he thought it his greatest and only happiness.'

For many years, his chief recreation was the building of Theo-

balds. There is no doubt that his own mind was the creative and
controlling influence behind the design, and yet, he admitted, 'not
without some special direction of Her Majesty. Upon fault found
with the small measure of her chamber (which was in good measure
for me) I was forced to enlarge a room for a larger chamber; which
need not be envied of any for riches in it, more than the shew of old
Oaks and such trees, with painted leaves and fruit.'

This must refer to the great chamber in the Fountain Court,
occupying the central position in the south front and commanding
the principal perspective of the gardens. Of its decorations, Jacob
Rathgeb in 1592 leaves the most detailed description. The oak trees
which lined the walls were so realistic 'that you could not dis-
tinguish between the natural and these artificial trees; and as far as I
could see, there was no difference at all, for when the Steward of the
house opened the windows, which looked upon the beautiful
pleasure garden, birds flew into the hall, perched themselves upon
the trees, and began to sing.'

As if to heighten the bizarre effect of this arboreal decoration, the
whole ceiling was laid out as a sort of astronomic clock, with the
signs of the zodiac, and the sun and stars performing their courses –
'which is without doubt contrived by some concealed ingenious
mechanism'. At one end of the room was an elaborate buffet consisting of 'a very high rock of all colours, made of real stones, out of
which gushes a splendid fountain that falls into a large circular bowl
supported by savages'. It is difficult to avoid the impression that the
great chamber was in extremely bad taste. It is possible that James I
was of this opinion, for under him, the oak trees were replaced by
panelling, the celestial ceiling by plaster fretwork and gilded pendants, and the fountain disappeared. Of Burghley's decorations,
there remained only the 'very large windows and several coats of
arms set in the same, opening south on the walk in the Great Garden
leading to the Green Gates going into the Park Walk of a mile long
between two rows of trees'.

West of the Fountain Court was the Long Gallery, one hundred
and twenty-three feet by twenty-one broad, panelled and frescoed
and lit by 'many large and spacious windows', some of them deeply
recessed so as to form square 'lobbies' into which one could retire

for intimate conversation. These windows were the great attraction of the gallery, 'making the rooms very delightful, looking into the Privy Gardens to the west, and east into the Fountain Court, and north into the Park, and so to Cheshunt'. Throughout its whole length, the gallery was 'set forth with a fret ceiling with divers pendants and roses and flower de luces, painted and gilded with gold'.

Another of the galleries – there were five in all – spanned the entrance front, being carried upon the arches of the loggia which backed the porter's lodge. Here in 1613 the Duke of Saxe-Weimar began his tour of the palace. 'His Princely Grace', writes Neumayr von Ramssla, his amanuensis, 'was first conducted into a Gallery, on either side of which the Shires of the Kingdom of England, with their Cities, Castles, Villages, Forests, Waters, Hills and Valleys are painted with great art. In each Shire stands a tree on which hang the shields and helmets of all the Lords, Nobles and Gentlemen who live in that province.' Here, evidently, Burghley's passion for maps, pedigrees and precise information found expression in the decorations of the Green Gallery.

Of the other rooms in the palace, some were entirely panelled – 'wainscoated round from ceiling to floor, with architrave, frieze and cornice' – and the rest, as Rathgeb recorded, 'were most magnificently decorated with splendid hangings and velvet bed and chairs'. Intricate plasterwork ceilings answered elaborate and often grotesque fire-places 'of carved freestone cut into Antiques and other wild beasts', adorned with coloured marbles and polished brass. But perhaps the most conspicuous features of the interior were the 'very large and fair windows' which looked out on to courts and gardens, their latticed panes embellished with colourful medallions of armorial glass.

Besides the main apartments, the house was a veritable warren of internal communications – of little 'pallet chambers' in which the servants slept, of lobbies and backstairs by means of which they passed unobtrusively about their business, and of larger staircases which gave the inmates frequent access down to the gardens or up on to the leads of the roof.

For it was a particular attraction of Theobalds that the roofs were 'laid almost level for walks'. The Duke of Stettin and his secretary

Rathgeb were able to walk round on the top, and the Commonwealth Commissioners, too, made use of the leads and found that
they afforded 'a very fine, pleasant and delightful walk'. Again and
again in their descriptions of the rooms we come upon doors which
gave direct access to the roofs, and it is clear that they were planned
deliberately for the pleasure and convenience of the household.
Some would have provided useful short cuts from one side of the
building to the other; others can only have been for the enjoyment
of the view they afforded.

The roofscape of an Elizabethan mansion is always one of its
most fascinating features, and it is worth imagining the scene in
some detail. We have now the whole fabric of the palace beneath us,
a pleasant medley of brick and stone and lead. Only the ornaments
are level with us now, the twenty cupolas, each with its gilded
weather-vane; the bell tower, now seen in all its elaborate detail,
'made of timber of excellent workmanship curiously wrought,
standing a great height, and divers pinnacles at each corner'. It is
described as being in the fashion of a lantern, but it was built to
contain a chime of twelve bells. Besides these more conspicuous
features, our chief companions are now the countless chimney-
stacks 'of sundry work and fashion'.

The walks were at three different levels, and to complete the circuit of the house, one would be repeatedly re-entering to mount
some spiral staircase and emerge again from the next storey.

At first floor level, there were the two walks that lay along the
colonnades east and west of the great hall. The one to the east was
the more elaborate affair, for one passed beneath, or behind, the
upper part of the hall porch, 'a goodly fair arch of freestone', which
was adorned with much painting and gilding, some of which could
even be discerned from the highway.

The next floor offered a walk over the Green Gallery and gatehouse block, between the two staircase towers which flanked the
entrance, and also over the south and west ranges of the Fountain
Court; the third storey took one onto the tops of the great pavilions,
'very high, with a fair prospect into the Great Garden'.

Standing on the leads of the great chamber and facing south, the
visitor would have overlooked a vast and formal layout of walks

and knots, their complex geometrical patterns centring upon a huge marble fountain which tossed its waters up as high as the house. This was the Great Garden, its many partitions 'compassed about with a quickset hedge of whitethorn and privet, and at every angle, a fair cherry tree of great growth'. Sheltered from the north and east by the house itself, it was the perfect situation for a garden; apricots and vines grew upon the south walls, the latter bearing 'excellent sweet grapes, and that in abundance', and dispersed amongst the knots were fifty-one cypress trees, which 'exceedingly adorn and set forth the Great Garden'.

Round the knots ran gravelled alleys, planted with lime and sycamore, 'being very pleasant, delightful and shady walks for summer'. At the ends of the walks were elaborate gazebos 'built with brick and turned over with arches, with towers of brick at each corner', and between these, the Great Green Gates gave access from the gardens into the long avenue to the south.

Around the gardens lay the park, well wooded and stocked with dappled deer. It was no easy task to people a forest with deer, and at Theobalds, the task was accomplished in a strange and almost incredible way. The Duke of Stettin was astonished to learn that some of the stags had been led 'from a large forest more than fifty German miles away, by some peasants marching before them with flutes and other instruments of music, the stags following the sounds'. This story he heard from the tailor who acted as German guide to Theobalds. There are other similar accounts known, and it is not improbable that they are true.

Lord Burghley was not himself a passionate hunter, and it is doubtful whether his own interest extended beyond the confines of his garden, in the making of which he certainly played a creative role. 'He greatly delighted in making gardens, fountains and walks, which, at Theobalds, were perfected most costly, beautifully and pleasantly.'

Besides the Great Garden, south of the house, there was the Maze Garden to the west, its complex patterns seen to their best advantage from the windows of the Long Gallery or from the leads above. In the middle of the maze was a typically Tudor feature, an artificial mound, described by Jean de Mandelslo in his *Voyages*

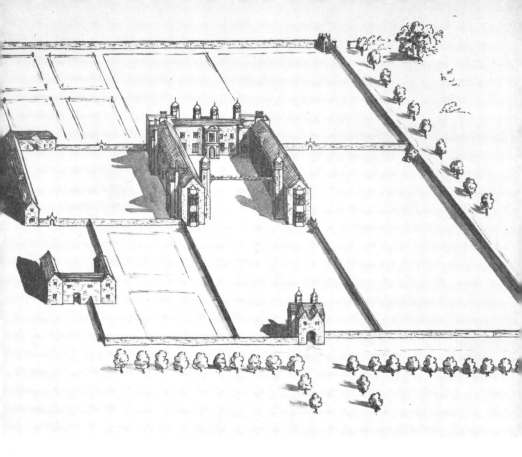

above: LONG MELFORD   BIRD'S EYE VIEW

below: KIRTLING   THE HOUSE AND GATE HOUSE FROM THE SOUTH

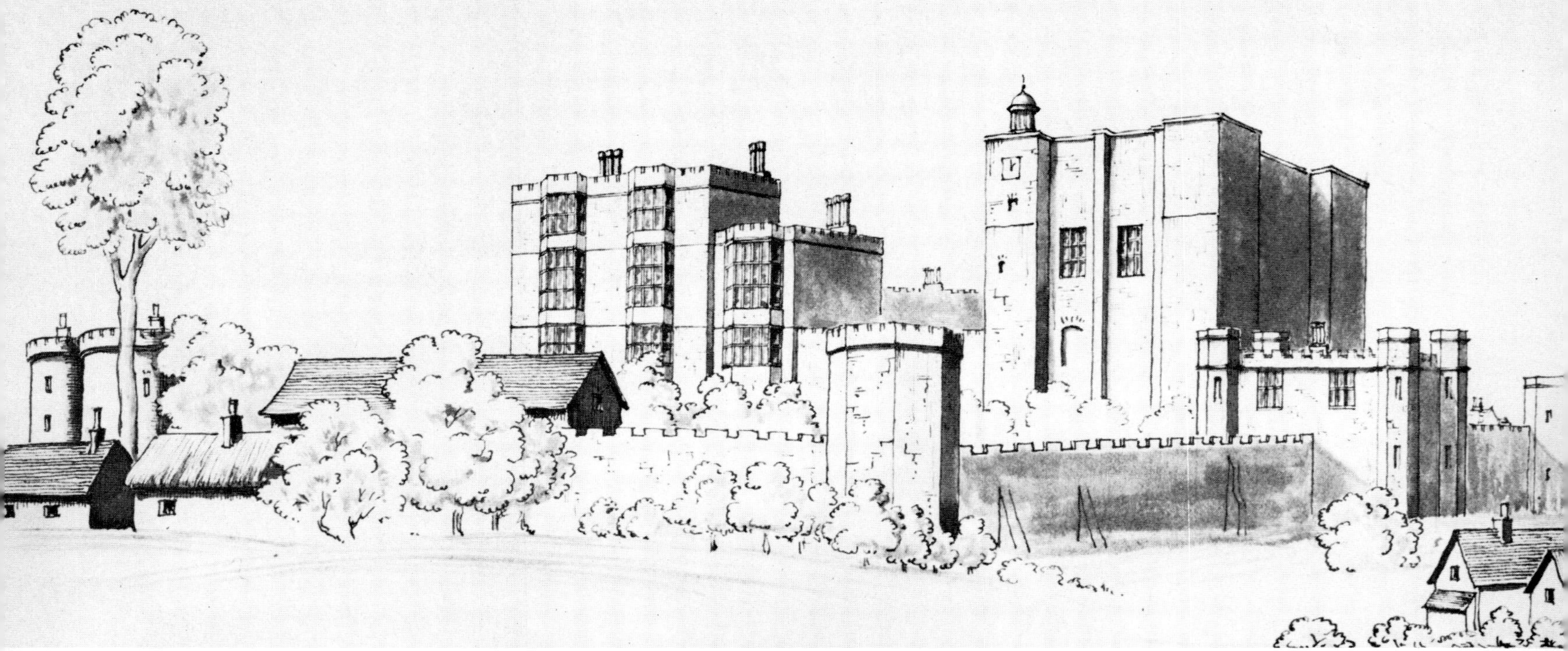

KENILWORTH THE CASTLE FROM THE EAST

Célèbres – 'une petite éminence que l'on appelle La Montagne de Vénus, au milieu du Labyrinthe, qui forme un des plus beaux lieux du monde'.

North of the house was the Privy Garden, an extremely sheltered and secluded spot, for it was deeply sunk and encompassed by a nine-foot hedge. Tulips, lilies and peonies coloured its borders, and apricots, figs and plums grew upon its walls. From this side of the house, too, ran the Mulberry Walk, 'a long, green and pleasant walk, set on both sides with mulberry trees' – there were seventy-two in all – lying between high brick walls, which led to the Great Pond in the park, and so to Cheshunt.

The creation and enjoyment of these gardens was Burghley's greatest pleasure, and they provided a diversity of relaxations for a much overworked man. In later years, 'when old age and gout sur-prised him', he had to refuse the throng of suitors whom he had so patiently and so impartially heard, and the focus of the household moved from the hall and the gardens to Burghley's chamber, where he continued to entertain as great a number of visitors as when he was abroad.

In his final illness, the Queen ministered to him with her own hand, and the old man was deeply moved. For forty years, they had enjoyed an unbroken partnership and when, months after his death, she spoke to Gilbert Talbot of her faithful minister, 'there was never a dry eye of the four.'

On Burghley's death, his estates were divided. Burghley House went, together with the title, to his elder son, later to be Earl of Exeter. Theobalds went, as it had always been intended, to his younger son, Robert, later to be Earl of Salisbury. These two houses were among the first to open their doors to James I as he travelled down to London on his accession. After visiting Burghley House, he lay at Broxbourne at Sir Henry Cox's, and, from thence, set out in the early afternoon with a great company of noblemen and a hundred and fifty followers 'in parti-coloured hats with red and yellow bands round rolled' preceded by trumpeters.

John Savile has left an enthusiastic account of the occasion. The new King was seen approaching Theobalds amidst a tremendous concourse of people, which continually added to its number as 'for

very joy, many ran from their carts, leaving their teams of horses to
their own unreasonable directions.' Round the entrance gates the
throng was terrific, for here the followers from Broxbourne were
met by the uninterrupted stream of sightseers that poured along the
London road. Savile himself, ensconced in a window at the Bell of
Edmonton with an hour glass, had attempted to number the
passers-by. Statistics are clearly not his *forte*, but he computed that,
if he had had a pin for every soul present, he would have had a
hundred and fifty pounds' worth.

At last, with ears deafened by the clamour of his subjects, King
James turned in at the gates, and saw for the first time the house
which was to become his favourite palace. So large a house, supported by so little land, was proving burdensome to Cecil, who
probably welcomed the opulent estate of Hatfield and the means to
build himself a smaller and compacter home. Theobalds on the
other hand, being a situation extremely favourable for hunting,
delighted James. Here he was to be, more than anywhere else, 'at
home', and here, twenty-two years later, he was to die, having forfeited much of that goodwill to which his first reception here bore
witness.

At the entrance to the base-court, the tumult began to thin out,
only the King proceeding thence on horseback. Here the master of
the house greeted him, and Sir Thomas Egerton delivered 'a
learned, brief and pithy oration', after which their host conducted
the royal party into the house. Outside, the crowds swarmed into
the courtyards and took up strategic points from which it might be
possible to see the King. It was a full hour before he reappeared to
show himself at one of the windows for some thirty minutes, after
which he withdrew to the gardens for some further respite, wandering in the shady alleys of the labyrinth and the meanders, where bay
and rosemary 'overshadowed his walk to defend him from the heat
of the sun'.

During supper, a prodigious quantity of money, meat and wine
was dispensed to the poor, none going away unsatisfied, and those
who had partaken of this liberal hospitality were not slow to 'blaze
it abroad' when they returned to London. However, in spite of
popular enthusiasm and pageantry, a note of disapproval of the

new regime was already present. Lady Anne Clifford recorded in her diary that they had been to 'Tibbals', where her mother and aunt had been most graciously received, 'but we all saw a great change between the fashion of the Court as it is now and that in the Queen's, for we were all lousy by sitting in Sir Thomas Erskine's Chamber.'

Four years later, when Theobalds had become a royal palace, it was the scene of entertainments which were far from edifying. During the reception of Christian IV of Denmark the revels were brought to a standstill by general drunkenness. First a lady who represented the Queen of Sheba 'overset her casket into his Danish Majesty's lap'; the King stood up to dance with her, but fell and had to be carried into an inner chamber. 'Now did appear Faith, Hope and Charity in rich dresses' – but the theological virtues, too, had succumbed to intemperance. 'Hope did essay to speak, but wine did render her efforts so feeble that she withdrew'. Nor was Victory to fare better, for 'after much lamentable utterance, she was led away like a silly captive.' It is unfortunate that the story of England's greatest Tudor house, which had begun in an atmosphere of such distinction, should end on such an undistinguished note.

XII

GORHAMBURY

ON THE seventeenth of July, 1572, while Lord Burghley was entertaining the Queen at Theobalds, a messenger arrived from his friend Sir Nicholas Bacon. The messenger was the bearer of a letter, in which Sir Nicholas sought the advice of the more experienced Burghley: 'Understanding by common speech that the Queen's Majesty means to come to my house, and knowing no certainty of the time of her coming nor of her abode, I have thought good to pray you that this bearer my servant might understand what you know therein.' To learn by hearsay of so important a visitation must have been a profoundly disturbing experience, but Bacon was not one to leave matters to chance. Burghley was of all men the most likely to be able to confirm or refute the truth of the rumour – 'and if it be true', continues the letter, 'then that I might understand your advice what you think to be the best way for me to deal in this matter (for in very deed no man is more raw in such a matter than myself)'. Bacon was a man of simple tastes, and the prospect of entertaining the Queen caused him no little consternation. 'I have wrote this', he added in a postscript, 'because I would gladly take that course that might best please Her Majesty, which I know not how better to understand than by your help'.

It would be extremely interesting to have Burghley's answer but, if he wrote it, it has not survived, and it is not known what preparations were made for the Queen's visit. Four years earlier, however, Bacon had completed the building of Gorhambury House, and it was no doubt to see how her Lord Keeper was seated that Elizabeth was planning this visit.

Like Cowdray, Gorhambury is only known today from eighteenth-century water-colours and engravings which give no idea of

above: THE CASTLE FROM THE EAST

KENILWORTH

below: THE RUINS IN THE EIGHTEENTH CENTURY, FROM THE SOUTH

above: THE ENTRANCE FRONT FROM THE WEST

COWDRAY

below: THE EAST RANGE OF THE GREAT COURT

the original Elizabethan setting. A map of the estate dated 1634, however, makes it possible to picture how the house was related to its landscape, and to take note of its characteristic features.

The great houses of the Tudors were often built at an easy proximity to their town or village; Gorhambury was set deep in the Hertfordshire countryside, and the long drive wandered with typically English inconsequence through the woody landscape until it reached a point somewhere between Prae Wood and the present Temple Cottage. Here it struck off to the right into the long straight 'Walk' which gave a direct frontal approach to Gorhambury House. There was no avenue and the façade must have been visible for the whole length of the approach. Before the house was a garden wall, and before the wall lay a green, enclosed and partitioned. A greater and a lesser ornamental archway gave access to the forecourt and to the gardens which lay to the left as one entered. To the right was a small plantation which was most probably the orchard. The whole plot, buildings, courts and gardens, was backed and overtopped by a noble plantation known as Oak Wood, which gave an atmosphere of trim and cosy seclusion difficult to recapture today.

The main front of the house (Plate 24) presented a white plaster façade one hundred and fifteen feet long. Three gables breaking the roofline and a central archway surmounted by a projecting bay window were its only features. This sober simplicity gave the house an unpretentious domestic appearance which made no terms with the great octagonal towers at either extremity. A further tower, rising from the angle formed by the projection of the chapel, carried its belfry high above the rest of the building, but these features, usually grouped into an impressive central gatehouse, lost much of their effect through being set so far apart.

Passing through the archway into the main quadrangle, the visitor would have been struck by a rather more deliberate architectural contrivance, for here Sir Nicholas had introduced some of the newfangled ideas borrowed from Italy. The courtyard was a happy mixture of Gothic and classic which deceived the sharp eye of Horace Walpole, who visited the place in 1751. He wrote that the porticoes and loggias 'though Italianized, artfully are prevented from swearing with the older parts of the buildings'.

They were, in fact, only older in style. The beautiful Renaissance porch (Plate 24), with an Ionic order surmounting the Doric, gave access to the hall, whose tall mullion and transom window was in the local and medieval tradition. Both, however, were built at the same time, for the date inscribed on the porch, 1568, agrees with that shown in the single sheet of building accounts as the year of the completion of the original structure. This document, 'a Brief of the whole charges of the money bestowed upon the building of Gorhambury between the first day of March anno dni 1563 and the last day of September A.D. 1568', is preserved in the library of Lambeth. It is arranged so as to show the relative cost of each of the various craftsmen during each of the six years of construction. What a story these simple rows of figures tell! One can picture the first year of digging and bricking in the foundations. Labourers, masons, carpenters, and bricklayers are in demand, but the greatest disbursement is for 'divers carriages' – as materials, many of them taken from the medieval house of the de Gorhams and the Abbey of St Albans, were collected on the site.

The second year sees the addition of brickmakers and tile-makers, and evidently the roofing was completed, for no further demands were made upon their services. The third year, glaziers, joiners and plasterers have swelled the throng, and we can picture the house in shell form, with its new windows set and the plaster still wet upon the walls. For Sir Nicholas had chosen this unusual external surface for his house. It is possible that the softness of the local stone, called 'clunch', had deterred him from using it, although there was a ready supply to hand from the dismantled Abbey of St Albans.

The fourth year marks the summit, and a total of nine hundred and fifty-two pounds was spent. Figures for carpenters and sawyers are the highest yet; the payment to joiners has risen from two pounds seventeen shillings to sixty-three pounds eleven shillings, and we can imagine the doors and wainscoting beginning to grace the rooms as the result of their labours. The fifth year shows a decline in expenditure all round as the great house nears its completion. Bricklayers and 'divers carriages' have dropped to a quarter of the sum paid in the previous year, and only joiners and plasterers continue at anything like the same rate. Paviours and plumbers make a modest appearance, suggesting the final arrangements for draining and laying out the courtyard.

The last year, during which £296.14.9 is accounted for, sees the significant addition of painters, and it is reasonable to picture the mansion complete in its internal decorations. It is interesting to notice a few comparative totals. Woodwork, including sawyers, carpenters and joiners, comes to £562.5.1, stonework and brick-work, together with carriage, £783.7.1, plastering £65.13.0, and glazing £35.0.2½, while labourers, exclusive of the specialists named, command £577.10.2½ of a total outlay of £3,177.11.9½. We are warned in a footnote that this takes no account of 'timber felled within your Lordship's woods'. A further saving would have been affected by the use of materials from the old house and the Abbey.

For this relatively modest price, a modest house was built. Its greatest charm was in the quiet little court around which the inmates lived their daily lives, crossing and recrossing it to get from one part of the house to another, for, like most houses of that date, Gorhambury was one room thick and had no corridors. The quad-rangle was only eighty feet deep and seventy-two feet across and mostly built in the homely Tudor vernacular. But the south range, with its shady cloister in the Italian style, and the north range with its Renaissance porch and the tall mullioned windows of the hall conferred a certain architectural dignity upon the court. Above the rooftops rose the battlements of the two towers, somewhat incon-gruous and only surpassed in height by the belfry, by whose sono-rous chimes the routine of the household was regulated. The bell, which still hangs in the stables of the new house, was engraved with the couplet:

> Anthony Bartlett made me
> In fifteen hundred and sixty-three.

The bell summoned the inmates to the communal functions of the household – to prayers in the chapel and to meals in the hall, the domestic servants reaching it through the door in the screens, the gentry coming across the courtyard and using the elegant entrance porch.

It was a modest hall, only thirty-five feet long, and not quite twenty across. The ceiling, for it was probably a plastered wagon vault, was some twenty-two feet from the floor. Its decoration, according to Aubrey, was in the form of emblematic paintings. Over the fire-place was depicted an oak with acorns falling from it, with the motto 'Nisi quid potius' ('What else is stronger?'); on the wall over the table – presumably behind the dais – Ceres teaching the sowing of corn, with the motto 'Moniti meliora' ('instruction bringeth improvement'),[1] while the main decorative feature of the hall was 'a large story very well painted of the feasts of the Gods where Mars is caught in a net by Vulcan'.

Like many Tudor houses, Gorhambury began as a simple quadrangle, but, in two generations, it had more than doubled its size. The first expansion was the direct outcome of the Queen's first visit. 'My Lord Keeper,' she said, after being shown round, 'what a little house you have gotten.' 'My house is well, Madam,' came the reply, 'but you have made me too great for my house.'

All the same, he took her criticism to heart. By her next visit, five years later, the buildings had been extended towards the west by the addition of a magnificent new gallery carried upon a Tuscan colonnade. This formed below a sunny loggia – 'a noble portico', as Aubrey describes it, 'which fronts the gardens to the South'. There were, as Pennant recorded in his *Journey from Chester to London*, two such cloisters to the house 'where the philosophic inhabitants walked and held their learned discourse': the south range of the original quadrangle, and the gallery just referred to, 'the one being intended for enjoying the shade, the other to catch in winter the comfortable warmth of the sun'.

That was the supreme virtue of Gorhambury; everything was done for a purpose, nothing for ostentation. It was this that won the unstinted praise of Walpole. 'It is a most respectable and agreeable retirement', he wrote, 'with an air of sober simplicity, yet calculated for great enjoyment.' It is just the house one would have expected from Sir Nicholas Bacon, 'a plain man', according to his more illustrious son, 'direct and constant, without all fineness and doubleness'. He was surely thinking of his father's home when he wrote in his essay, 'houses are built to live in, not to look on;

---

[1] The translations of the two mottoes are Aubrey's.

therefore let use be preferred before uniformity, except where both may be had.'

If Bacon was to be able to entertain his sovereign, however, at least one really noble apartment was necessary, and to provide this the west gallery was designed. It was a building one hundred and twenty feet long by eighteen wide, broken in the centre by a slightly projecting frontispiece and having a return of some twenty feet at the extremity. The ground floor was taken up by the open loggia already referred to. The wall which backed the colonnade was arcaded, the arches answering to the thirteen bays. Three of them were hollowed into niches, that in the centre containing a gilded statue of Henry VIII in armour, flanked by painted terracotta busts of Sir Nicholas and his lady. The remainder of the wall spaces were painted with the adventures of Ulysses. These were the 'curious pictures all emblematical with mottoes under each' noted by Aubrey. They were painted 'by an excellent hand (but the mischief of it is in water-colours)'. Pennant identifies the 'excellent hand' as that of Van Koepen.

Above this loggia was the gallery, panelled in oak with compartments picked out in gilt and adorned by the Lord Keeper with Latin texts 'selected by him out of divers authors'. The ceiling, painted with heads of Greek and Roman emperors, spanned the apartment with a spacious barrel vault, but the paintings – 'done only in umber and shell gold, all the heightening and illuminated part being burnished gold, and the shadowed umber' – seem, from Aubrey's description, to have dated only from the days of Sir Francis. The windows of the gallery were of painted glass, some of which survives in the present Gorhambury House, 'every pane with several figures of beast, bird and flower'.

Such was the addition made to the house in time for the second visit of Elizabeth in 1577, on May 27th. She came for a long week-end, 'coming thither on Saturday ... before supper and continuing until Wednesday after dinner following'. In the library at Lambeth are accounts of 'the charges expended at Gorhambury by reason of her Majestie's coming thither'. They give an insight into the gastronomic side of such an entertainment.

Eight oxen, sixty sheep, thirty-four lambs, eighteen calves and ten kids were purchased for the table, besides thirty bucks and two stags taken from the park. The bill for meat came to £77.15.2; for game, £105.7.11; while fish, which appeared in great variety, added a further £36.18.0. Twenty-four pounds were spent on beer and fifty-seven on wine. The list of wildfowl comes more within the range of the ornithologist than the poulterer. Twelve dozen herons and thirteen dozen bitterns were supplemented by godwits, dotterels, shovellers, curlews and knots, until it seemed that the whole population of the sea-shore had come under the fowler's snare. Gammons of bacon, neat's-tongues, cow's udders and calves' feet all figure in the bill of fare, which made a grand total of £377.7.8 for food and drink. An additional twenty pounds was paid 'for them of the revels'. Now the Bacons were somewhat puritan in their tastes. 'I trust you will not mime nor mask nor sinfully revel', Lady Bacon had written to her sons while they were sharing rooms at Gray's Inn. Perhaps it was only as a reluctant concession to royalty that the revels were ever admitted to Gorhambury.

Other items of interest in the account show that Sir Nicholas had got in special caterers from London for the occasion. Ten pounds were laid out in 'carriages from London to Gorhambury', and twelve to 'the cooks of London for their wages'. The extraordinary numbers gathered for the occasion made it difficult to keep a careful check on everything, and £6.15.6 were entered in the accounts for 'loss of pewter' and two pounds for 'loss of napery'. Whether this was a reflection on the honesty of the Queen's household or of the extra personnel taken on for the occasion, history does not relate.

The whole five days' entertainment cost Sir Nicholas £577.6.7½, exclusive of a cup presented to the Queen. Although no mean sum, this was less than what other, more prodigal noblemen were outlaying in the same cause. Considering that he went to Burghley for advice on how to entertain Elizabeth, Bacon seems to have got off fairly lightly.

The year 1602 brought a new lustre to the life of Gorhambury, when Sir Francis Bacon inherited the estate and enriched the home of his father with his own distinguished presence. It was probably he who added the second courtyard to the north of the mansion. By moving the offices to this court, he made all four sides of the original quadrangle available for lodgings and greatly increased his household.

Sir Francis is too well known to require any introduction, but it is worth looking at Aubrey's picture of him, for it shows the great philosopher in close relation to the background of his home at Gorhambury.

Apparently, he was not free from those little unreasonable foibles which are the privilege of genius. For instance, Aubrey records that none of his servants dared appear before him but in boots of Spanish leather, 'for he would smell the neat's leather, which offended him'. He seems to have paid considerable attention to questions of smell, and the flowers of his garden were disposed with as much regard for their perfume as for colour. We find, in his own handwriting, notes for the construction of an 'arbour of musk-roses set all with double violets for scent in autumn', and at all times in the year, his table was strewn with flowers and sweet herbs 'which he said did refresh his spirits and his memory'. With similar finesse he would often have music played in the next room to stimulate meditation.

It is probable that much of his writing was done at his country house for, like many other pensive people, Bacon liked to do his thinking in the open air, and, during the period of his ownership, much care was given to the embellishment of the gardens and grounds of Gorhambury.

Of the gardens which immediately surrounded the mansion we know nothing, but must be content with Aubrey's conjecture that they were 'no doubt rare planted in his Lordship's time'. From these gardens, a handsome gateway led to a noble plantation of oak trees, 'very great and shady', and, beneath their shade, the ground was planted with tulips and peonies. This was one of the philosopher's favourite haunts, and here he would pace up and down with Mr Bushell at hand to commit the fruits of his meditation to paper.

Some of his secretaries found this a wellnigh impossible task, for 'when he read their notes, he scarce understood what they writ, because they understood not clearly themselves.' It took someone of the intellectual calibre of Thomas Hobbes to do this, and he soon endeared himself to the Lord Chancellor by his ability in this respect. Sir Francis was 'wont to have him walk with him in the delicate groves where he did meditate, and when a notion darted into his mind, Mr Hobbes was presently to write it down'.

Besides the groves, much of the park was planted in straight avenues, some wide enough for three coaches to pass, and 'at several good views were erected elegant summer houses, built of Roman architecture, well wainscoted and ceiled.' We have Bacon's own notes for a 'plot to be made … of the walk through Prae Wood and the stand there on the hill for prospect'. These pavilions, when Aubrey visited them, were so defaced that he exclaimed 'one would have thought the barbarians had made a conquest here', and where there had been 'in his lordship's prosperity a Paradise, now is a large ploughed field'.

But Sir Francis's most important additions to his estate were neither in the vicinity of the house, nor in Prae Wood. They were down in the valley, about a mile to eastward of the house, adjoining Watling Street. The reason for this departure from the precincts of the mansion was probably the lack of water, an element of which he made the fullest use in his new creation.

Sir Nicholas Bacon had gone to great lengths to obtain an adequate water supply for the house. There are references to a 'force' which raised the waters of the River Ver, and later to reservoirs in Prae Wood with three-quarters of a mile of lead piping to bring the water to the house. This was no mean achievement for its day, and Dr Rawley, chaplain to Sir Francis, leaves no doubt as to the efficiency of the Prae Wood line. 'When Sir Nicholas Bacon, the Lord Keeper, lived,' he writes, 'every room in Gorhambury was served with a pipe of water from the ponds distant about a mile off. In the lifetime of Mr Anthony Bacon, the water ceased, after whose death, his Lordship coming to the inheritance, could not recover the water without infinite charge.'

Being unable to bring water to his house and garden, Sir Francis was obliged to take both these to the water, and it was in the valley bottom that he made his new gardens, later to be adorned with Verulam House – 'the most ingeniously contrived little pile', according to Aubrey, 'that ever I saw'.

Some notes in Bacon's own hand are preserved in the British

COWDRAY THE GREAT HALL

above: THE ENTRANCE FRONT FROM THE SOUTH

GORHAMBURY

below: THE RUINS OF THE QUADRANGLE IN 1842

Museum which give a clear account of his scheme for a charming Water Garden, covering in all about four acres of land: 'To turn the Pond Yard into a place of Pleasure, and to speak thereof to my Lord of Salisbury ... ' The Bacons were frequently consulting the Cecils about the details of country life, and the gardens of Gorhambury probably owed much to those of Theobalds.

The directions were that all the ground was to be 'cast into a lake, with a fair rail with images gilt round about it, and some low flowers, especially strawberries and violets ... then a fair hedge of timber work till it touch the water, with some glasses coloured for the eye'. The Elizabethans had an almost childish love of gold and all that glittered, and Sir Francis Bacon was true to his Tudor up-bringing. His practice here conforms closely with his precept, for in his essay on gardening, he recommends that ponds should be 'finely paved with images, the sides likewise, and withal embellished with coloured glass and such things of lustre'. The ponds, Aubrey noted, were 'pitched in the bottoms with pebbles of several colours, which were worked into several figures, as of fishes, etc.', and 'many a poor body had brought his Lordship half a dozen pebbles of a curious colour' and received a shilling for his pains.

The Water Garden was set all about with islands, 'an island with a Grott', 'an island mounted with flowers in ascents', 'an island where the fair Hornbeam grows', and the island of musk-roses already referred to. Each island had its guardian statue of nymph or Triton to keep it. There were no communications between the islands except for a 'fair bridge to the Middle Great Island only, the rest by boat'. On the Middle Great Island was built a 'house for freshness, with an upper gallery open to the water, a terrace above that and a supping room below that'. Aubrey describes this as a 'curious Banqueting House of Roman architecture, paved with black and white marble, covered with Cornish slate and neatly wainscoated'.

By the time that Aubrey examined the Water Garden, it was already in full decay. The 'fine little stream run upon gravel' was silted up, and the pebbled figures 'which in his Lordship's time were plainly to be seen through the clear water, now overgrown with flags and rushes'.

The Civil War, in fact, was kinder to Gorhambury itself than to the more recent embellishments of the park. The Countess of Sussex was tenant in those troubled times, and was ready to withstand a minor siege. 'My servants give me hopes', she wrote to Sir Ralph Verney, 'they were able to keep out one hundred if they should come upon us.' Fortunately, they never came, for Gorhambury would have stood but a frail chance against Cromwell's cannon. A few weeks later, she wrote again, 'I am thinking to put my hangings and best stuff in one of the round turrets over my chamber and wall it up.' The house, however, survived with nothing worse than the loss of some of its charming appendages, and became the property of the Grimston family, later to be Earls of Verulam.

An amusing anecdote is told of Sir Samuel Grimston by his descendant Charlotte. This gentleman had married a Lady Anne Tufton 'whose violent temper occasioned the misery of the latter part of his life'. To escape from her tantrums, he appropriated for his use a small room, approachable only by a narrow spiral staircase, and called it 'Mount Pleasant', because the Lady Anne 'being extremely corpulent, found the ascent of the stairs too difficult to interrupt his retirement by her presence'.

The later history of Gorhambury is a tale of unsuccessful attempts to adapt the house to eighteenth-century needs and to preserve its crumbling fabric. For, unlike Cowdray, whose very solidity contributed to its downfall, Gorhambury was not a building of sufficient strength to endure; much of the brickwork was of poor quality, and the earlier additions had been made with no bond. Even in Aubrey's days, the murals, which were only water-colours, were beginning to fade, and, by 1773, despite the buttressing of the hall, 'the extreme want of repair of the old house rendered it quite unfit for habitation.' Eleven years later, when Robert Taylor's new mansion had been completed, the home of the Bacons was abandoned and fell into rapid decay, its remains becoming 'almost enshrouded by an evergreen wreath of affectionate ivy'. In 1799, Baskerfield, surveying the place that had been the residence of the great philosopher, found it impossible to avoid 'the contrary impressions of joy and grief. Joy, that so great a genius should have been the product of our island; grief, that such a favourite of Nature and prodigy of Learning should expire in want and contempt.'

The same emotions might be evoked by the ruins of his house. The more one admires – with Horace Walpole – the way it was 'built to live in', the more one regrets that it has not survived as a memorial to its distinguished inhabitants. But, like so many houses of the sixteenth century, Gorhambury was hastily and shoddily built.

EPILOGUE
DEATH AND RECONSTRUCTION

ON FEBRUARY 2ND, 1603, the Venetian ambassador, Giovanni Scaramelli, arrived in London and found that the Queen had gone to Richmond, 'a Palace suited to the season'. A week or two earlier, the Court had removed thither 'in very foul and wet weather', and the wind, moving round into the north-east, had brought on one of the sharpest spells within living memory. Nevertheless, the Queen was in excellent health when she received the new ambassador. 'She was clad in taffety of silver and white trimmed with gold', he writes; 'her dress was somewhat open in front and showed her throat encircled with pearls and rubies down to her breast. Her hair was of a light colour never made by nature, and she wore great pearls like pears round the forehead ... and displayed a vast quantity of gems and pearls upon her person.'

In the Presence Chamber, she was surrounded by the great officers of the Kingdom, and behind them thronged the gentlemen and ladies of the Court. In the background musicians were playing, but they stopped as Scaramelli approached. Elizabeth rose to greet him with the words, 'Welcome to England, Mr Secretary.'

Elizabeth was now in her seventieth year, in excellent health and in full possession of all her senses. Almost to the end of her life, she kept up a high pitch of gaiety. 'We are frolick here at Court,' Lord Worcester had written from Oatlands that autumn, 'much dancing in the Privy Chamber before the Queen's Majesty, who is exceedingly pleased therewith.' A few days later, Sir Fulke Greville wrote to the Countess of Shrewsbury of the Queen's continuing health: 'The best news I can yet write your Ladyship is of the Queen's health and disposition ... I have not seen her everyway better disposed these many years.'

It was not to last. During the winter, Elizabeth was having trouble with slight swellings in her throat. She was also having trouble with Arabella Stuart – 'a lady of great beauty and remarkable qualities', but in an uncomfortable proximity to the succession. She was at that time undergoing a sort of house arrest at Hardwick. In March, she was transferred to the closer custody of Woodstock Manor. Scaramelli saw this as the beginning of the mischief with Elizabeth. 'She has suddenly withdrawn into herself' – he wrote – 'she, who was wont to live so gaily, especially in these last years of her life.'

A week later the situation was getting serious. 'I was right when, in my last despatch, I said that Her Majesty's mind was overwhelmed by a grief greater than she could bear. It reached such a pitch that she passed three days and three nights without sleep and scarcely any food.'

Scaramelli watched, perforce, as an outsider. Within the precincts of the palace, Sir Robert Carey, newly arrived from the borders, was able to take a closer view of events. Summoned by the Queen on his arrival, he had expressed his happiness to see her in safety and in health. 'She took my hand', he wrote, 'and wrung it hard, saying "No, Robin, I am not well." ' She told him of her indisposition, how she had been heavy and sad these ten days since, 'and in her discourse she fetched not so few as forty or fifty great sighs.'

The next day, she failed to attend the chapel, but, after much delay, had cushions laid in the Privy Chamber 'hard by the Closet door', and so heard the service sung. On these cushions she spent the next four days, refusing all food, until, at last, the Lord Admiral persuaded her to take to her bed. Even now, there was little wrong with her that could not have been easily remedied, but she was a prey to a 'settled and unremovable melancholy, insomuch that she could not be won or persuaded, neither by Councils, Divines, Physicians, nor the women about her, once to sup or touch any physic'.

Back in London, Scaramelli records: 'Her Majesty's life is absolutely despaired of ... for the last six days she has become quite silly ... London is all in arms for fear of the Catholics ... Every house and everybody is in movement and alarm.' The French ambassador, Camden asserts, was stirring up what trouble he could, and 'as the report now grew daily stronger and stronger that her sickness increased upon her', it was incredible to see 'with what great speed the Puritans, Papists, Ambitious Persons and Flatterers of all kinds ... posted night and day by sea and land to Scotland'.

Meanwhile, the Queen was sinking fast. 'A heavy dullness' began to seize upon her and she relapsed into an ever profounder silence, 'fixing her mind wholly upon her meditations'; people were not slow to guess at the subject of her thoughts. She was pining for Essex; she was worried about Arabella; she was regretting the pardon of Tyrone; she was incensed at the departure of so many 'to adore the rising sun'.

Of the latter, there were not a few, and among them was Sir Robert Carey. Within her chamber, he had been 'full of tears to see that heavy sight'; once away from it, self-interest was uppermost. 'I could not but think', he confessed, 'in what a wretched estate I should be left, most of my livelihood depending on her life. And hereupon I bethought myself with what grace and favour I was ever received by the King of Scots. I did assure myself it was neither unjust nor dishonest for me to do for myself, if God at that time should call her to his mercy.'

At this critical moment, Scaramelli came a second time to Richmond and 'found all the Palace, outside and in, full of an extraordinary crowd, almost in uproar and on the tiptoe of expectation'. Carey, anxious to be the first with the news to Scotland, had a private arrangement with the cofferer to keep him informed, and had tipped the porter an angel to let him in at any time.

Within the Queen's chamber, peace and quiet reigned. There were musicians playing; and the Archbishop of Canterbury, her beloved Whitgift, with a few other divines, was praying with her, Elizabeth meanwhile making signs 'of the sweet comfort she took in their presence and assistance'. Twice the old man rose from his knees, and twice she signalled him to continue. And so she lay, her hand in his, in the gathering darkness of the night, and at three in the morning she departed this life 'like a ripe apple from a tree'.

Thus died the Queen, and with her died the inspiration of an age. It is appropriate that in her last moments she was attended by her musicians, for of all the forms of art whose flowering gave lustre to her reign the most significant was music, and of all the forms of music the most typical was madrigal – several voices singing different tunes in harmony. It is a fitting thought with which to review her reign. In so far as Elizabeth was successful, it was because her aim was harmony and not uniformity. Her ideal, unlike that of her sister, was something organic and comprehensive, a blending together of differences so as to form an intelligible whole.

The social expression of harmony is community, which combines a sense of belonging with a sense of individual worth. Community comprehends difference, and differences if they can be held together result in mutually fruitful intercourse and generate vitality. Vitality will be for ever sparking off in new directions. So the age of Elizabeth, conceived in harmony, issued in originality, and is remembered supremely as an age of expansion and discovery.

The measure in which Elizabeth achieved political harmony is the measure of her greatness. England was divided at her accession; it was divided again within a generation of her death, this time with a rift so devastating that to men such as Aubrey, looking back across years of bloodshed and destruction with nostalgic reminiscence to the days of their childhood, this was the Great Divide. When Charles I stepped from one of the windows of Whitehall on to the scaffold before the Banqueting House, a part of English history died with him, and the destruction, started in the Reformation, was all but completed in the Revolution. It ranged from acts of light-hearted iconoclasm to systematic and mercenary vandalism. Of the former type had been the action of Mr Forde, usher of Winchester College. Conceiving a dislike for the statues round about the chapel, he attached cords to them, and 'being in his chamber after midnight, he plucked the cords' end, and all the golden gods came down with *heyho rumbelow.*' A century later the job was being completed with business-like efficiency, and Aubrey tells of a man in Croydon 'hired for half a crown per day to break the painted glass, which were formerly very fine'.

By the end of the Commonwealth, the England of Elizabeth had been to a large extent destroyed. A whole host of buildings, stained glass windows, paintings and manuscripts had been swept away before the tide of triumphant Puritanism, and with them went an odd miscellany of quaint and often lovable traditions.

The pointless severing of so many links with the past is symbolized, perhaps unconsciously, by Aubrey in his tale of the Raven of Fawsby: 'At Fawsby, in Northamptonshire, a raven did build her nest on the leads between the tower and the steeple. The oldest people's grandfathers here did never remember but that this raven yearly made her nest here; and in the late civil wars, the soldiers killed her. I am sorry for the tragical end of this old Church-bird, that lived in so many changes of government and religion.'

The Raven of Fawsby, however, lasted for longer than many of the Tudor palaces. Theobalds, acquired by the Crown in 1607, was among the first to go. 'Our fathers saw it built,' lamented Fuller, 'we behold it unbuilt.' For years its mutilated carcass lingered on, leased out for tenements or left to pilfering hands and eroding elements. By the time that antiquarian interest was fully aroused, nothing significant was left.

Before the end of the Commonwealth the fate of Richmond, Greenwich, Oatlands, Woodstock, Kenilworth and Holdenby was likewise sealed. But in spite of the Restoration the destruction continued. In 1682 Nonsuch fell. The house which had been the architectural sensation of its age was sacrificed to the financial needs of the Duchess of Cleveland, and its passing was hardly noticed. No longer wanted, it was sold to brokers and gradually demolished. Whitehall, purged of its 'superstitious pictures', survived a little longer, but fire was to destroy what bigotry had spared, and by the end of the century Hampton Court and Newhall were the only Tudor palaces to survive in anything like their entirety. These, together with many private houses, were not demolished, but altered to conform with the requirements of another age. Hampton Court retains enough to be of great interest. Newhall, reduced to one-tenth of its original size, has little to tell us about the Tudor way of life.

The historian who approaches the houses of the Elizabethan age must face the task of reconstruction. Most of his subjects have disappeared, and amongst them the most important. Some have vanished completely, leaving only a legend, and, if luck will have it, a plan or a drawing or two to illuminate and guide. Some have survived in part or in ruins, and to these the antiquary instinctively turns. A fragment is perhaps the greatest stimulant to the mind – 'as Pythagoras did guess at the vastness of Hercules' stature by the length of his foot,' Aubrey observed, 'so amongst these ruins are remains enough left for a man to give a guess what noble buildings were made by the piety, charity and magnanimity of our forefathers.' He even saw a psychological advantage in leaving something to the imagination, for ruins 'breed in generous minds a kind of pity and set the thoughts a-work to make out their magnificence as they were when in perfection'. This is the true calling of the antiquary.

Can we, then, reconstruct the houses of Elizabethan England, or are they for ever lost behind the destructions of time and the improvements of later generations? Scholarship can provide the foundations; it can also sharpen the mind and inform the imagination, and it is to the imagination thus trained that the final stage must be left.

We must begin with the land itself, with even a flora and a fauna that are no longer familiar. We must see it wild, menacing and deserted, with its undrained fens and tangled undergrowth; we must penetrate its great oak forests and rolling woodland and feel their emptiness and their silence – a silence emphasized rather than broken by the call of rutting deer and the 'wheeling kite's wild solitary cry'. Against this background we must see the rich and fertile valleys where man has made his conquest, and we must glory in them as only a man could glory who has felt the barrenness and the loneliness of the wilds. If the Elizabethan was inspired to his most lyrical mood by meadows and orchards and spring, it was because winter and woods and mountains still frightened him.

In these happy valleys we must set our gardens, laid out by men who were rich enough to plant lands only for delight, and delighted to plant them with every conceit and variety that fancy could suggest. We must not dismiss them with Dallaway's disdainful smile as 'quaint and sumptuous departures from nature and simplicity', but enjoy their mixture of trim formality, artificial wildness, practical joking and delightful surprises. Whether we come upon a maze which baffles us, a fountain which souses us, or 'a little turret with belly enough to receive a cage full of birds', we must revel in their riotous invention, in the insatiability of a man who has just discovered mastery over nature.

In these gardens we must set the houses – and here we find our real problem. For in the new passion for exploring after ways and means, the diversity is so great that it is impossible to imagine such a thing as a typical Tudor house. What is the thread which links the black-and-white houses of the north and west with the stone masonry of Derbyshire and the Wolds or the brick quadrangles of East Anglia? What has the moated and embattled manor house in common with the pilastered front and balustraded skyline of the Renaissance palace?

But we must not look for uniformity. The whole tenor of the age should warn us against that. We must look for harmony and for community. It is in the patron, the future owner and occupant of the house, that we shall find the key to both. The creative, integrating role was his, and it is through his eyes that we must see our house take ghostly shape.

He himself, as patron, is one of a community. The Reformation Parliament had been a great marriage-market, and where there were broad lands and opulent houses there were also intricate family connections. Not unnaturally there was interchange of architectural ideas and borrowing of craftsmen. Our patron knows what Sharington is doing at Lacock, Thynne at Longleat, and Cecil at Theobalds. He naturally consults with his more experienced friends as to his projected buildings, and together they ride out into the park to consider its site and orientation. The importance of these was fully recognized by the Elizabethans. 'In the seating of ourselves (which is a kind of marriage to the place),' advised Sir Henry Wotton, 'builders should be as circumspect as wooers.' Due consideration will be given to the proximity of woods and water, to protection from wind and rain, to the wholesomeness of the air and to the attractions of the prospect. In placing his house 'with a singular regard to the nature of the region,' the patron makes his first contribution to harmony – the matching of architecture to landscape which is often so conspicuous a feature of the Tudor house.

Two important factors, the materials and the scale, are already determined for the patron; the former by the locality of his estate, the latter by the size of his household.

This household is also a community. It is significantly known as the 'family' – a word interpreted in the widest sense by the Elizabethans. 'Their vast mansions', wrote Horace Walpole, 'received and harboured all the younger branches, the dowagers and maiden aunts', so that the family proper was often present in its entirety. But instead of one clear division between family and servants, the Tudor household offered the picture of a complex social structure. Its great officers, the Steward, the Chamberlain or the Treasurer, were frequently relatives – sometimes even brothers – of the lord. Nor were their activities confined to the narrow sphere of domestic duties, for their posts could be held in plurality with public office. In 1588 Lord Derby's Clerk of the Kitchen was returned to Parliament for Preston.

Our patron has several attendants who keep their coaches and number their incomes in four figures. They belong to the ornament rather than the structure of the household. Of those whose work maintains the family, there were gentlemen, yeomen, and underlings to each office, and on their number the size of the mansion will depend.

The structure of the household is reflected in the fabric of the mansion – hall and chapel, kitchen and offices, lodgings and state rooms being clearly articulated on the plan. Here the patron makes his second contribution to harmony, for he is sufficiently in touch with the new humanism to seek a unifying principle in Nature and to find one in the human body, in which 'we see that diversity doth not destroy uniformity, and that the limbs of a noble fabric may be correspondant enough, though they be various.' This organic conception of a mansion will nowhere be better illustrated than in his treatment of the kitchen. It will no longer be a separate unit, as at Richmond or Cowdray, but will be incorporated in the main façade, balancing the great hall and repeating its oriel window. By according them architecturally a place of honour, the patron will give the kitchen and its dependencies their full value as members; he would not have approved 'the willingness in the Italian artisans to distribute the kitchens underground' even though it might 'by the elevation of the front, add majesty to the whole aspect'.

Already the ground plan is beginning to take shape in the patron's mind. A front of some two hundred feet, with a porch in the centre, hall and chapel to the left, kitchen and surveying place to the right. Behind the centre of this front, a great quadrangle with lodgings for the noble and gentle members of the household; behind the kitchen, a little courtyard with bakehouse, pantry, dry-larder and lodgings for their staff; behind the chapel, the state rooms ranged about a corresponding court. Across these three courts on the far side, the entrance front, built low to reveal the architecture of the quadrangle, with a Renaissance archway instead of a gatehouse. It is essentially the plan of a college.

The general disposition being now determined, questions of orientation will be carefully considered, for this is the age of domestic convenience. 'Let all the principal chambers of delight, all studies and libraries, be towards the east,' suggested one critic, 'for the morning is a friend to the muses.' Offices which require heat may face the south; those which prefer an even coolness, the north – and here may be included 'such rooms as are appointed for gentle motion, as galleries'.

The gallery is another feature in which the collegiate nature of the house is shown. Its length is designed to provide indoor exercise, especially for the ladies of the household, and the gardens are laid out to afford a rich and delightful outlook from its windows. Many of these will be deeply recessed and imbowed to lend a note of privacy to an otherwise public apartment.

These bay windows, together with those of the great chamber, hall and surveying place, will provide the most important features in the façade. The general appearance of the house is in fact controlled by the plan. In particular it will be affected by the treatment of staircases. There will be several handsome newel stairs in the lordlier parts of the mansion, but with over a hundred domestics about the place, a considerable number of smaller communications are required. So the earlier method of building spiral stairs in square towers is retained. These towers, marking the corners of the house, will make a distinctive contribution to its outward aspect. Thus far has the building materialized in the patron's mind.

The time has now come for him to make his contracts. The plural is significant. He may make three or four separate contracts, one for the shell of masonry; one for special ornamental features, such as oriels, porches and fire-places; another for ceilings and plasterwork. For the masons, the carpenters and the plasterers have their separate traditions; they form another community, and the ultimate appearance of the house will be the result of their artistic collaboration rather than the expression of a single, all-embracing design.

The harmonious integration of the decorative elements is the patron's business, but it will not be achieved in advance. In his contracts he refers to parts of other buildings which are to serve as models, but all that he is tied to is the 'platt' or ground plan. This he has drawn under his directions, paying John Symandes of London forty shillings for his pains. As the building progresses and his ideas develop with it, he will frequently have new plans and designs made, not necessarily by the same draughtsmen. In all cases his own taste will be the creative, governing force.

Meanwhile, down on the selected site, all is preparation. Thatched huts have been put up for the workmen, and the contractors are busy collecting their materials.

The first period may be one of inactivity for the patron, but as the walls rise from their foundations he comes increasingly into his own. At ground floor level he makes an alteration in the design, introducing a 'stone gallery' – a Doric colonnade – to the main façade of the great quadrangle. This forms a south-facing loggia, delightful as a sun trap in winter, and providing also a most attractive leaded walk above.

This will not be done by the present contractor, it is a job for the foreign craftsmen who are providing the fire-places. At the same time the pillars and pediments for the central doorways to either side of the quadrangle are ordered, and one side of the court is completed, to try the effect, before the other is begun.

Already the character of the house is emerging. The colonnade and porches give the great court a classical dignity, but the little entrances in its corners retain the Tudor arch. The kitchen court has no Italian flavour because it has no ornament, and the state rooms, relying on their enormous windows for distinction, are still in the vernacular.

As the walls grow higher, the ornamental features become more numerous, and the patron is busier than ever, inspecting, selecting and even designing. If his mason should write to him and ask for the 'upright' of some gable or dormer, he will supply it from his own hand. He has various sources of inspiration on which to draw: his own artistic sensibility, his neighbours' achievements or the books of Serlio, John Shute, Dietterlin or de Vries.

The statelier parts of the house, the whole of the north range containing kitchen, hall and chapel, are to be finished with a balustrade, but in the humbler quarters the gable has still its place and offers scope for a variety of ornament; our patron will make his scrolled and spiked after the Flemish fashion.

Meanwhile the plasterers have begun their work upon the interior. Their richly interlacing patterns, criss-crossing about the ceiling and dropping in graceful pendants at their ganglions, are too involved for the patron's pencil, but he knows his workmen and gives them a free hand. The joiners, too, setting up their wainscoats and hanging the doors, are left to their own conventions. The patron is more concerned with the purchase of tapestry from abroad, whose verdure and 'forrest work' will insulate him from the cold stone walls.

Then will come the cupboards for the hall, on which his gold and silver plate will make their impressive display, the squat four-posters, velvet-upholstered chairs, the cabinets, chests and musical instruments for the Gallery, the cloth of Estate and almost throne-like trapping of the great chamber, the pothooks and chopping blocks for the kitchen, down to the cushions and posset cups and the smallest accessories which make a house not just a specimen of architecture, but a place to live in.

For the patron, life will be a blend of calculated ease and almost liturgical ceremony. The books of nurture and treatises on health of the period show that the Tudors took their pleasure seriously. From Hugh Rhodes we have a glimpse of the Chamberlain dressing

his master on a winter morning; his petticoat, doublet and hose are
brought warmed from the fire. In an earlier book of nurture, a versi-
fied account of the bedtime bath shows a similar attention to detail:

> If your sovereign will to the bath,
> His body to wash clean ...
> Look he have sponges, five or six,
> Whereon to sit or lean.

A basin of hot herbs and douche of rose-water added fragrance
to cleanliness, and the account ends with the patron drying luxu-
riously before an ample fire. At meals he was served with a ritual
scarcely inferior to that of the Court, but if he had noticed any such
bobbings and genuflectings in his church, he would have fulmi-
nated against such detestable enormities.

For him, the routine of the household was merely the background to a richer life – richer intellectually, for he is a lover of
books and learned discourse, he has his library and his university
friends; richer recreationally, for he has his falconers at command to
ride out with him into the park and match his tiercels against the
ducks and herons. His lady, though sharing his interests, is confined to a narrower circuit. Her life is a placid alternation of walks
in the garden, walks in the loggia, walks in the gallery, embroidery
by the fireside or music at the virginals, set in the framework' of
prayer and introspection which puritan piety demanded.

From his position of ease and honour, the patron dispensed
abundant hospitality. 'He always kept his greatness by his charity',
wrote Donald Lupton. 'He loved three things, an open cellar, a full
hall and a sweating cook ... There are four sorts who pray for him,
the poor, the passenger, his tenants and servants ... Lusty, able men
well maintained were his delight, with whom he would be familiar
... Well, we can say that once such a charitable practitioner there
was, but now he is dead, to the grief of all England, and 'tis
shrewdly suspected that he will never rise again in our climate.'
That was written in 1632. Already the Tudor ideal of a household
was beginning to savour of the past. Both its architecture and its
way of life were under attack.

The architecture of the house and the life of the household had this in common: they both depended for their quality on the capacity of the patron. It is not everyone who could design Longleat; it is not everyone who could acquit himself as warden of a college. In the hands of a Thynne, a Bacon or a Cecil, the design-as-you-build method could produce a masterpiece. The glimpses we have of their family life also are attractive. But with less capable persons there was no telling what folly they might not beget. In the following century Henry Wotton and Balthazar Gerbier were to complain of columns swelling in the middle 'as if they were sick of some tympany or dropsy', or placed 'like things patched or glued against a wall'. With an inadequate patron, beauty would be replaced by ornament, magnificence by ostentation and scholarship by thoughtless plagiarism. The crossing of local and Renaissance traditions would issue in that heavy, bastard style censured by Walpole, that 'lost all grace by wanting simplicity'.

In their domestic life, the same tendency to gravitate towards the dull and the formal was observed by Aubrey. 'The conversation and habits of those times were as stiff and starched as their bands and square beards.' Pompousness passed for dignity, gravity for wisdom, quibbles for wit; parents were as heavy-handed as schoolmasters, and schoolmasters as the warders at Bridewell; 'the child perfectly loathed the sight of his parents.' Daughters were made to kneel in the parental presence, and sons, their forelocks stiffened with spittle, 'were to stand mannerly thus ... one hand at the bandstring, the other on the breech or codpiece'.

It is remarkable that the attack on the houses was concentrated against the Elizabethan method of building, rather than any effect which it produced. Sir Henry Wotton began with a plea for stylistic purity, castigating the light-hearted use of classical orders, 'as if the very terms of architraves and friezes and cornices ... were enough to graduate a master in this art'. The Civil War, decreeing the ruin of the finest specimens, left their survivors to the mercy of a new fashion and an altered way of life. Balthazar Gerbier turned his attack upon the remnant: 'No curious eye can well endure the barn-like roofs of many noble persons' palaces ... Let any good eye judge whether it be not true that the extreme height of a room takes not away from the greatness of the company that is in the same.'

Harmony was to be replaced by uniformity, and the aristocracy was advised 'not to build at random, as the custom is of too many ill builders.' The age of the patron is over; the age of the architect has arrived. 'No building is begun before a mature resolve on a complete finished model of the entire structure.'

A civil war, a new fashion in building, a new conception of the role of the country house, and the operation of time upon an often flimsy construction have combined to rob England of a priceless part of its Elizabethan inheritance. Perhaps most serious of all has been the lack of appreciation for the proper character of the architecture of the age. Protagonists of the Gothic and classic schools are common, but the Elizabethan, partaking of both styles, fails to appeal to the purists of either.

In the Elizabethan house, English architecture had lost the unsophisticated charm of the Gothic, but had not yet attained the settled maturity of the classic; it had reached, in fact, its awkward age. This age has few attributes of its own, but holds in an uneasy synthesis the unrelinquished past with the unrealized future. Delightful when it succeeds, irritating when it fails, it is always interesting to those who judge it aright. Sometimes the houses have a physical beauty which is not strictly architectural, but depends on a strange and undefinable affinity with the landscape; perhaps their diversity is more consonant with the forms of nature than the more rigid uniformity of later buildings. Sometimes they succeed by mere audacity, dominating their surroundings like some great castle or cathedral. But whether there is real aesthetic quality, or whether its place is taken by pretentious ornament, they are out to impress, and their display was seldom backed by the solidity of a castle or a cathedral.

William Harrison, comparing the architecture of Elizabeth to that of her father, made the significant comment: 'Certes, masonry did never better flourish in England than in his time. Albeit that, in these days, there are many goodly houses constructed in the sundry quarters of this island, yet are they rather curious to the eye (like paper work) than substantial for continuance; whereas such as he did set up did excell in both.'

Sometimes the Elizabethans give the impression that they were not building for posterity. Perhaps, for all their self-assurance, they felt too insecure. Their lands depended on the Protestant succession, and up till 1587 the heir presumptive was a Roman Catholic. They were nouveaux riches, and their hold upon their wealth was precarious. This made them spendthrift and ostentatious in their use of it; their houses were built for immediate enjoyment, hastily constructed and garishly decorated. In times of greater security men build on firmer foundations and in serener styles.

But it was this ephemeral beauty that gave the houses of the Elizabethans their distinctive quality and which linked them to the person of the Queen. Built or enlarged specially for her entertainment, many of them outlived her reign by less than half a century. It is this association that has made the few which survive so quick to captivate the minds of those who look on them today – some, as Vanbrugh so rightly discerned, for their quaint and curious workmanship, and others because they move such lively and pleasing reflections upon the persons who have inhabited them.

BIBLIOGRAPHY

BIBLIOGRAPHY

GENERAL

CUNNINGHAM, P.
Extracts from the Accounts of the Revels at Court (1842).

JONES, P. VAN B.
The Household of a Tudor Nobleman, University of Illinois Studies, vol. VI (1917).

KLARWILL, V. VON
Queen Elizabeth and some Foreigners (1928).

MALFATTI, C. V.
Two Italian Accounts of Tudor England (1953).

NICHOLS, J.
Progresses and Public Processions of Queen Elizabeth, 3 vols (1823).

ROBSON-SCOTT, W. D.
German Travellers in England (1953).

RYE, W. B.
England as seen by Foreigners (1865).

SALTER, E. GURNEY
Tudor England through Venetian Eyes (1930).

SUMMERSON, SIR J.
Architecture in Britain, 1530–1830 (1953).

SPECIAL (*by chapter*)

Prologue: WOODSTOCK. The quotations from Vanbrugh and the account of the Gentleman of the Army at Norwich (British Museum, Lansdowne MSS 313) are from D. Green, *Blenheim Palace* (1951). Most of the material is collected in E. Marshall, *The Early History of Woodstock Manor and its Environs* (1875). The account of Elizabeth's imprisonment is in C. R. Manning, *State Papers relating to the Custody of the Princess Elizabeth at Woodstock in 1554*, in the

Transactions of the Norfolk and Norwich Archaeological Society, vol. IV, part 2 (1855).

Chapter One: INTRODUCTORY. For Oatlands, see E. W. Brayley, *Topographical History of Surrey*, vol. II (1850); *Notes and Queries*, August and September 1922; *Surrey Archaeological Collections*, vol. XXVIII (1915). For Newhall, see *Vetusta Monumenta*, vol. II (1789), Society of Antiquaries, and the *Essex Review*, vol. XXVII (1908). For Hatfield, the author has used, by kind permission of the Marquess of Salisbury, the typescript of R. Gunton, formerly librarian at Hatfield House. Quotations are from 'Cecil Family Papers', vols. I, II, III, and 'Hatfield Manor Papers', vol. III. For the palaces mentioned other than Oatlands, Newhall and Hatfield, see the special sources listed below for each palace.

Chapter Two: GREENWICH. The account of Elizabeth's baptism is from Nichols, *Progresses*, vol. I; the reception of Lambarde from vol. III. Quotations from the building accounts are from J. W. Kirby, *Building work at Placentia 1532–1533*, and *Building work at Placentia 1543–1544* in the Transactions of the Greenwich and Lewisham Antiquarian Society, vols V and VI respectively (1954). John Barclay's description, translated from his *Icon Animorum* (1614), is from vol. IV (1936). For Holbein's work on the banqueting house see A. B. Chamberlain, *Hans Holbein the Younger* (1913).

Chapter Three: WHITEHALL. The main source is the L. C. C. *Survey of London*, edited by M. H. Cox and P. Norman, vols XIII (1930) and XIV (1931). Details of jousting come from Nichols, *Progresses*, vol. II. The descriptions of Holbein's murals are quoted from P. Ganz, *Hans Holbein* (1912); the pamphlet 'The Children of the Chapel Stripped and Whipped' is quoted from E. K. Chambers, *The Elizabethan Stage*, vol. II (1923). The theatrical productions of 1578 are from P. Cunningham, *Extracts from the Accounts of the Revels at Court* (1842); those of 1601 from L. Hotson, *The First Night of Twelfth Night* (1954).

Chapter Four: RICHMOND. The anonymous description written in Henry VII's reign and the Commonwealth Commissioner's Survey of 1650 and the extracts from the account books come from E.

Beresford Chancellor, *Historical Richmond* (1885). Details of Henry VII's life are from Sir F. Bacon, *History of Henry VII*, edited by E. Lumby (1881), and the story of Prince Henry from T. Birch, *Life of Henry, Prince of Wales* (1760). The Ordinances of Eltham are printed in the *Antiquarian Repository*, vol. III (1808).

Chapter Five: HAMPTON COURT. Most of the material is collected in E. Law, *History of Hampton Court Palace* (1885); references to the building accounts and inventories are quoted from this. Theatrical productions are from Cunningham (see above under Whitehall). Further details are from G. Cavendish, *The Life of Cardinal Wolsey*, and G. Wyatt, *Some Particulars of the Life of Queen Anne Boleyn*, both edited by S. W. Singer (1827).

Chapter Six: NONSUCH. The Commonwealth Survey of 1650 is printed in *Archaeologia*, vol. V (1779). The Latin description by A. Watson (*circa* 1590) is in the Library of Trinity College, Cambridge (MS R.7.22). A typescript translation by C. F. Bell and A. W. Carr has been used, by courtesy of the Nonsuch Palace Excavation Committee. Sir J. Wallop's letter (Nov. 17th, 1540) is in *Letters and Papers Foreign and Domestic, Henry VIII*, vol. XVI, 1540–4. *The Quest for Nonsuch* by John Dent (1962).

Chapter Seven: THE QUEEN IN PROGRESS. Details of Elizabeth's visits come from Nichols, *Progresses*. For Holdenby, almost all the material is collected in E. Hartshorne, *Memorials of Holdenby* (1867).

Chapter Eight: A PROGRESS INTO EAST ANGLIA. The account of the progress, Topclyffe's letters and Churchyard's entertainments are from Nichols, *Progresses*, vol. II. Further details of Long Melford are from Sir W. Parker, *History of Long Melford* (1873); of Hawstead from Sir J. Cullum, *History and Antiquities of Hawstead and Hardwick* (1813), and of Kirtling from *Topographical Miscellanies* (1792). Biographical notes on Roger, 2nd Lord North, are from Lady Frances Buckley, *Three Men of the Tudor Time*.

Chapter Nine: KENILWORTH. Most of the material, including the quotation from Bishop Hurd, is from *Kenilworth Festivities: comprising Laneham's description of the Pageantry and Gascoigne's Masques,*

presented before Queen Elizabeth at Kenilworth Castle anno 1575 (1825).
E. H. Knowles, *The Castle of Kenilworth* (1872), and Sir W. Dugdale,
The Antiquities of Warwickshire, edited by W. Thomas (1730), have
also been used.

Chapter Ten: COWDRAY. Most of the material is from C. Roundell,
Cowdray (1884). Details of Elizabeth's entertainment are from
Nichols, *Progresses*, vol. III. The full text of the household book is
in Sir S. Scott's article, 'A Book of Orders and Rules of Anthony,
Viscount Montague', in *Sussex Archaeological Collections*, vol. III
(1854). The account by the anonymous Italian visitor is in C. V.
Malfatti, *Two Italian Accounts of Tudor England* (1953).

Chapter Eleven: THEOBALDS. The chief source is Sir J. Summerson,
'The Building of Theobalds, 1564–1585', in *Archaeologia*, vol.
XCVII (1954). Details of Lord Burghley's life are from an anonymous biography thought to be by one of his household, printed in
F. Peck, *Desiderata Curiosa* (1732). Accounts of James I at Theobalds are from J. Nichols, *Progresses and Public Processions of James I*
(1828).

Chapter Twelve: GORHAMBURY. Most of the material, the building
accounts, the expenses for the Queen's visit, the quotations from
Dr Rawley, are in C. Grimston, *History of Gorhambury* (1821). See
also H. M. M. Lane in the *St Albans and Hertfordshire Architectural
and Archaeological Society Transactions* (1930–2), and J. C. Rogers in
the same (1933). Sir F. Bacon's notes for the Water Garden are in
the British Museum (Add. MSS 27.278). Quotation is also made
from T. Baskerfield's manuscript edition of H. Chauncy, *The
Historical Antiquities of Hertford-shire* (1799).

Epilogue: DEATH AND RECONSTRUCTION. Sir R. Carey's account of
the death of Elizabeth is from Nichols, *Progresses*, vol. III. Details of
the building of a Tudor house are based on Sir J. Summerson,
Architecture in Britain 1530–1830 (1953). Details of a Tudor household, including the reference to Lord Derby's Clerk of the Kitchen,
are taken from P. van B. Jones, *The Household of a Tudor Nobleman*
(1917). The books on architecture which were often used by
Elizabethan builders were: J. V. de Vries, *Architectura* (1563), W.

Dietterlin, *Architectura* (1594), J. Shute, *The First and Chief Grounds of Architecture* (1563), and S. Serlio, *Libro Primo d'Architettura*.

MISCELLANEOUS QUOTATIONS

Aubrey, John: *Aubrey's Brief Lives*, edited by O. L. Dick (1949).

Bacon, Sir Francis: *Essays*, edited by R. Whateley (1856).

Barclay, John: *Icon Animorum* (1614), in Transactions of the Greenwich and Lewisham Antiquarian Society, vol. IV, no. 1 (1936).

Braun, Georgius, and Franz Hohenberg (sometimes spelled Hogenberg), *Urbium Praecipuarum Theatrum Quintum* (1572).

Breuner, Baron Kaspar von (Chamberlain to Archduke Charles of Austria, 1559): in Klarwill (see above, General).

Buchenbach, Breuning von (Ambassador from the Duke of Württemberg, 1595): in Klarwill (see above, General).

Camden, William: *The History of the most renowned and victorious Princess Elizabeth, late Queen of England* (1675).

Cavendish, George (Gentleman Usher to Wolsey): *The Life of Cardinal Wolsey*, edited by S. W. Singer (1827).

Chapuys, Eustace (Imperial Ambassador 1529–33): *Calendar of Letters, Spanish*, vol. IV, pt 2, 1531–3.

Churchyard, Thomas: *The Entertainment of the Queen's Majesty into Suffolk and Norfolk*, in Nichols (see above, General).

Clifford, Lady Anne: *The Diary of the Lady Anne Clifford*, edited by V. Sackville-West (1923).

Enriquez, Pedro de: in M. Hume, *Two English Queens and Philip* (1908).

Evelyn, John: *The Diary of John Evelyn*, edited by E. S. de Beer (1955).

Fuller, Thomas: *The History of the Worthies of England* (1662).

Gerbier d'Ouvilly, Balthazar: *Counsel and Advice to all Builders* (1663).

Gerschow, Friedrich (Secretary to the Duke of Stettin-Pomerania, 1602): in Transactions of the Royal Historical Society, new series, vol. VI (1892).

Giustiniani, Sebastian (Venetian ambassador): *Calendar of State Papers, Venetian*, 1509–19.

Harington, Sir John: *The Metamorphosis of Ajax*, edited by P. Warlock and J. Lindsay (1927).
Letters, in Nichols (see above, General).

Harrison, William: *A Description of England*, 1577, edited by F. J. Furnivall (1877).

Hentzner, Paul: *Paul Hentzner's Travels in England during the Reign of Queen Elizabeth* (1598), translated by Horace, late Earl of Orford (1797).

Heylyn, Peter: *Ecclesia Restorata; or, the History of the Reformation of the Church of England* (1661).

Holinshed, Ralph. *The Third Volume of Chronicles, beginning at Duke William the Norman, commonly called the Conqueror; and descending by degrees of years to all the Kings and Queens of England in their orderly Successions; first compiled by Raphaell Holinshed, and by him extended to the year 1577. Now newly recognised, augmented and continued to the year 1586.*

Howes, Edmund: *Annals, or, a General Chronicle of England. Begun by John Stow: continued and augmented with matters foreign and domestic, ancient and modern, unto the end of the present year, 1631. By Edmund Howes, Gent.*

Kiechel, Samuel: *England and the English, 1585*, in Rye (see above, General).

Lambarde, William: *A Perambulation of Kent, written in the year 1570* (1826).

Lemnius, Levinus: *Notes on England, 1560*, in Rye (see above, General).

Litolfi, Annibale: in *Cal.S.P. Venetian*, 1557.

Lupton, Donald: *London and the Country Carbonadoed* (1632).

Machyn, Henry: *The Diary of Henry Machyn, Citizen and Merchant-Tailor of London, 1550–1563*, edited by J. Nichols, Camden Society, series I, vol. XLII (1848).

Magalotti, Count: *Travels of Cosmo III, Grand Duke of Tuscany, through England in 1669* (1821).

Mandelslo, Jean de: *Voyages Célèbres* (1640), French translation edited by H. Wicquefort (1727).

Mander, Carel van: *Het Schilder-Boek* (1604), French translation edited by H. Hymans (1884).

Monconys, Balthasar de: *Journal des Voyages de M. de Monconys* (1666).

Moryson, Fynes: *Itinerary* (1617).

Norden, John: *Speculi Britanniae Pars: An Historical and Chorographical Description of the County of Essex* (1594), edited by Sir H. Ellis, Camden Society, vol. IX (1840).
 Speculum Britanniae, the first Part; An Historical & Chorographical Description of Middlesex (1593). Manuscript notes on Westminster, omitted from this, are printed in Rye (see above, General).

Orsino, Virginio, Duke of Bracciano (1601): in L. Hotson, *The First Night of Twelfth Night* (1954).

Pennant, Thomas: *The Journey from Chester to London* (1782).

Pepys, Samuel: *The Diary of Samuel Pepys*, edited by H. B. Wheatley (1897).

Ramelius, Henry (Danish ambassador, 1587): in Nichols (see above, General).

Ramssla, Neumayr von (Secretary to the Duke of Saxe-Weimar, 1613): *Des Durchlauchtigen Hochgebornen Fürsten und Herrn, Herrn Johann Ernsten des Jüngeren, Herzogen zu Sachsen Reise in Frankreich, Engelland und Nederland*, edited by J. G. Pagendarm (1734).

Rathgeb, Jacob (Secretary to the Duke of Württemberg, 1592): in Rye (see above, General).

Rhodes, Hugh: *Book of Nurture* (1577), Early English Text Society, vol. XXXII (1868).

Rich, Barnaby: *His Farewell to the Military Profession* (1581), Shakespeare Society (1846).

Sagudino, Niccolo (Secretary to Giustiniani): *Cal.S.P. Venetian*, 1515.

Savorgnano, Mario, Count of Belgrade: *Cal.S.P. Venetian*, 1531.

Scaramelli, Giovanni (Venetian Secretary): *Cal.S.P. Venetian*, 1603.

Schifanoya, Il (Venetian ambassador): *Cal.S.P. Venetian*, 1559.

Soranzo, Giacomo (Venetian ambassador): *Cal.S.P. Venetian*, 1554.

Sorbière, Samuel de: *Relation d'un voyage en Angleterre* (1664).

Soriano, Michael (Venetian ambassador): *Cal.S.P. Venetian*, 1561.

Spinelli, Gasparo (Venetian Secretary): *Cal.S.P. Venetian*, 1527–1533.

Stow, John: *A Survey of the Cities of London and Westminster* (1598), edited by J. Strype (1720).

    Annals (see above, under Howes).

Wedel, Lupold von: *Beschreibung seiner Reisen und Kriegserlebnisse* (in England, 1584–5), in Klarwill (see above, General).

Wotton, Sir Henry: *The Elements of Architecture* (1624).

Wyatt, George: *Some Particulars of the Life of Queen Anne Boleyn*, edited by S. W. Singer (1827).

Zinzerling, Justus: *Description of England* (*circa* 1610), in Rye (see above, General).

INDEX

Westminster, 25, 117; Abbey, 59, 74; Henry VII's Chapel, 28, 35, 81; Palace of, 59, 144; St Margaret's, 35, 117
West Wycombe, 14
White, Roland, 112
Whitehall, 33, ch. III, 87, 195, 196; pls 9, 10, 11
Whitgift, Archbishop, 194
Winchester College, 195
Winchester, Marquis of, 116
Windsor, 14, 29, 32, 65, 116
Williams, Lord, 14
Wolsey, Cardinal, 28, 60, 64, 87 ff
Woodstock, 13 ff, 80, 96; pl. 1

Wotton, Sir Henry, 198
Wren, Sir Christopher, 172
Württemberg, Duke of, 24, 32, 36, 53
Wyatt, George, 93
Wyatt, Sir Thomas, 14, 62
Wyngaerde, Antonius van den, 18, 30, 50, 63
Wythiam, 119

YEOMAN OF THE CHAMBERS, his office, 161
York House, 60

ZINZERLING, JUSTUS, 98

The
PROGRESS TO
EAST ANGLIA
and to
KENILWORTH

Stamford

Burghley

Kirby

Kenilworth

Holdenby

Warwick

Northampton

BEDFORD

Banbury

BUCKINGHAM
SHIRE

Woodstock

Gorhambury

Hatfield

OXFORD

S⁺ ALBANS

Theobalds

LONDON

Whitehall

Windsor

READING

Gr

D152435I